A COUNTRY BOY
From Owl Hollow

By

Clyde Lyon

A story about a boy's life on a farm
without telephones, radios, running water
or electricity from 1913 to 1929 in what is now
known as the "Land Between the Lakes"

Second Printing, 1995

Published in Nashville, Tennessee by
Country Life Publishers
P. O. Box 92108
Nashville, TN, 37209

ISBN 0-9640691-0-5

Printed in the United States by
Vaughan Printing Company
411 Cowan
Nashville, Tennessee, 37207

Cover design by

Jack Cornett

Highlights of Contents

Preface

In his book "Land Between The Rivers", Dr. J. Milton Henry, Professor of History at Austin Peay State University, wrote that "Characteristics of the American frontier appear to linger longer between the Cumberland and Tennessee than in other areas of America". The Cumberland and Tennessee he mentions were rivers that have been replaced by the Barkley and Kentucky Lakes, and the area is now known as "Land Between The Lakes", a sportsman's paradise that is visited each year by thousands of people from all over the world.

The land between the rivers was settled mostly by Scotch-Irish decendants from the early part of the nineteenth century and before. Most of them were Protestants, devoted to their religion, yet fiercely independent. They tolerated the whiskey maker and the bootleggers, although they considered them tools of the Devil. Some of the finest moonshine ever made came from the land between those rivers, and Al Capone, the notorious Chicago gangster, was one of the area's best customers.

Many generations had grown up in the land between the rivers before I was born so it was only natural for me to be a part of it just like those before me. Most of my teen years were spent in the area of Blue Spring, Owl Hollow, Panther Creek, Hickory Hollow, the White Hills and on the banks of the Tennessee. I learned where the deer grazed, where the wild turkeys roosted, where the fox squirrels were more plentiful, and where the swamp rabbits grew bigger.

In the early and mid-thirties I wrote some articles for our local paper about experiences on the farm, and somehow they came to the attention of Silliman Evans, the late publisher of THE NASHVILLE TENNESSEAN. He wrote a letter asking me to come by his office the next time I was in Nashville. Later when I visited him, he suggested that these experiences be written down for publication and said he would personally see that they were published. He explained that true events needed to be published instead of the "comic" versions that were becoming popular, and giving people the wrong impression of what it was like to live a *real* country life. He said he had discussed one of my articles with a reporter and wanted me to talk to him also. It was the first time I had met Mr. Evans or his reporter, J. Percy Priest. I promised to give it thought, but in my mind did not believe I could meet their expectations. Soon World War II was in full sway and the idea was dropped. Through all the years, however, those farm life memories were kept fresh in my mind, hoping that some day they could be put down in writing, so that my sons and grandchildren would know what it was like when we live without radios, telephones, cars, running water, plumbing, air conditioning, or electricity. Hopefully, I can make them realize that it was not a dull life.

I have never considered myself a writer nor a story teller. I have never been accused of using the English language perfectly, and my grammar may have caused some teachers to wish they had chosen some other profession. I became nervous when it came my turn to diagram a sentence and it was my opinion that a part of speech was a portion of some orator's address.

It is my hope to dispel any idea that those early days were dull. If you think it was dull making your own toys, being chased up a tree by wild hogs, tracking a big bobcat all day in the snow, skinning a polecat (skunk to city folks), making friends with a wild fox, or pulling a big catfish from the river, you just may be in for a surprise.

It will be noted that there is an absence of sex in this book. The reason is simple. Sex was a private matter in the twenties and was not discussed in public. There were "necessary" weddings, but they were kept secret and I will let them remain that way.

NOTE: For some reason unknown to me, the TVA changed the name of Owl Hollow to Wildcat Hollow and Bailey's Creek to Hughes' Creek. I hope this will not be confusing

Acknowledgements

Many thanks go to a lot of people, some are listed below

Virginia
Sadie
Barbara
Alvin Earl
Duncan
Lee
Tim
Ken
Bill

and
A special thanks to my parents,
E. A. (Gus) Lyons
and
Thetus Barbee Lyons
(Papa added the s to Lyon)
for instilling in me a love and respect of Nature, and
for allowing me to roam the hills and hollows; to fish
the creeks and river; or do whatever I wanted to do
as long as it was in harmony with God, Nature and my fellowman.
That is why I was fortunate to enjoy so many things
that most other farm boys never experienced.

Also to the
Oscar Farris Agricultural Museum
at the
Ellington Agricultural Center
Nashville, TN 37204
for allowing me to take pictures of the
old farm machinery they have on display.

i

*When the Government decided to build the Kentucky Dam and flood the
river bottoms of the land between the Tennessee and Cumberland Rivers,
they ended a peaceful way of life and caused*

Trouble in
Paradise

It was in the Fall of 1940 or 41 when I last saw the Tennessee River
bottom land and my heart sank. I was visiting my grandparents and had
walked around the hill to where I could see the river bottoms, but instead
of the fertile fields surrounded by trees, the land was cleared as far as I
could see. Huge piles of wood were burning and the wisps of smoke were
winding their way toward the heavens as if searching for a place to rest.
The lone cypress which had stood in Campbell Slough for hundreds of
years was gone. It had been a landmark and was the only cypress along
the river for many miles. I wondered where the hawks and buzzards were
roosting now or where they sat to rest or watch for prey.

The Tennessee Valley Authority (TVA) wanted the land so it could
be flooded by waters from the Kentucky Dam that was being built several
miles down the river. This is where I had hunted swamp rabbits, and
caught fish from the creek and river. It is where the Indians had hunted
and fished for a thousand years before me. They had left two big mounds
that Grandpappy said might be sacred, and that I was never to disturb
them. The farmers that owned the land had plowed around the mounds
for a hundred years, but now they were going to be under several feet of
water. I gazed on the destruction for awhile, turned and followed the path
back to Grandpappy's house.

1

A COUNTRY BOY *From Owl Hollow*

Many times I had watched as the Tennessee went on a rampage and sent her floodwaters up the creeks to spill out over the fields to the foothills. I would set notched sticks in the water to see how fast it was rising, knowing that it would soon go back within her banks and be calm again. But now she was going to be forced to the foothills to stay. Grandpappy use to say that the Tennessee had a right to go on a rampage once in awhile after carrying boats and rafts peacefully along her waters for all those years. To him the river was an old friend and adversary that was going to be tamed like a horse, and he was disturbed about it. Then too, like thousands of others, he and Grandmammy would have to move to higher ground

Later they did move out of the path of the rising waters. Blue Spring Church of Christ and the Boyd Graveyard were moved to a location that would be safe from the flood. Grandpappy built a small house beside the church and settled down again. It was only a few years before the government decided to take all of the land between the rivers and again the people had to move. Many had been born there and had spent all their lives in this gentle land but now they were forced to start all over again for the second time in less than a generation.

Most of the people of Owl Hollow, Panther Creek, Blue Spring and Fort Henry were poor by the standards of the outside world, but they were rich in happiness and honesty. They had plenty to eat, and warm clothing to wear. They were an independent lot, and nothing except the government could have driven them from their land. A preacher once made the remark that there were God-fearing people in those hills and hollows that were unequaled any other place he had visited. He could have added that God was about the only thing they feared. No one could have ever dreamed that these gentle people would one day be driven from their land, and their houses destroyed so there would be no evidence of the quietness that was once there.

I entered the land between these rivers in January of 1913 without the aid of a doctor. There was a Dr. Giles living at the Boswell farm about three miles away and Papa had gone to fetch him. I must have gotten tired of waiting for when they arrived I had already made my appearance and was doing fine. Mama, who weighed less than a hundred pounds, wasn't feeling too good. My Great-Aunt Fanny Hosford delivered me, and more than twenty years later, had to sign papers for me to get a birth certificate.

2

Abraham Lincoln and I have one thing in common. We were both born in log cabins, but that is where the resemblance ends. He split rails and became president and I never did either one. I have been luckier than Abe though because as far as I know, nobody has ever taken a shot at me, or at least up until now. Although Lincoln was born about 100 years before me, our early teen years were not so different, as indicated by Dr. Henry, in his book, *"Land Between the Rivers"*. I was one of the last to be born into a quiet and unspoiled generation and there is probably no other time in the history of the human race when so many advances in technology have been made in the span of one lifetime.

Papa worked at a sawmill and farmed a little, but he was never a farmer at heart. He wanted to be, as they say, where the action was, and when I was about one year old, we moved to Paducah and he got a job with the streetcar company as a motorman. The first house we lived in was on Clay Street, but I guess my memory hadn't kicked in because I have no memory of the place. Our second house was across the street from where the Guthrie Avenue streetcar line ended and that is where the first incident of memory began. It was during the Summer of 1915 and I was playing out in the back yard. I was watching big drops of rain as they hit in the road, causing the dust to scatter like a miniature bomb. A couple of older boys came by and warned me that if one of the raindrops hit me, it would drive me into the ground like a fence post. I almost tore down the back steps getting into the house and Mama said it was the next day before she could get me to go outside again. I was two and a half years old, because we moved to Guthrie Avenue in the Fall of 1915.

Grandpappy Visits Us in Paducah

In the Spring of 1918 a letter arrived with the news that Grandpappy was bringing a raft down the Tennessee and would be visiting us. The letter said that he wanted to get the raft to Paducah while the water was still high enough to come down the "shoot". As they read the letter the word "shoot" must have dug a hole in my brain, and I could see Grandpappy coming up Guthrie Avenue with guns ablazing and shooting up the neighborhood in general. It was a letdown when I learned that the "shoot" was a small stream of the Tennessee that separated Paducah from an island. Instead of the gun-toter I had imagined, Grandpappy turned out to

3

be the most gentle person I had ever known. When there was talk of him returning to Owl Hollow, I wanted to go with him and it was agreed that I could go and spend the Summer there. Mama and Papa would come for me in the Fall.

On Saturday afternoon we went down to lower Broadway where we would board the packet *Paducah* later in the day. The drays, pulled by big horses, were rushing to the wharf with loads of freight to be shipped up the river. The sound of hoofs and wagons on the wood block streets of Broadway was something I will never forget. Now and then a truck with big solid rubber tires came rumbling down the street and some of the horses were afraid of them. Grandpappy had brought a friend, Tom Herndon, along with him on the raft and we met him at the wharf. They bought some presents to take back home, and before we went aboard the *Paducah,* they went into a place where each of them bought a bottle of something, and put it in their coat pockets.

About dark we went on board the *Paducah* and I was greeted by Aunt Julia, a black maid. When she saw me she held out her arms and yelled "Here comes my baby" and gave me a great big hug. I had been on the packet before but can't remember it, although am sure I remembered her at the time. On that trip, and others that would follow, Aunt Julia took

Sunday Morning Steamboat, *Paducah*

4

good care of me. She would let me go into the restrooms at the rear of the boat where I could look down through the holes at the huge paddle wheel below. If the big wheel was turning, sometimes she would have to come in after me. She also saw to it that I was well fed, and tucked me in bed at night. She would warn Grandpappy to take good care of me or she would "feed him to the fishes".

I was asleep when the *Paducah* pulled out from the wharf and headed up the Tennessee. The river was so full that most of the landings were covered with water, and freight could not be unloaded on the trip up-river. Because of this the packet ran ahead of schedule and we reached Iron Landing, near the mouth of Bailey's Creek, before daylight. Aunt Julia woke and dressed me and took me out to where Grandpappy, Mr. Herndon and a man they called Pat, were standing. I wanted to see what was going on below our deck and hung over the railing for a better look. The water fascinated me as it rushed along the gunnels of the boat in the floodlights. Grandpappy would pull me back to where he considered it safer, but it would not be long until I was hanging over the rails again. The man they called Pat solved the problem by telling me that he had two big dogs in a cage down below, and if I didn't stay away from the railing he would put me in the cage with them. After that I stayed back and watched the boat's powerful searchlight as it probed the river banks, giving the pilot information about the location of the channel. Soon the *Paducah's* whistle was blowing for our landing.

Aunt Julia came out and gave me a big hug and warned Grandpappy again to take good care of me. I watched the willows brush along the side of the boat as the pilot maneuvered for a landing. Several feet of water covered the bank where we were to be put off, and the only dry place was a pile of crossties that had been hauled in and stacked before the river went out of her banks. The *Paducah* was tied up to a tree and began a series of whistles, a signal for someone to come and take off passengers. After a while a light was spotted coming across the backwater toward us and the gangplank was lowered and we walked out in the bright lights of the boat and stepped off on to the pile of ties. The *Paducah* lifted the gangplank and backed out into the river and went on her way up the Tennessee.

For the first time on the trip I was scared, although Grandpappy and Mr. Herndon were with me. It was dark and the water rustled as it hurried around the pile of crossties. The light on the rowboat came closer and a voice called out wanting to know who we were. Grandpappy recognized the voice as that of Mr. Cephas Barnes and told him who we were, and soon we were being rowed to dry land.

It was getting daylight by the time we reached Mr. Barnes' house and Mrs. Barnes cooked breakfast for us. The men seemed to show an unusual amount of interest in the two bottles that Grandpappy and Mr. Herndon had brought along and I suppose, to get me out of the house, Mr. Barnes told me there was a dog and several puppies out in the back yard. He suggested I might like to play with them and I was soon lost in a world of fun and puppy dogs. When we left, Mr. Barnes told me I could have one of the pups and Grandpappy said it was alright with him for me to take one. We headed up Bailey's Creek, across the White Hills, past the Boyd Pond and down a hollow to Owl Hollow, where I would spend the Summer. My puppy Ceef, named after Mr. Cephas Barnes, and me had a whole new world to discover.

Standing: Aunts Mavis, Tince and Gladys
Seated: Grandmammy, me and Grandpappy and my dog, Ikey.

Summer of 1918 in Owl Hollow

We were greeted by Grandmammy and three aunts, Gladys, Mavis and Tince. Tince's real name was Esther but nobody ever called her that. Another member of the family, Uncle Milford, was over in France helping to fight the Kaiser in World War I. Maybe I had gotten the idea that all the family was like Grandpappy, easy-going and gentle and was not prepared to deal with Grandmammy's burst of pretended anger. She could fly off the handle at some little thing and before you knew it, had forgotten all about whatever it was that made her all riled up. I soon learned that Grandmammy's bark was the extent of her anger and there was no bite at all. To be on the safe side, I found an opening under the house that was big enough for me, but too small for Grandmammy. Sometimes she would light into Grandpappy until it looked like she was ready to kill him then suddenly walk away and go about her business. He would just sit in his old chair, eyes half closed, smoking his pipe as if he was enjoying tongue-lashing.

My aunts felt they were too young for me to call them "Aunt" so I was told to call them by their first names only. Gladys was the oldest girl and was courting Willie Kennerly that summer. She was the motherly type and was always like a second mother to me. Mavis was the dresser of the family and spent hours looking at the fancy clothes pictured in the catalogs. She was at the awkward age, old enough to like the boys but too young to date them. Tince was only seven years older than me and was an expert at cutting out paper dolls, cooking mud pies and hiding from Grandmammy. We got along great that summer in Owl Hollow when I became *A Country Boy.*

If Grandpappy had been a person to hold a grudge, he probably would have had little to do with me. I told Grandmammy about him and Mr. Herndon drinking out of a bottle before we got home and that I was thirsty but they refused to give me a drink. Grandmammy was not an educated woman, but she sure could put two and two together and come up with four every time. She wanted to know if I had seen them hide the bottles before we got to the house and I assured her I had. We went out to a patch of sage grass across the hollow at the edge of a field. There was no bottle but there was the tell-tail evidence that something had been taken from there not too long before. Grandpappy had removed the bottle just in time, but he got a tongue-lashing anyway.

Because Tince and I were closer in age, she was closer to me than the others. She was the tomboy of the family, but she could also be the little girl any time it was to her advantage. We cut paper dolls from Sears & Roebuck or Montgomery Ward catalogs, played school, and we played house. Somehow I was always the pupil and she was the teacher when we played school. We cooked hoecakes, made mud pies and once we even fried a mouse. Our cooking stove was a piece of iron skillet resting on a couple of rocks. A fire was built underneath and she could make some of the best hoecakes I have ever had, although they were made without lard or salt. If Grandmammy had put them on her table I would probably have turned up my nose at them, but cooked by Tince outside, they were delicious.

Fresh meat was a scarce table item in Owl Hollow so one day when Grandmammy smelled meat cooking, she knew something was going on that required her immediate attention. I don't know just where she was when the tantalizing smell of fresh frying meat reached her nose, but it wasn't long before she was standing over us. Pointing a menacing finger, she explained in detail what nitwits we were and confiscated our main dish of fried mouse. Tince had been frying hoecakes when one of the cats sauntered by with a freshly killed dinner, headed for some quiet place to eat the animal in peace. Tince relieved the cat of its catch, skinned and cleaned the rodent, cut it up into little pieces and put it in the skillet. It smelled good and many times I have wondered what would have happened if Grandmammy had not had such a good smeller for fresh meat cooking.

Mavis did most all of the milking the cow and I went along with her most of the times. Another guest that went along every time was one of her cats, and as we stood nearby with our mouths wide open, Mavis squirted milk directly from the teat into our mouths. No doubt but that was the freshest milk I have ever drunk. She tried to teach me how to milk the cow but it was one of the many things I could not master. The cow wasn't too happy with my efforts either, so Mavis gave up the idea.

8

Tooth Brushes and Sassafras Tea

Several times during the spring and summer Grandmammy took me with her on forays in the woods and fields, looking for blackgum or sassafras for making toothbrushes or tea. She taught me how to choose just the right size of blackgum, about half the size of a pencil, cut to four or five inches long. After removing about half an inch of bark from the larger end, it was chewed until the fiber became a mop. When a soft mop was formed, Grandmammy dipped it in snuff and placed it in her cheek. It was my job to do the chewing because her teeth were not as solid as they once were. Most of the women either dipped snuff, chewed tobacco or sometimes smoked a pipe. At one time or another Grandmammy used tobacco in all three forms. The men usually chewed, smoked a pipe or rolled their own cigarettes from-home grown or store-bought tobacco. If money was scarce, home-grown tobacco was rolled in pieces of the thin sheets from a Sears catalog. When looking for sassafras for making tea, Grandmammy somehow knew which bushes had red roots. These were dug and the bark stripped from the root, boiled in water until the liquid was an amber color. When sweetened, it was not only delicious to drink, but many believed it to be a good Spring tonic that thinned the blood.

Grandmammy was a clean housekeeper and when the floor needed a good scrubbing she used sand to do the job. Her source of sand is still sort of a mystery because it was so unusual. She and I went out in the hills near where the Morgans lived, to a big sandstone rock that protruded a few feet out of the ground. Local people called it the "meteor" because it appeared to have fallen there and splattered over the ground. There was not another rock like it anywhere in the area. Grandmammy brought a small hammer along with her and she pecked on the rock until the hard crust broke, and underneath was pure clean sand that she used for cleaning her floors. I suppose the sand rock is still there, waiting for someone to explain how it got there.

Ceef and Buck

Ceef, my young puppy and I did a lot of exploring together, but we were limited as to how far away from the house we could go. We were told to stay within a distance that we could hear the rooster crowing, but when Grandpappy would go with us, there was no limit. Sometimes we went as far as the Boyd Pond, Humphries Field, the Love Place or Summers Spring. Each of these places would become a landmark for me in later years when these hills became my second home. On one of our trips we found the fresh carcass of a ewe that was being devoured by buzzards, and nearby was her lamb that was two or three days old. Grandpappy said the ewe had died from the birth of her lamb because if she had been killed by dogs they would have killed the lamb also. We took the lamb home and somebody gave him the name Buck and soon he was a regular member of the family. Grandmammy fussed at Grandpappy, accusing him of bringing home everything that was not tied down or penned up. He just looked at me, puffed on his pipe and grinned. Of course it was Grandmammy who rigged up a bottle and took on full responsibility of feeding Buck. She would never admit there was a soft spot in her heart. Said she wanted Buck to grow big enough so she could shear him and use the wool for making socks. She also said that he would make some fresh mutton, but we knew she could never butcher Buck.

Ceef and Buck spent a lot of time playing a game that was their version of follow the leader. Buck would go up on the back porch, walk to the edge next to the garden, bow his back and leap high into the air, landing several feet out in the yard. Ceef would follow, except that he didn't stop to bow his back. Sometimes Ceef chased some imaginary prey and Buck would chase Ceef until they were both exhausted. Once when the three of us were up on the hill above the tobacco barn, a rabbit jumped from his nest and headed down the hill toward the road. It was Ceef's nature to chase anything that ran away from him so he took out after the rabbit, and Buck took out after Ceef. Some fellow from over around Tharpe was walking down the road and had maybe had been hitting the bottle pretty hard, and when he saw a rabbit being chased by a dog and a sheep, he decided to go back to where things were more normal. He told about seeing a sheep chasing a dog and a rabbit and they said he laid off booze for several months.

It seemed there was almost always company in Owl Hollow. There were relatives scattered all over the hills, and most of them lived just far enough away to have to spend the night, and were always welcomed. To live as far away as Tharpe, Byrd's or Bailey's Creeks meant walking several miles through the hills and following old tie roads or animal trails. News from other communities was interesting, and the only way it could travel was by foot and word of mouth. There was the U.S. mail, but all too often one person could not write, and if they could, the receiver might not be able to read. Once Grandmammy got a letter from some relative who had moved to Kentucky and they said they were running a cafe. Grandmammy was puzzled and wondered why anyone would go all the way to Kentucky just to chase a calf.

Grandpappy, the Dentist

Grandpappy owned the only dentist's forceps closer than Dover, and if anyone needed to have a tooth pulled, and was unable to go to a dentist, he pulled it for them. This happened before my time but I have heard some stories that would tend to make one keep his toothache to himself. It was said that some of the victims whetted their nerves with an ample supply of whiskey and there were even times when Grandmammy tolerated the drinking. It was considered better than hearing the screams of the sober patients. I have seen the forceps, but nobody ever wanted to talk much about them or Grandpappy's dental episodes.

Because there were three pretty girls, two of them were either at the courting stage or getting near it, there were boys of all sizes and shapes visiting in Owl Hollow. Gladys and Bill Kennerly were getting serious and Grandmammy was not too happy about it. Somebody had told her that there were some Kennerlys that lived above Fort Henry that were pretty rough at times if they were drinking, and all Kennerlys were no good as far as she was concerned. Bill was not one of the bunch that got rough at times but he did have the same name. Their courting place was out by the cistern which just happened to be my favorite playing place until Bill would slip me an orange, apple or once a nickel to go find another favorite playing spot. One day Bill gave me the biggest orange I had ever seen and I went inside to show it to Grandmammy. She suggested that it was probably full of whiskey. That upset me and I went back and asked Bill if there was whiskey in the orange and that didn't set too well with Gladys and she suggested that Grandmammy keep her opinion to herself. Bill didn't mind though, for he had a great sense of humor.

The Pack Peddler

One visitor that I enjoyed most of all was, I believe, a pack peddler, who had a wooden leg. He had lots of interesting stories to tell and I spent every minute I could listening to them. They were about all the strange places he had been and the sights he had seen. Either he had done a lot of traveling or had a great imagination, and either way, he was my hero. Pack peddlers carried an assortment of pots and trinkets for sale, stopping at each farm house to show their wares. They also brought news of the outside world and were often the only source of news farther away than Dover. Wherever darkness caught up with them, they would spend the night and were always welcomed in Owl Hollow.

Most of the stories he told have long been forgotten, but some of them remain clear as the day he told them. One in particular, about a trip through the jungles of South America, has stayed with me because I was so intrigued that there was a feeling that I went along on the trip. One day while they were hacking their way through the jungle, someone spotted a huge boa constrictor that must have been over 40 feet long. My friend decided to kill the big snake, but the native guides begged him to leave it alone because if he killed the animal, its mate would follow them and kill one of them for revenge. He laughed at their superstition and went ahead and shot the snake. As predicted, next morning one of the natives was found dead, squeezed to death while he slept, by a big snake.

My hero's peg leg was a sensitive subject and he did not want to discuss it. Occasionally when someone innocently asked him how he had lost the leg he would answer by asking them a question. If he would tell them, would they promise never to mention the subject again, and of course the person promised. Then my friend would tell them that it was "bitten off", making the mystery even deeper.

Uncle Milford Comes Home

Sometime during the Summer of 1918 Uncle Milford was seen coming down the hill from toward the old Greenup Place. It was the most excitement I had seen in Owl Hollow as everyone rushed up the hill to meet him. In his uniform he was the most handsome man I had ever seen, and I was awed by all the brass buttons that decorated it. He had gotten a ride with the Dover-to-Model mailcarrier and then walked through the hills from Brandon Springs. Uncle Milford had visited with us in Paducah and had given me a lot of attention while he was there. At that time I was his only nephew and was probably spoiled by him.

The two of us slept in the loft which could only be reached by climbing a wall ladder. He was so strong that he would tuck me under an arm, and carry me up the ladder as easily as if I were a kitten. Mornings we would scuffle before getting out of bed and he was careful not to hurt me, but one morning something went wrong and I got a bloody nose. Tucking me under an arm, he rushed down the ladder and out into the yard. Holding me in a horizontal position I watched the drops of blood as they fell to the ground, and tried to be brave about it because I didn't want Uncle Milford to see me cry.

While he was home, friends and relatives came from miles around to see him and visit awhile. The many stories about Uncle Milford, Papa, Ira and Tot Lyon, Wheeler Love and others were repeated over and over. One of my favorites was about the time Uncle Milford got up one morning complaining about being tired. Said he dreamed that he had worked all night at Bill Biggs' sawmill where all of them were working at the time. On the way to work that morning they found barefoot tracks in the dust going to and from the mill. When they arrived at the sawmill there was a head of steam in the boiler, and Papa always believed that Uncle Milford went to the mill while sleeping and fired up the boiler.

On the day he had to leave for the journey back to France and the fighting, Uncle Milford told Grandmammy that he had a feeling that he would not come back alive. On October 12, 1918, one month before the war was over, he was killed in action. He was posthumously awarded the Distinguished Service Cross for bravery beyond the call of duty. He is buried in the National Cemetery at Dover, Tennessee.

13

Fourth of July At Tharpe

The biggest event of the Summer of 1918 was going to the annual Fourth of July picnic at Tharpe on the Cumberland River side of the divide. It was one of the two occasions during the year when Grandpappy could be persuaded to hitch Blanch and Mike to the wagon for an all day trip. Those two animals were the most mismatched critters I have ever seen, Blanch being a frisky mare and Mike the most stubborn mule that ever lived. He was always willing to let Blanch pull more than her share of a load. The wagon was old and creaky and Grandmammy always predicted that it would never make the trip without breaking down.

Heading out through the hills, following old tie roads that were often grown over with small saplings and blackberry briers, we joined the road that ran between Tharpe and Fort Henry. We passed the Morgans and I remember Grandmammy saying that they were the only family she knew that were poorer than we were. There were children playing out in the yard, their clothes were ragged and I wondered if they had anything to eat. From the Morgan's place we followed the road down a long hollow until we came to Claude Wilkerson's store, one of the two stores in Tharpe. The other, much larger, was owned by W. D. Sykes who also operated a flour and grist mill and a blacksmith shop, in addition to the general store. Tharpe also had a doctor and a post office.

Grandpappy parked the wagon near a creek that had clear water in it. Blanch and Mike were led down for a drink and then tied to the wagon. The wagon would act as a meeting place while the members of the family did whatever they were supposed to do. Gladys helped Grandmammy and they shopped for necessary things like pots, pans, dress materials, thread, snuff and goodies like sugar, salt, lard and coffee. Mavis, the dresser of the family, looked over the fashions of the day and bought a pretty hat to wear on Sundays. Tince divided her time with everybody because she was just as interested in plow lines and singletrees as she was in dresses and the other frilly stuff. I was more interested in the creek with running water than any of the other things, and spent most of my time wading and looking for frogs, or watching the minnows in the creek and was elated when I found a duck egg. I took my prized egg to the wagon and put in a safe place so it wouldn't be broken.

14

The afternoon sun was still high when we started back to Owl Hollow. I sat up front with Grandpappy because he would let me hold the lines to Blanch and Mike. Grandmammy and my aunts sat in the back where straw had been laid to make riding in a bumpy wagon more comfortable. There was a lot of talk going on about things they had bought. Suddenly my aunts started laughing so loud that I could hardly hear Grandmammy's fussing and looking back I saw egg yolk running down her face and knew there was trouble brewing and I was smack dab in the middle of it. When I was looking for a safe place to hide the duck egg, Grandmammy's parasol was the ideal place but I forgot to tell her about it. When Grandmammy wanted some protection from the hot sun, she had opened the parasol and the egg fell out on her head and broke. By the time we got home she had begun to see the funny side of the ordeal and I didn't even have to go under the house for protection.

Soured New Orleans Molasses

Grandpappy was not one to turn down a bargain, and when Claude Wilkerson offered him a ten gallon keg of soured New Orleans molasses for fifty cents, he took it. Because of the war, sugar had gone from six cents a pound to as much as thirty-five cents and was a scarce item in the house. With almost ten gallons of molasses, we had them on hot biscuits, in coffee, pies or anything that needed to be sweetened. Grandmammy even showed off and gave some to the neighbors.

It takes a long time to use ten gallons of molasses and Grandmammy didn't know that soured and fermented meant about the same thing. Given time, fermented meant they were ready to make into rum and rum meant an alcohol drink that had strange effects on people, especially a five-year-old boy if he got into the molasses and ate a lot of them. Grandmammy was proud of me when I climbed up on the fence and started singing songs I had heard at church, but when I fell off and started laughing and wouldn't stop, she began to worry that maybe I had fallen on my head. After a while she became suspicious that I was drunk, and maybe had found a bottle that somebody had failed to empty, and that I had done the job for them. It was sometime later when she learned about the molasses, and from then on she doled them out by the spoonful for coffee, or to put on hot biscuits.

Tharpe Picnic Tales

Many stories have been told about events that were supposed to have happened at the Tharpe Fourth of July picnic, but most of them were before my time, and I cannot say if they were true, partly true or out-right made-up lies. It is sometimes difficult to determine where truth ends and speculation begins. Without today's modern communication systems people made up their own stories, and they were experts at doing it. Likely some local person's name was attached to the tale and it fit perfectly. One story that I heard was about a local man and a telephone.

Most of the people of the area had never seen a telephone until one Fourth of July the two stores installed a phone at each place, and stretched a wire between them. It was a popular attraction and soon people were lined up at each store, waiting for an opportunity to talk on the gadget. They were eager to hear a voice coming over a distance through what looked like a piece of bailing wire. Sam Lancaster refused to try the thing, insisting nobody was going to make a fool out of him, and stuck to his guns until the usual Fourth of July thunderstorm drove him and every-body else inside the stores. Once inside, pressure was put on Sam until he gave in and agreed to try if he could talk to his wife, Wrett, because he knew she was at the other store and couldn't fool him. After some conversation back and forth, his wife Wrett was on the line and the phone was handed to Sam. He awkwardly placed the receiver against his ear and getting as close to the mouthpiece as he could, yelled "Hello". At that instant lightning struck the line somewhere between the stores, knocking Sam several feet out on the floor. They said that Sam raised up on one elbow and smiling, told the crowd "By god that was her, alright"!

Another story involving the name of a local person concerned a new repeating shotgun. A popular event at the picnic was a clay-pigeon shoot where men, who considered themselves experts at shooting, would bring their best shoot'n irons to show off their skills. This fellow had a new repeating shotgun, the first one in the area, and it was the envy of every-one. He was an expert marksman and considered a shoo-in to win the contest. When his turn came, he walked to his post and was encouraged by a number of ladies present to cheer-on their favorite contestant. He was struck suddenly by a severe pain in the lower part of his body, the

16

result of a can of pork and beans he had eaten for dinner. There was no way of letting the gas escape without a noise that would be very embarrassing, but some quick-thinking made him feel secure. He would just hold tight until the gun fired and the noise of the gun would drown out his own impending explosion. It would have been a good idea if the gun had fired. It was said that he went out and sold the gun real cheap.

People were pretty much confined to within a few miles of their homes and the Fourth of July picnic was the only time they had a chance to visit, swap ideas and sometimes fight. A person could swap knives, guns, livestock and even tracts of land were transferred from one to another. If there was some difference of opinion between two boys who happened to be courting the same girl, it could be settled fair and square with a fist-fight in front of an audience. Sometimes money or other belongings were wagered on the outcome. It was said that Dr. Scarborough did a thriving business patching up fighters and selling pills to the people. The linament peddlers were there and claiming their product could cure any ailment that happened to be plagueing the population at the time. A photographer was always present to take pictures of families or sweethearts. The first picture ever made of me was on the Fourth of July, 1913, at Tharpe.

Dinner on the Ground

If there was such a thing as the social event of the year, it was the "Dinner on the ground" that was observed on the last Sunday of the annual revival, or "Meeting" as it was called. Grandmammy and my aunts worked all day Saturday and into the night cooking such delightful food as fried chicken, pies, cakes and all kinds of vegetables for the occasion. This was always in September when there were signs of Fall in the air and the crops were laid by. Early Sunday morning Grandpappy hitched Blanch and Mike to the wagon, all the goodies were loaded, and we headed down the hollow to Blue Spring Church of Christ.

After several songs, prayers and a sermon that lasted entirely too long, church was let out and a dash made to the wagons. After sitting and listening to a preacher carry on for what seemed to be an eternity and all the time the odor of fried chicken oozed from a dozen wagons, a boy's appetite has a tendency to overcome the preaching, but that was just one of the tortures a boy had to endure.   When the preacher finally unwound and slowed to a stop, it was one of the greatest moments in a youngster's life.   Several of the best bedsheets were spread on the ground and each family chose a place to display their finest dishes of food.   After a blessing of the food that lasted too long, the starving crowd was allowed to start eating.   Plates were piled high with chicken, ham, vegetables, and then later one could return for the cakes and pies.   A barrel of spring water was hauled in to quench the thirst for there was no coffee, tea or pop.   There was one fellow in the neighborhood that didn't take much interest in religion except when there was dinner on the ground.   He could eat more than two ordinary people and once it was said that he ate until he couldn't stand up, went and sat down and asked somebody to bring him another plate.

Bible, Food and Water

During the meeting and at all other services, Grandpappy sat in the amen corner, second row back and next to the wall, and I sat with him. One hot night during the meeting the preacher started telling about Moses leading the children of Israel through the wilderness and how they were hungry and God fed them manna.   I pictured manna as some sort of cookie and got real hungry, but there was nothing I could do about it and it passed away. Then he went on to describe how hot it was and water was scarce and that Moses struck a rock, causing cool water to gush forth. That did it!   I got so thirsty that I just had to have some water, and knowing there was a bucket of cool spring water just beyond the preacher, I went to quench my thirst.   Grandpappy was so absorbed in what the preacher was saying that he paid no attention to what I was doing, or that I was wearing his "specs".   His glasses were difficult to see through, so I flipped them up on my forehead the way he did.   I stood on the pulpit along side of the preacher, sipping water from the dipper, and looking out over the crowd and seeing things from a parson's point of view.   There was a ripple of giggles, but when I pulled the specs down on my nose and tried to look out over them, it turned into a roar of laughter.   Suddenly I realized the preacher had stopped his preaching and was staring down at me, and he wasn't smiling.   The next thing I knew he was marching me to where Grandpappy was sitting.

The annual meeting was a series of religious services held to bring in new members and bring back those who had back-slid. A preacher with a reputation of adding new members would be hired to conduct the services which lasted two weeks. There were two services each day, one at night and one in the afternoon for the women's bible study. As a rule the men were too busy to attend the daytime service and were working in the fields. At night I enjoyed the long walk to church, but by the time the service was over I was too sleepy to walk, and Grandpappy would put me on his shoulder, back of his head, with a leg dangling on either side of his neck. The sound of thousands of bugs and the rhythm of his walk soon put me to sleep and I would wake up next morning at home and in my bed.

Kittens get Baptized

At the end of the meeting there would be several to be baptized. Watching the preacher take people down into the creek and push them under the water fascinated me. I knew it was supposed to be a good thing, and one day when Grandmammy and Gladys were working in the garden I decided to do some good myself.   There was nearly always a litter of kittens around the house and at this time there were three about half grown, and I decided they should be baptized.   There was a washtub with water, sitting in the hallway and soon there were three wet and unhappy kittens trying to escape from being drowned. Grandmammy and Gladys came in from the garden just in time to bring back three animals into this world, and kept them from passing into wherever good kittens go when held under water too long.   Fortunately for me I was able to beat them to the hole where I went under the house to bide my time while two unhappy women cooled off.

The Hop Vine

Grandmammy loved to grow things and always grew lots of flowers and had a good vegetable garden. She had a favorite vine that grew around the cistern shed that kept it shaded from the hot summer sun. She had no idea what the vine was, or what its fruit was used for until one day she found a bucket of liquid in the hallway that seemed to be eternally boiling without fire under it. Sampling the concoction she found it to be rather pleasant to the taste and she wanted to know what it was, but nobody seemed to have the answer. Wheeler Love and Ira Lyon were spending a few days with us and when she questioned them they tried to evade answering and that made her suspicious. When she caught them trying to take the mixture away she demanded some answers, and they confessed they had mixed the liquid and with the aid of her hops, were making some brew. When she learned her vine was furnishing fruit for making an alcohol mixture, its fate was sealed and before another day was over, the vine was destroyed. Morning Glories replaced the hops vine from that time on.

Grandmammy Takes Me Visiting

Sometimes Grandmammy would get the urge to go visit one of the neighbors and often took me along. The Herndons, Bill and "Miss Della", owned the farm next to us and they had two tenant houses and a hand-dug well. One of the tenants was Alex Hosford whose wife, Catherine, was related to Grandpappy. There were seven Hosford children and one of them, Hazel, was about my age and I enjoyed playing with her. We smoked rabbit tobacco and played like grownups. Gertie, Kirby and Pauline would join us sometimes.

"Miss Della" Herndon was one of the sweetest and kindest ladies I have ever known, but for some reason known only to Grandmammy, I was told to never ask for anything to eat when visiting her. Bill Herndon was more interested in mules, tobacco, or other crops than he was in visiting. I remember that he had no teeth but could bite into an apple with his gums and chew anything he chose to eat. Once after visiting Miss Della, as we passed the Herndons' tobacco barn, I picked up a broken stick, straddled it and pretended it was my galloping steed.   When we reached the gate that separated the two farms, Grandmammy opened it for me, and I spurred my horse toward the opening.   Suddenly I was pawing the earth but was going nowhere.   Her hand was holding on to my collar and when I settled down, Grandmammy told me that the stick I was riding belonged to Mr. Herndon and to leave it on his farm.   She probably never heard of the word "psychology", but she sure knew how to use it.

The Nances lived on the next farm down the hollow from the Herndons, where Owl and Stilly Hollows came together.   Miss Emma Nance seemed to me to be grouchy and I was afraid of her, but Grandmammy would let me ask her for something to eat.   I soon learned to love and respect Miss Emma because she was the nice lady who gave me lots of goodies to eat.

Helping Grandmammy

Grandmammy had an old-fashion spinning wheel that attracted my attention right off because anything that moved was interesting.   The big wheel had to be powered by hand and she was an expert at turning the wheel with her left hand while holding a batt of cotton or wool in her right.   I begged her to let me turn the wheel and am sure she would rather have done the job herself.   A belt ran from the big wheel to a small spindle that turned at a high speed.   The batts were made by placing wool or cotton between two large wire brushes that were pulled against each other resulting in a piece of material about five inches wide, eight inches long and half an inch thick. The wire brushes combed the fiber until the strands were all in one direction.   Somehow Grandmammy started a bit of material from the batt to the spindle that resulted in a large thread.   The more times through the spindle, the smaller the thread.

Grandpappy and Grandmammy had no sheep, but that was no problem when the time came to harvest wool.   Livestock was permitted to run anywhere they chose, and instead of keeping them inside, they were fenced out of the fields where they could do damage.   There were always some stray sheep or other livestock on the farm, and Grandmammy was accused of sowing some timothy grass in spots near the house to attract them.   Wool or milk was yours when sheep or cows wandered onto your property for food.   Some said that she enticed the sheep into the yard where the grass was more plentiful, and the animal was sent on its way without its wool coat. Grandmammy planted a small patch of cotton, picked it and removed the seed and carded it into batts. The wool and cotton thread was used to knit socks, toboggans or mittens for the family.

Making Lye Soap

It was usually in the Spring when Grandmammy made lye soap, probably because there was more washing done in Summer than any other time of year   All winter the ashes from the two fireplaces and cook stove had been dumped into an ash hopper that stood near the garden gate.   The hopper was a V-shaped wooden container with one end slightly lower, so a liquid would flow to one end of the trough.   A rainproof top kept the ashes dry until she was ready to make the soap and hominy.   One day Grandmammy would pour buckets of water over the ashes, and sometime later a strong alkaline liquid dripped from the hopper. The liquid was collected and stored in a crock, and kept until she was ready to use it.

For a year Grandmammy had been saving grease that she considered unfit to eat but used for making soap. Every family had a big iron pot that would hold up to twenty gallons that was used to boil clothes, cook out lard and make soap.   The lye water was heated and the grease added and stirred until the liquid began to thicken. A portion was removed from the pot, and when cooled it was a thick liquid used for removing tobacco gum from the hands or overalls.   The rest was allowed to boil longer and when cooled, was a hard substance, and cut into bars for convenience. There were a few complaints that her liquid soap was capable of removing a layer of skin if the hand was exposed to it too long.   The alkaline solution was also used to make hominy. After soaking for an extended time the outer crust of corn was removed, or softened, leaving a tasty morsel to be served as a vegetable.

Quilting

Quilts were not something just to look pretty, they were necessary to keep you from freezing in Winter. There were quilting frames hanging from the ceiling of the main room and they usually held a quilt in some stage of completion.   The frame was made with four pieces of wood about one-by-four, and eight feet long.   Two pieces of the frame were smooth except for a one-eighth inch hole about six inches from each end. The other two pieces had holes of the same size every three or four inches apart.   As work on the quilt progressed, it was rolled up on the smooth frame, and a wooden peg pushed through the holes to hold it firmly in place.

The quilt top was made by sewing scrapes of cloth together in a pattern that was usually original.   The scraps were leftovers from material used for making dresses or bought from a rag man that came around once or twice a year.   Once somebody made a cover from discarded tobacco sacks that were collected from roll-your-own smokers. When a top was completed, a bottom made from bleached or unbleached muslin was attached with cotton batts placed between them.   The quilt was now ready to be "quilted".

Word went around that there was to be a quilting on a certain day and the neighborhood ladies came together for a day of work, play and gossip. The quilters brought a covered dish of their favorite recipe.   A stitching pattern was chosen and each lady tried to out-do the others by making neater stitches.   Often the quilt was finished in one day, depending on the quantity of food consumed or the amount of gossip available. After it was hemmed and all the edges were trimmed, another call went out to all the young women of marrying age to come for the initiation.   The young women held the quilt between them, stretching it tightly, and some disinterested person threw a cat in the middle.   The girl lucky enough to be closest to the terrified cat when he escaped to freedom, was sure to be the next to marry.   Maybe it didn't work every time, but the young ladies thought it worth the try.

Gladys and Willie Kennerly were doing some serious courting and Grandmammy helped in making quilts for her.   She was more or less in training to become a housewife in the near future, and a girl needed all the training she could get on how to feed a hungry man.   No mother wanted her daughter to be considered a failure in married life.   Gladys spent a lot of time in the garden where she learned the art of growing food for the table.

Mavis and Tince, being too young for married-life training, worked with Grandpappy in the field when needed.   They didn't want people to know they were still working in the fields and out in the sun, for that was a sure sign they were not being considered for marrying. Protective clothing was worn, including a big hat, to protect the face and neck and mittens to cover the hands. Black stockings covered the legs and after a summer of working out in the sun, they would be as white as if they had not been outside the house.

Cloud Watching

One of my favorite pastimes that Summer was watching clouds. A special place for this sport was a little knoll between the house and tobacco barn where there was a good view, and also it was out of Grandmammy's sight. The clouds seemed to follow a path across the hollow above the barn, and it was amazing how many familiar faces and objects one could see as the clouds played follow the leader across the sky. There were faces of pirates, people who were laughing, dogs of all sizes, cows, mules and lots of sheep with their white fluffy wool and a host of other things. One that I remember was a cloud that looked like a big steamboat, and reminded me of the *Paducah,* that I had ridden on when I came with Grandpappy to Owl Hollow.

There were no all-weather springs on Grandpappy's farm and the creeks were dry most of the time. Once he did show me where a spring used to be, but it had dried up. There was a little moisture at the spot, but the water had ceased to flow a long time before. When there was enough rain to cause the creeks to flow, I took advantage and waded as much as I could before they dried up again. I also built paddle wheels from the pith of dried corn stalks, and placed them so the running water powered them. A favorite spot was where the water rushed around a large moss-covered rock and many hours were spent there. The rock is still there, but doesn't look as big as it did many years ago.

Grandpappy Kills a Waterbird

One day Grandmammy started fussing at Grandpappy about not having fresh meat on the table. In his younger days, Grandmammy said he was always out in the woods killing some kind of wild game and now he rarely went hunting.   Grandpappy's gun had been a muzzle loader at one time and had been converted into a breach loader.   When that shotgun belched forth a load of shot through about 40 inches of barrel, anything that was in its sights died, either from wounds or sheer fright.   It was somewhere between a 10 and 12 gauge, too small for ten gauge shells and too large for twelve.   I don't know where the name originated, but the gun was called Zulu.   It was getting toward Fall when Grandpappy took Zulu and headed down the hollow.   Nobody knew where he was headed or what he had in mind.   Later that afternoon he returned carrying a big bluish-grey waterfowl that he had killed down on Panther Creek.

Grandmammy scalded the bird just like she would a chicken, plucked off the feathers and cleaned out the insides. She complained that the meat was too dark and that it also stank but she was always fussing about something so nobody paid any attention to her. When she started boiling the critter, we were all thankful the kitchen was separated from the main house by an open hallway.   Even Grandpappy admitted that the bird smelled bad and didn't think it would be "fittin" to eat.   When Grandmammy went in the kitchen and came out gagging, and about to puke, it was agreed the thing should be thrown out. She threw the stinking mess out in the corner of the yard hoping some animal would drag it away. She said the meat was tougher than when it was raw.   Ceef was curious and went almost up to the bird, but when he got a whiff of it, turned and went under the house.   Next morning there was no sign that the bird had been disturbed and someone took it way out in the woods and left it.   I believe that was the last time Grandmammy asked Grandpappy to go hunting for wild game.

Pet Terrapin

I have always loved animals, especially wild ones, and tried many times to make pets out of them.   During the summer of 1918 I had two dogs, a lamb, a host of cats and a terrapin. Somebody found the terrapin out in the woods, and because it was misshapen, brought it home. Either through a freak of nature or an accident in his younger life, the terrapin's shell was cocked to one side.   Of course I kept playing with him until he started to eat tomatoes from my hand and soon everyone was feeding the reptile. The name "Whomperside" was suggested and it stuck. The terrapin became a member of the family and was even accepted by the other animals. Hot days he would make his way into Grandmammy's kitchen and bury himself in the fireplace ashes where it was cool and away from Ceef and the other pets that might want to tease him.

When Fall came, Whomperside returned to the wild, and we were certain that we would never see him again. One warm day the next Spring one of my aunts was walking from the stables to the house and spied the terrapin making his way toward the house so she picked him up and gave him a ride the rest of the way. Whomperside spent the Summer with us but each Fall returned to the woods to hibernate, and then show up next Spring. When the family moved to the river place in the Fall of 1920, they forgot to tell the new people about Whomperside, and when he showed up next Spring, and insisted on coming inside the kitchen, they killed him.

My Aunts Read and Sing

It was during the Summer of 1918 that I learned to love and appreciate books. Gladys would read stories to me that I had never heard before, and I became fascinated with so many wonderful places out in the

Aunt Mavis standing; Tince and Mama, with Ikey, Buck and Ceef

world that were waiting for me to visit one day. *Swiss Family Robinson* was my favorite, and as she read I became one of the family and was shipwrecked along with them. I helped them build every lean-to and helped rescue the animals from the sinking ship. I searched for wood and other items that might be brought from the ship to the island. I watched in horror as the big snake swallowed some of the animals we had worked so hard to save, and I hunted game for food. It was fun to be one of the Swiss Family.

Sometimes my aunts would sing songs, mostly of the West, including "Springtime in the Rockies" and another that had words that went "We'll build a little nest, somewhere in the West and let the rest of the world go by". They sang religious hymns that they had learned at church and were good at it. When there was company, it was not unusual for a group to sing for an hour or more.

If there was a staple food, it was Grandmammy's hot biscuits for breakfast and cornbread for dinner and supper. Lunch was an in-between snack and not the noon meal. To go with hot biscuits we had sorghum molasses, some form of fried pork or what was called thickening gravy made with flour, water and bacon grease. Grandpappy grew a small amount of wheat for making flour, but there was never enough to last the year. His farm was too rough for a wheat binder and even if the field had been level, a binder could never have made it on the roads up Owl Hollow. Grandpappy used a "cradle", a scythe with an attachment to catch the wheat stalks, and held them in an orderly way until they were tied into bundles. He hauled the wheat to a thrasher that came to the Boyd Farm and then took the grain to Tharpe to be ground into flour. Grandmammy said she was glad when the flour Grandpappy grew was used up so she could buy some that was white, but I think she was just fussing about it like she fussed about a lot of things.
.

Return to Paducah

In late September Papa and Mama came to visit a few days, and then take me back to Paducah with them. They had only been in Owl Hollow a short time when Papa received word from his draft board in that he was expected to report on a certain day in Paducah for his physical. There was not time enough to wait for the next packet going down river, and the only way he could be on time was to walk to Murray, Kentucky, and catch the train. Bill Herndon decided to join Papa, and they set out across the hills to Pine Bluff, where they would cross the Tennessee. It was getting dark by the time they reached the ferry and headed toward Murray.

For years Papa told the story about them walking along a road near Concord when they came upon a small creek that flowed across the road. Testing the water with their fingers, they were certain that it came from a nearby spring, because the water was cold and the weather was hot. They were both plenty thirsty and got down on their knees and began drinking from the stream. Just as Bill got a big mouthful of water, some geese started to complain about being disturbed, and they were in the creek just above where they were drinking. Knowing how dirty geese can be, Papa said Bill spurted water all over the road and some went all the way to the other side. They continued on their trip, hot and thirsty, but the next drink of water was when they reached the train station in Murray. Papa made it to Paducah and the draft board on time, but was rejected because of a heart murmur. Everyone thought the war would soon be over, anyway.

A few days later Mama, Tince, and I started on the return trip to Paducah. Grandpappy went with us to the river, and taking somebody's boat, ferried us around the foot of Panther Creek Island, and put us out near where his brother, John Lyon lived. He went back across the river and we walked the short distance to Uncle John's house. We were to wait there until a boat came down the river to take us on down to Paducah.

Because of my love for animals I was intrigued by a big gander that I soon discovered was not playful like a dog but seemed to enjoy taking bites out of my behind. We spent the night while members of the family took turns keeping an open ear for the sound of a boat whistle somewhere up the river. It was late the next afternoon before a packet came down, and there was a rush to get to the landing. By the time we went on board a fog was settling in, and soon had gotten so bad that the captain decided to remain tied up until morning. There was a band on board and soon the packet was using her whistle to let people know she was staying overnight at the landing. Everyone knew there was entertainment and shortly people began to arrive. I recall that there was music and dancing and food for everybody and that all were having a good time. I was put to bed early and next morning we went on down river to Paducah.

Rivers Freeze Over

We had made a trip to Blue Spring in January, 1918, but much of the trip escapes my memory. The winter of 1917-18 is still remembered as one of the worst on record. With almost two feet of snow and ice on the ground and the rivers frozen over so thickly that teams and wagons were driven across, transportation was at a standstill. River packets, including the *Paducah,* were encased in ice alongside the wharf.

Somehow a message reached us that Mama's father, Grandpa Barbee, was in critical condition and was not expected to live. While taking the harness off a mule he had been using to drag wood to the house, the weight of the snow and ice on the roof caved it in and trapped him. According to a witness, Charlie Reeder, the mule escaped when he heard the timbers giving way to the load. Somehow Charlie pulled Grampa from beneath the shed, but Charlie was unable to get out of bed for two weeks. It was said that he lifted the shed while Grandpa crawled out, a feat that seemed impossible.

Papa made arrangements for us to go to Blue Spring by way of train, mail boat, and open shay. Because the train for Paris, Tennessee left early, we spent the night in a hotel near the train station. The only thing I recall about the hotel was that we had pork and beans as a vegetable for supper and I insisted, and got them for breakfast next morning. Both Papa and Mama were embarrassed because of my love of the vegetable.

We went by train to Paris and changed to a L&N train from Paris to Cumberland City, a small town on the Cumberland River a few miles above Dover. The ice on the Cumberland had started to break up, and I remember standing on the porch of the hotel, a two story building overlooking the river. Next morning we boarded the mail boat to Dover. It was the first trip the boat had made since the freeze-up a month before. Grandpappy Lyon was waiting for us at Dover, driving an open shay.

Grandpa Barbee died shortly after we arrived, and all that I recall was the day he was buried. Papa and Mama thought I was too young to understand the funeral, and I stayed at a house near the Crook Graveyard. I remember standing on the front porch of the house and watching the procession go up the steep hill with the coffin. I knew it was Grandpa Barbee, and that I would never see him again and I was very sad.

Life in Paducah

Although most of my early memories are about living in Owl Hollow, there are many pleasant ones of when we lived on Guthrie Avenue in Paducah. The house is still there, but many improvements have been made since we moved from there in the Spring of 1919. Our water supply was a hydrant in the back yard. An outhouse was located at the back of the lot next to the coal shed, and our lighting was furnished by a single bulb hanging from the ceiling of each room. Heating and cooking were done with coal-burning stoves. The Gillums lived across the street from us and my favorite friend was "Uncle" Tip Gillum, a policeman, who was a big man and carried a big pistol on his side. They had a daughter, Margaret, who was about my age, and we played together in an old barn in back of their house. Mrs. Gillum was popular among the children because she was always giving us homemade candy. Later the family started the Gillum Candy Company.

Guthrie Avenue was not paved, but there was no traffic to stir up the dust except the streetcar that ran down the middle of the street, and an occasional wagon or buggy. Phelps' grocery was located at the end of Guthrie Avenue, and Mama would send me there with a list of items that were charged. She gave me a penny to spend for candy, and that was the best part of the trip. I liked to walk the streetcar tracks, and one day when Mama saw me walking them she warned me not to walk them again. Memory has a tendency to be short when you are young, and soon she caught me on the tracks again. She yelled at me loud enough for the entire neighborhood to hear, that I was going to get a whipping when I got home. Knowing that Mama never failed to keep a promise, that was one of the longest trips I have ever made.

Papa and Mama were good at keeping me supplied with playthings that would keep me entertained. I had a scooter and tricycle that I was allowed to ride on the sidewalk as long as I didn't cross a street. Not that the traffic was dangerous, but rather an invisible boundary to keep me in sight of the house. I don't recall ever seeing a car or truck passing our house. Going toward town I could go as far as a big persimmon tree on the edge of a pasture where people tied out their cows to graze. I also had

30

jacks, a game of skill, a 22-caliber pistol that shot real blank shells, and a small cannon that could send a projectile 30 or 40 feet by the use of ignited carbide. It was one toy my parents regretted giving me because it was as loud as a shotgun, and Papa and Mama never got use to the noise.

Papa Buys A Graph-O-Phone

Soon after we moved to Guthrie Avenue Papa bought one of the new-fangled talking machines called a Graph-O-Phone. It was one of the newer machines that played a 78rpm record instead of the old hollow disk type. It must have been a RCA, because I recall the little dog sitting with his head cocked and listening to "His Master's Voice" pictured on the speaker. The speaker was a big horn-like thing that caused me to wonder what was inside that made it talk, sing and make music. The unit holding the turntable had a spring inside that had to be wound each time a record was played. It used throw-away needles nearly an inch long that had to be replaced every two to four records. They came in packages of 100 for about twenty-five cents. I was only four when Papa bought it, and was warned to keep my hands off the thing, and it was a difficult order to obey. Anything that turned, moved or made a noise was fascinating and I wanted to know what made it work. It was many years before I found out.

Papa and Mama must have liked marches and comedy because we had lots of Sousa and Uncle Josh records. We also had Negro Spirituals and Uncle Milford had bought an extra large record of "Maggie", his favorite song. Uncle Josh was a favorite of mine, and I would ask for his records to be played every chance I got. He was very country and always running up against things that baffled him in the city. He went to New York and all the sights were foreign to him. He saw bananas for the first time and thought they were big butterbeans, and wondered where the land was rich enough to grow them so large. When he registered at the hotel, the clerk asked if he wanted an inside or outside room, and Uncle Josh told him he would take the inside room because it was a little chilly outside. When asked if he wanted a room with a bath, he became indignant and said he would take his own bath if they didn't mind. Some of the songs were "Are You From Dixie?", "Alabama Bound", "When You Wore A

31

Tulip", "Swing Low Sweet Chariot", "Nobody Knows the Trouble I've Seen" and several instrumentals.

Papa was a motorman on the Guthrie Avenue streetcar when we first moved to Paducah, and sometimes on his last run would take me with him to the car barn. There was a huge man that often sat out in front of the car barn and he was about the ugliest man I have ever seen but was kind and gentle. He would put me on his knees and start talking about ice cream until my mouth was watering then take me to a nearby store and buy me an ice cream cone. I didn't know his name at the time, but Papa told me later that he was Irvin S. Cobb, the famous writer. Papa said that he would hang around the car barn looking for stories to write about the everyday working man.

Papa and Guthrie Avenue Streetcar -- about 1915

Back of our house, and just across a street was a big gravel pit that was full of water and must have been the favorite swimming hole for a lot of people in Paducah. Mama would let me go there and watch the people swim or dive off the high bank. It was fun tossing pebbles into the water, and watching the little ringlets of waves spread into the lake.

Another special memory was a man that would come down the street pushing a cart and yelling "Hot Tamales". Papa would give me a quarter and send me out to buy three of the tasty morsels. I have never lost my taste for the Mexican delicacy, but have never found one that tasted as good as those tamales that were wrapped in real corn shucks. I'm sure that a person's taste buds change to some extent, but am equally sure that cooking methods have change also.

During the winter of 1917 or 1918 I saw my first airplane that landed in a field near Guthrie Avenue. I don't recall whether or not it was a forced landing, but do remember it was awfully cold when Papa and Mama and I went to see it. There was a big crowd to see the contraption and Papa said he believed most of Paducah came out to see the airplane. He said they all came back to watch it take off a few days later.

Mama had a special friend who was black and she lived somewhere in back of the Gillums. I was never to call anyone by their first name if they were older grownups, and that included blacks. I was told to call her "aunt" so-and-so. Her name has long slipped away from my memory but a lesson she taught me has lingered. One day when she came to visit Mama I was playing in the front yard, and she asked me where my mother was, and knowing she was in the back yard I yelled out "Mama, there is a Nigger here to see you". That was the last time I ever called a black person a Nigger. Mama was going to give me a spanking for using the word, but the black lady suggested she be allowed to do the job and Mama agreed. She then asked Mama if she could use Papa's razor strop, and when she got it, started slapping the piece of leather against her hand and making a noise that scared the heck out of me. I ran to Mama for protection from certain mutilation, but she handed me back to the black lady like a lamb to be sacrificed on an altar. After a few more slaps on her hand she put me over her knees and gently slapped my behind, and told me to never call her Nigger again. Later I learned to love her and we became great friends.

Early on the morning of November 11, 1918, I was awakened by the loudest noise I had ever heard. The quietness of Owl Hollow had tuned my ears to the stillness, except for the hoot of an owl, the whistle of a rabbit, or some other sounds of nature. All at once it seemed that every siren in Paducah had joined every whistle of the boats and trains, and I was scared half to death. I was sure that the world was coming to an end. The war was over, and was being celebrated by any way that a loud noise could be made.

Back to Owl Hollow

I can't remember just when the message arrived that Uncle Milford had been killed in France, but it was to change the lives of a lot of people, including us. Papa was the only son left and he felt it was his duty to return to Owl Hollow to be near his parents. After working for the street car company he had gone to work for the Illinois Central Railroad as a carpenter and was happy with his job. Even though he disliked farming, his loyalty was to his parents and that was his first concern.

Sometime in the early Spring of 1919 Papa quit his job with the railroad and moved back to Owl Hollow, taking our belongings on the packet *Paducah.* We were met at Boswell Landing by two wagons, one driven by Grandpappy and the other one by Bill Herndon, Grandpappy's neighbor. Our furniture was loaded and Bill and his team were out of sight before Grandpappy and Blanch and Mike could get started. Bill had gotten home, unloaded his wagon and was back to his house by the time we got to the Herndon farm.

Grandmammy and my aunts were glad to see us even though we would be living with them for awhile. The house was an original of the area and consisted of two large log rooms with an open space between them. One of the rooms had a loft, a lean-to, and back porch and served as the living and sleeping area. The other was the kitchen and the space between them was to protect each room in the event there was a fire. When the house was built, the loss of all the house by fire could cause considerable trouble, especially in Winter.

I was too young to understand how the extra furniture and eight people could be crowded into the space, but somehow we did. The main room had two beds where Grandpappy, Grandmammy and two of my aunts slept, and I slept in the loft where Uncle Milford and I had slept together last Summer. Papa and Mama slept in the lean-to. Gladys and Bill Kennerly had gotten married and were living away off in some town called McEwen

Chewing Tobacco

Most memories of that first year of Papa's farming are about my first year of school. However, there was one incident that is not likely to ever escape from me, and it too was a first, my first chew of tobacco. Sometimes Papa would take me with him to the field, especially if he was "boating" with a wooden contraption that had a slanted front like a jon boat, but was used to burst clods instead of waves. It was the only piece of field equipment Grandpappy owned that could be ridden, and was pulled by Blanch and Mike. Once while I was riding with Papa, and feeling like a grownup behind that team, Papa took a plug of tobacco out of his pocket and cut off a chew. I asked for a chew, and without a word he obliged by cutting off another piece for me. I put the tobacco in my mouth, and right away was ready to spit the awful-tasting stuff out, but held on because I didn't want Papa to think I was too young to handle it. When we reached the edge of the field Papa said he thought he heard Grandmammy calling me, and that I should go home and see what she wanted. He knew the right size chew to give me for if it had been any bigger I would have never made it to the house. Any desire I might have had to grow up as a tobacco chewer ended right there. Many years later I reminded Papa of the incident and told him he had missed his calling as an engineer because if that chew had been larger I would not have made it.

The Summer of 1919 was not much different from that of 1918 except that Mama and Papa were there, Ceef had grown to be a big dog and Buck and died from unknown causes. I would start to school in August, but that was a long way off so Ceef and I spent a lot of time exploring again, the woods around Grandpappy's place. Three days a week someone went to the mail box about two miles down the hollow and we often went along. Arb Rutland was the mail carrier who brought the mail from the Fort Henry Post Office, and usually came by our box in the early afternoon. I remember him riding what I thought was the prettiest horse in the world. Meeting the mail carrier was an event everyone looked forward to because getting mail from anybody was welcomed.

Mama and my aunts often helped out in the field and I went along for no special reason except to be where the others were. While they were busy suckering tobacco one day, I entertained myself by tossing my straw hat high into the branches of a tree, and tried to catch it as it worked its way down through the limbs. Once while looking up and following the hat, my foot came down on something too soft to be a rock or piece of wood. Looking down I saw that my foot was on a copperhead snake, and even a six-year-old boy doesn't have to wait to be told to move to safer ground in this situation. It is amazing how fast one can move from one place to another when he is standing on a copperhead. I yelled that I had stepped on a snake, and everyone came running and started looking for the culprit. It was nowhere to be found and someone decided it must have crawled into a nearby pile of rocks, and started removing them one by one. They found the copperhead and killed it. It remained a puzzle as to why I was not bitten but I guess a guardian angel protects little boys, and mine must have been kept kinda busy.

First Year At School

Papa and Mama had been preparing me for school even before we moved from Paducah. They spent a lot of time teaching me the ABCs, and I was up to the fifth multiplication table and could read simple stories. The letter "D" gave me more problems than all the rest, and Papa solved the problem by telling me to just remember Dee Bishop, a fellow he knew. My school equipment included a slate, slate pencil, a primer that had belonged to Tince, and a lard bucket to carry my lunch in. Miss Betty Crutcher was the teacher of the one-room school and I sat with her younger brother Jim, that first year.

Papa and Mama had promised that if the teacher gave me a whipping at school they would give me another one when I got home. They could be depended on to keep a promise, and the fear of getting a whipping subdued any desire I might have had to get into trouble. As time went on, I became braver, and before I knew it was in trouble. Jim and I thought it was real funny when I cut a hole in Layton Rowlett's hat to give it some ventilation, but Miss Betty was either in a bad mood or had no sense of humor that day, and I got lashed with a hickory switch. Dreading the thrashing that Papa and Mama had promised when I got home, I found more things than usual on the way home that needed my immediate attention, and it was getting dark when I got to the house. I never knew, even until now, why they did not give me the punishment as promised, and had no desire to bring up the subject. I hoped they would forgive and forget and I like to think they did.

When school started in August, it had opened another world for me. There were more than two miles of road to walk through woods, crossing creeks, following creek beds and around the edges of fields before reaching Blue Spring School. I had been over the road many times going to and from church, but was restricted as to activities because of my Sunday clothes. With everyday school clothes on I could get down on my knees to get a closer look at a bug or rock, and being barefooted could wade in the ponds or creeks looking for frogs or tadpoles. I was like taking the bridle off a mule and sending it out in the pasture. Mavis and Tince were still going to school, and there were lots of other kids to join us along the way so my aunts paid little attention to me. Then too, they may have been embarrassed that they were in school with a nephew.

Miss Betty Gets Married

While school was in session one day Mr. Sid Callicott came by, and Miss Betty went out to talk to him. He was driving a car which meant he was rich, and it was said he also owned a big farm over in Henry County where the land was level, and that you couldn't find a rock anywhere on his place. Miss Betty gave us orders to be quite and stay in our seats, but that was too much to ask of a room full of kids who hardly ever got a chance to look at a car. We knew that they had been courting for a long time and thought nothing of another visit. Miss Betty stayed longer than she usually did and when she came back into the room, she told us we could all go home and that she and Mr. Callicott were going off somewhere and get married. It was a week or more before we got another teacher and we could go back to school.

Grandpappy's Pipe

Satan himself must have been walking right beside me one morning as I left the house to go to school. Laying on the gate post in plain view was one of Grandpappy's used pipes just waiting to be taken to school and disaster. I slipped the smelly pipe into my pocket, and all that was needed now was some tobacco. Mr. Herndon's barn was on the way to school and was full of fresh cured dark-fired tobacco, the strongest type grown, and I put a good supply in my pocket.

No boy can keep such a thing secret for long and soon nearly every boy in school wanted to borrow my pipe and tobacco. I let Kennedy Mathis carry them in exchange for a big red apple he had brought for lunch. Awhile after dinner recess, Kennedy held up his hand, a signal to the teacher that nature was calling for him to go up into the woods for awhile. She nodded her approval and he went out the door. This sort of trip ordinarily took ten or fifteen minutes, and after half an hour had passed, the teacher asked Claudy Rushing to go check on him. Another half-hour went by and the teacher, (I can't recall her name), became concerned and sent Raymond Mathis out to find them and report back to her. Raymond did come back, but the boys were not with him. He said both boys were very sick and had to go home. Said they had done a lot of puking and were white as a sheet, but they should be alright by next morning. There were rumors among the girls that some monster was lurking outside, and they were afraid to leave the room.

The area where the boys had vanished was off limits to the girls and the teacher, and she had to rely on what was told her. I had an idea that my pipe and tobacco were involved and could see myself being beaten up with something like a two-by-four. Raymond told us boys that he found the two boys lying on the ground, wallowing, moaning and vomiting, and that they were two of the sickest boys he had ever seen. Seems Kennedy had tried to smoke Grandpappy's pipe and became very sick. The boy that was sent to fetch him wanted to prove he could handle it and also got very sick. Both of them went home but were back at school the next day. I doubt that either of them ever had a desire to smoke a pipe again.

Stick and Dirt Chimney

In winter Grandpappy's house could get very cold as the winter winds found their way inside through cracks in the walls. A fireplace in the main room, like most fireplaces, could keep you warm on one side while the other side about froze. There was also one in the kitchen where Grandmammy spent much of her time, and a lot of her cooking was done over the fire in the fireplace. The first chimneys were made with sticks of wood and clay because limestone rock, that was suitable for building chimneys was too far away. Brick cost too much, and had to be substituted with the sticks and dirt, the most handy material at the time. The wood in the chimney was covered with a thick layer of clay mud, and when it dried protected the sticks from the fire. When it was extremely cold, and a hot fire was necessary, sometimes the clay crumbled off exposing the wood. The wood would catch fire, and buckets of water had to be carried up and poured down the chimney until the blaze was extinguished. A bad side-effect was that the fire in the fireplace was also put out, and dry wood had to be brought in and a new fire started but the house would become very cold while all this activity was going on. As soon as a warm day came the exposed wood was covered again with clay, and the whole process was repeated several times during a cold winter. As heating stoves became available, many people who could afford them changed from fireplace to stoves.

The Night Riders

Even peaceful communities like Blue Spring were not immune to turmoil, and during the Summer of 1919 there was a threat of bloodshed between a few rowdies above Fort Henry and the people around Blue Spring. There was a rumor that the trouble started between two churches of different faiths, but that was not true. Seems there was a man and woman living on a shanty boat at Fort Henry Landing, and the woman had a reputation that was on the shady side and the man was a bootlegger. A fellow from the Blue Spring area started hanging around the shanty boat and neglecting his family. Things like that didn't set too well with most of the neighborhood people, and they decided to go to the shanty boat and suggest the couple find some other place to anchor. The shanty boat people knew that those men did not kid around with idle words, and the next day they were on their way down the river. Some of the fellows that liked to hang out on the shanty boat and drink liquor were upset when they learned what had happened. A few nights later about half a dozen of them rode to Blue Spring, called a man out of his house and gave him a beating.

What those fellows didn't know was that those religious God-fearing people were not afraid of anybody except God. They sent word to the gang that they would be more healthy if they stayed out of the Blue Spring community. Things really began to heat up after that, and a rumor went around that the group was planning on coming to Blue Spring on a Saturday night and teach the folks a lesson. The sheriff was notified that things were getting out of hand and there might be some trouble brewing, but he paid no attention, and didn't check on the rumor. It was a tense situation about to explode.

I remember that Saturday afternoon well when the bunch from above Fort Henry were supposed to ride down with trouble on their minds. I was too young to realize the full meaning of what was going on, but when Papa and Grandpappy got out their guns, and started checking them out, and the women started crying like they were at a funeral I knew they were not going on a coon hunt. Later I learned that twelve or fifteen of those God-fearing citizens met after dark and took up positions behind logs, trees, or rocks on a hillside overlooking the road where the riders would have to pass. They had agreed that when the nightriders were right below them, on signal each man would aim and fire at the rider closest to him.

Somehow word reached the sheriff about what was going on, and realizing a slaughter was in the making, made one of the fastest horseback rides to Fort Henry that had ever been made and just in time to warn the invaders. Not knowing about the sheriffs action, the men at Blue Spring stayed at their posts until almost day-light. When the sheriff arrived at Fort Henry, he found the group of fellows getting their courage worked up by hitting the fruit jars of home-made whiskey. When they realized what was in store for them if they made the raid, there was some fast sobering up, and it was reported that two of them passed out when they learned how close they were to sudden death.

Grapevine Swings

There were lots of pleasant days in Owl Hollow that year. Papa taught me things like making grapevine swings, hunting ginseng or may-apple root, or taking me to old sawmill sights where he and Uncle Milford had worked. There were still mounds of sawdust, or some slabs laying on the ground that had not been taken by farmer for firewood. There was

40

always plenty of water nearby in the form of a pond or a spring that furnished water for the steam boiler. He showed me where he and Wheeler Love had hid a dead skunk among some logs, and it took Mr. Bill Biggs, owner of the sawmill, a week to find it. They were always playing tricks on each other and on Mr. Biggs.

It was a grapevine swing that got me into trouble with Papa that summer, although I did not plan it that way. A grapevine swing was made by locating a vine that reached high into the branches of a tree, and cutting it off about three feet above the roots. By taking hold of the vine and backing up as far as possible and running, one could swing a distance out in the air. I found one on top of a high bank beside the road, and when swinging out over the road was high up in the air and that was much more fun. One day Papa had been somewhere down the hollow in the wagon, and as he drove along the high bank heard me calling him, but I was nowhere to be seen. He finally looked up, and there several feet above him was his son dangling from a grapevine. He stopped Blanch and Mike, picked up his ax and climbed up the bank to where the swing was, and cut it off too high for me to reach. He also gave me a good lesson in safety that would be much help in the future.

My First Hunt!

Once when Grandpappy had been somewhere with his gun, "Zulu", I met him before he got to the house and asked him to let me take the gun and go hunting. Grandpappy put a shell in the monster and handed it to me without even telling me to be careful. I went up the hollow to the tobacco barn and into a small field that straddled a ridge. Beyond the ridge at the edge of the field, I had seen rabbits several times and was walking by some brush piles, when a rabbit jumped from its nest and ran up the hill in the direction of the house. As I tried to follow the fleeing animal in the gun's sights, three objects came into view just above me on the ridge. It was Mama, Mavis and Tince, and when they saw the gun pointing in their direction, they hit the dirt and lay there, yelling for me to put the weapon down. Someone had asked where I had gone, and when Grandpappy told them I had taken his gun and gone hunting, a posse was

41

formed to capture me alive. Grandpappy failed to tell them that the shell he had put in Zulu was a dud that would not explode.

Above: Blue Spring Church of Christ
Below: Grandpappy and Uncle Walter at the Spring

Moved to Graveyard Place

Sometime in late 1919 or early 1920 Mama received some money from a settlement of Grandpa Barbee's farm, and it was used to buy two frisky white mules, complete with work and fancy harness, a wagon, a No. 9 Vulcan turning plow, a double shovel plow, and a coonfoot harrow. The two mules, which were named Kate and Nell, were young and full of the devil, and with dispositions as different as day and night. Nell had a gentle disposition and was always willing to do more than her share of the work, and it showed in her ears, which were pointed forward or flopping back and forth as she walked. She would let Papa or me ride her to and from the fields and was always easy to handle. Kate hated work and kept her ears laid back on her neck, a sign she was angry, and anyone who attempted to ride her was sent on a trip toward the sky and ended up on the ground. I was too young to be around the mules when they first came to us, but later I spent many days following them behind a plow in the fields, or driving them hitched to a wagon on the road.

Now that Papa had his own team and farm equipment, he was ready to try sharecropping on a bigger scale and he talked to Mr. Boyd Gorham, who lived in Clarksville and owned the Boyd Farm about sharecropping. It was agreed that we would live in the house next to the graveyard and keep Kate and Nell in his stables; Papa would get two-thirds of what he grew. Most tenant farmers used the landlord's mules and equipment and received half of what they grew.

Boyd House built in 1810. Picture taken about 1900

43

Right after New Years' Day of 1920 we moved into our new home. The house had two log rooms with an enclosed hall between them, that was big enough for me to sleep in. After sharing Grandpappy's house with four others, our place seemed like a big house. It had a fireplace and chimney that was made from stone and we could have a roaring fire without the chimney catching on fire. There was no cistern, but just down the hill, about a hundred yards, was a hand-dug well with plenty of good water. There is nothing more refreshing than a big dipper full of cool well-water on a hot summer day. There was a wellhouse and a long bench where Mama could put her washtubs when she did the laundry, and she would not have to skimp on water. The water did have to be pulled up forty or fifty feet, two gallons at a time, but that was no big job.

The well was located at the Boyd House where the number one tenant lived and acted as a caretaker of the farm. The house consisted of two large log rooms with an open hallway between them, and a lean-to in back of the house. The first room was built about 1810 and there were holes cut into the walls in the shape of an hour glass to be used in the event of an Indian attack. The barrel of a gun could be put through the hole without a lot of exposure to enemy fire. There was a big loft and I use to play up there and make believe I was defending myself against the Indians. At the head of the stairs was a big trunk, filled to the top with clothing from the last century and several letters that were very old. Mr. Sam Lancaster, his wife Wrett, and the two boys lived in the Boyd House.

Spring Is Moving Time

Spring was the time of year when you could see many wagons loaded with families and their belongings as they moved from one farm to another. Some tenant farmers were better than others and often lived on one farm for many years. Those who were on the shiftless side moved to a new farm nearly every Spring at the request of the landowner. There was one family in our area who moved so often it was said that every time they went out to feed, the chickens cross their legs to be tied up.

The Graveyard Place got its name from the Boyd Graveyard that was just behind the house with only a garden between them. There were three other tenant houses on the Boyd Farm, but one of them, The Point, was not in use and was in a run down condition. It was at the upper end of the farm and next to the Nance farm.   Farther down the creek was the Gardner place that was occupied, but I don't recall who lived there. There were two children's graves in the front yard of the Gardner house and another grave out in the field some distance away from the house. There were no names on the graves, but the information had been handed down from one generation to another for nearly a hundred years.   The tenant at the Gardner house would keep the small graves cleaned and a stone marker placed at the head of each grave.   Later a concrete wall enclosed the grave out in the field.

The Funerals

When there was a funeral our house was the center of activity until the body arrived at the grave where the service was held.   When there was a death, neighbors would make a coffin from rough lumber, furnished by a local sawmill.   Papa was a good carpenter and usually helped make the coffin.   The more well-to-do were buried in a factory-built coffin bought from Cherry & McElroy Hardware store in Dover.   Papa said they were not as good as the ones that were homemade but just more fancy looking. Most of the time there was no preacher available and the rites would be performed by some member of the local church.   If the deceased was a decent church-going person, they were "preached into Heaven," but pity the poor devil who was a known chicken thief, made or bootlegged whiskey, cheated his fellow man or beat his wife more than needed.   He was preached "straight into hell", depending on which person preached the funeral.   There was a lot of weeping, especially for those who were destined to be barred from entering through the Pearly Gates.

Some of the local people were reluctant to talk about the departed soul unless they could say something good about them.   A story was told about one man who had died and had been just about everything a man shouldn't be while on this earth.   At his funeral, several of the local men were discussing his past, one telling about how the departed had stolen corn from him, another said he passed the departed's house one time and he was beating his wife, and the stories continued about all the bad things of his life.   One fellow just sat and whittled, not saying anything one way or another until he was asked his opinion.   He said he didn't know much to tell except that "He shore could play a french harp good".

A Message To Deliver

One day during the first Spring we lived at the Graveyard Place, a message was delivered to us late in the afternoon that concerned Uncle Milford who had been killed in France. I believe it had something to do about his remains being shipped from France back to America. I do remember that Papa thought the message was important, and should be delivered to Grandpappy and Grandmammy that evening. Papa and Mama had been working hard all day and decided that they would send me to deliver it. After being inactive during the winter months, the first few days of Spring work resulted in being tired and sore much like an athlete when he goes out for Spring training. It was not a quick decision because there were some doubts in their minds about sending a seven-year old boy nearly two miles up Owl Hollow after dark.

There were only two families living on the road between us and Grandpappy's place and they were near each other, leaving most of the road without protection. Trees lined the road most of the way and it was dark even when the road cut through a field. Papa warned me to be on the lookout for rattlesnakes and copperheads because they were more active in the Spring. He also told me to listen for the growls of animals and if I heard an animal in front of me, to stand perfectly still until it moved away. Papa wasn't trying to scare me but was only giving me some good advice on how to get along in the wilds. It was also the time of year bobcats had their young and they would usually stay away from humans but could be very protective of their young kittens.

I cannot remember ever being afraid in the dark, but Papa's warnings did make every dead tree look like a "bugger" and every sound could be that of a tiger laying in wait to pounce on me, but I knew those things did not exist along the road. The first house I would pass had been vacant for a few years. The two houses where people lived were dark and quiet because the people were tired and went to bed early to get a good rest. The only sign of life was the movement of cows, hogs and mules as they went searching for something to eat. The Spring frogs were so loud when I passed a pond that I could not have heard a wild hog if it had been next to me. There was also an occasional sound of a bullfrog' s harsh croaking, or the rustle of a rabbit as he ran to safety, not knowing whether or not I was some animal looking for a meal.

When I reached Grandpappy's there were no lights, and as was the local custom, I yelled a loud "Hello" from the front gate and waited for a response. When you live in the last house up a hollow, it is not often you are awakened at night by someone at your front gate. It usually meant that somebody was sick and help was needed by a neighbor. When Grandpappy came out to the cistern house, I had a little trouble making myself known above the barking of Ikey the dog, and when they finally realized it was me, they were scared something awful had happened to Papa or Mama. I gave one of them the message and after reading it aloud, there was some sobbing from Mavis and Tince. That's why I am certain the message was about Uncle Milford. Sometime after I arrived, there was another "Hello" from the front gate and it was Papa and Mama. They had gotten worried about me and could not sleep, so they got up and came to see that I arrived safely. I believe that was the last time they ever worried about me being out in the woods at night. If they worried they kept it to themselves, and I am grateful they had so much trust in me.

A Cousin Arrives

I had been the only grandchiled on Papa's side of the family for over seven years but it ended in June, 1920, when my cousin Duncan Kinnerly was born. Aunt Gladys and Uncle Bill Kennerly had moved to McEwen, a small town several miles up the river, across from Camden and near Waverly. Grandmammy knew that Gladys was expecting her first child in early summer and wanted to go and be with her. When she left, she spent the night with Uncle Sam and Aunt Fanny Hosford, and boarded the Thursday morning packet, *Saint Louis* at Fort Henry. Uncle Sam went on the boat and helped her with buying a ticket to a landing across from Camden. Some fellow met her in a wagon and took her the rest of the way to McEwen. Later, Gladys and Uncle Willie moved to our area and within the next few years, Hill and Ward were added to the family. After we moved away from Blue Spring two girls, Cherry Mae and Kathleen were born at the Louis Herndon Place. (Picture on front cover).

Going Barefooted

Spring has always been a favorite time of year for me because it meant I could go barefooted, as we called it. I feel sorry for those people who have never had the opportunity to walk barefooted through a puddle of mud and feel it squeezing up between the toes. It's a sensation that comes only to those who live in the country and go without shoes in the spring and summer. It was also the time of year Mama would give me a bar of P&G soap and send me to the creek to take a good bath. There had been a few baths taken in the kitchen in a washtub by the stove, but they were not as much fun as going to the creek and jumping in the swimming hole with nothing on except my birthday suit.

There was a mystery about Mama that I was never able to solve. When the days got longer and warmer in spring, every day I would ask if I could go barefooted, and day after day she would say it was not warm enough yet. Then one day that was no different from the others, as far as I could tell, she would tell me yes, I could take off my shoes. Science has its secrets and I suppose Mama was entitled to her secret way of knowing when the day came to go barefooted. There were a few grown men who pulled off their shoes and enjoyed Nature's great gift of going shoeless in the summertime.

Going barefooted in spring had its drawbacks. After being squeezed into shoes for several months, feet became tender, and those first days of going without them could be miserable. Every small twig, rock or clod felt like I was walking on knives and most of those first days you walked as if tiptoeing through a bed of flowers. By fall, however, I could run over a rocky creek bed at full speed and never feel pain. Thorns were always a problem, even for tough feet. There were locust trees everywhere and nearly all of them were protected by long sharp thorns that could be as much as six inches long. They seemed to fall to the ground with the pointed end up, just waiting for some barefooted boy to come along. Seldom a day passed that my feet were not stuck with one or more thorns, but except for a slight sting when removed, they went unnoticed. Nature has a way of building up a resistance to those things that were harmful. Only if a thorn went deep and broke off in the flesh would Papa cut it out with his pocket knife which he always kept handy. Then he would soak the wound in coal oil and it healed within a few days.

A COUNTRY BOY *From Owl Hollow*

One barefooted incident did almost cost me my life, but it might have been the same if I had been wearing shoes. Mama sent me to the Welkers', neighbors on the opposite side from the Lancasters, on some errand which has been forgotten. There was a well-worn path between the two houses, but a deep ditch forced the path to detour to where it could be crossed easily. For some reason that would only make sense to a boy, I decided to get a running start and jump the ditch, saving those extra steps around the path. I made the jump with room to spare, but waiting on the other side in the weeds was a board about two feet long and six or eight inches wide with a long nail in it where my left foot landed. The nail went all the way through my foot with an inch or more exposed above the skin. Pulling as hard as I could, the nail would not budge. I yelled for someone to come and help me, but there was nobody in hearing distance. I hobbled back to the house, and when Mama saw the trouble she tried to remove the board and nail but did not have the strength to get it loose. She ran to the Lancasters and one of them went to the field and got Papa. He pulled the nail out by standing on the board and pulling on my leg. By the time my foot was freed, the pain was so bad that I passed out and was in and out of a coma for awhile. I'm sure that Papa soaked my foot in coal oil, but my foot had swollen so badly that the oil may not have penetrated the wound.

My memory is fuzzy about most of that time, and I can only repeat what was told to me afterwards. My foot was swollen to two or three times its normal size and was hot with fever. Mama said I sweated a lot and they kept a bucket of cool water handy; so she could wipe my face and try to keep me comfortable. A few days later Doctor Ryan was passing by, riding his horse and someone went out and asked him to come in and take a look at my foot. It was swollen too bad for him to tell what had happened, and he had to be told. He asked for a piece of trotline string about three feet long and inserted a piece of cotton between the strands near the middle just like we did to clean a rifle barrel. After soaking the cotton in iodine, he forced one end of the string through the hole in my foot and pulled it back and forth until the pus and other impurities were cleaned from the wound. The pain was already so bad that the treatment made little difference. I was up and walking in a few days although Doctor Ryan was afraid the infection had gone too far for me to recover. He charged Papa fifty cents for his services.

Moving to The Boyd farm was like moving from one world to another. Grandpappy's farm at the head of Owl Hollow was rocky, rough and made up of small fields. The Boyd farm had more level creek bottom land and some of the fields had twenty acres or more in them. They grew more small grain and cut it with a binder. Later, a wheat thrasher came and thrashed the wheat and left a big stack of straw. The other tenants used a riding cultivator that could plow both sides of a row at one time and it looked like a lot of fun riding behind a good team of mules.

Cutting and Thrashing Wheat

The wheat binder was one of the most fascinating machines I had ever seen. It cut a six-foot swath, and the stalks fell on a wide conveyer belt that carried them to a "binder" that bundled and wrapped a string of twin around it, and then pushed the bundle out onto the ground. Two men followed, picking up the bundles and stacking several together in shocks. Another bundle was spread over the top of the shock to help protect the wheat from rain. I walked along beside the binder and watched as it did its thing, like it was supposed to do, and it looked easy except that part where it tied the string around the bundle. Like the hand is sometimes quicker than the eye, that thing tied a knot in the string too quick for me to figure out how it happened. I spent hours watching, but to this day I don't know how it worked

A few weeks after the grain was cut, a thrasher arrived, pulled by a steam tractor which also furnished power to the machine when thrashing. Both were large when compared to equipment that used the roads at that time, and it was a feat unequaled in modern times to bring them over the steep hills and sharp curves of the roads. I followed them once from the Gardner Place to where they set up in a field across the road from our house. The speed was no more than a mile per hour on level ground and was less when going down steep grades or on sharp curves. I followed close by and was amazed that the whole thing didn't turn over and crash to pieces. Once the equipment was set up on a spot near a pond where a supply of water was available for the steam engine, farmers from all around the neighborhood brought their grain to be thrashed. Grandpappy was always the one to bag the grain as it came from the machine's innards, and divide it between the grower and the thrasher owner. The owner received a portion of the grain instead of cash. Two men stood on a platform and as the bundles of wheat were pitched up to them, they cut the twine and fed the stalks into the gaping mouth of the thrasher. The stalks were pounded somewhere inside the machine and then pushed into a big fan wheel that blew the straw onto a conveyer and allowed the heavier grain to make its way to where Grandpappy was holding a bag to receive it. The conveyer carried the straw twenty or thirty feet away and dropped it on a stack where one or two men scattered it over a larger area. Most everyone agreed that working on a strawstack on a hot summer day was one of the hottest jobs in farm work. Long after the thrasher had gone, the strawstack remained as a place to play and neighbors to come for straw to make beds for the hot summer months.

Making Sorghum

About the time the first frost was due, and the heads of the sorghum cane began to turn a reddish brown, it was time for Moody Mathis to bring his "sorghum mill" to the Boyd Farm. Papa fashioned two sticks, a large one for him and a smaller one for me, and we went down the rows of cane, beating the narrow leaves off the stalks. He would take two rows and I would take one, and I made a game out if it by imagining the stalks were an enemy and I was defending myself against an attack from the tall monster. It was fun and I wondered why Papa called it work. After stripping off the leaves, the stalks were cut off near the ground and hauled to where the sorghum mill was to be set up. A few days later Mr. Moody arrived with his equipment and turned the juice from the stalks into a thick sweet syrup we called sorghum molasses.

The sorghum mill was made up of three main parts. The rollers that pressed the juice from the cane, a mule to furnish power to the rollers, and the cooking pan. The juice was piped by gravity from where the rollers squeezed it out to a barrel a few feet away. Another pipe ran to the cooking pan which might be 50 feet away. The heat of the pan and the person doing the cooking were the most important part of the operation because the quality of the final product depended on them. One man fed the cane in between the heavy rollers that were powered by the reluctant mule that walked around in a big circle all day, hitched to a long lever that extended twenty to twenty-five feet from the center. The person doing the cooking kept a fire under the pan that was about three by six feet and the temperature had to be constant, which was difficult because there were no thermostats in those days. The pan was divided into six-inch sections with a six-inch opening at alternate ends of the dividers. The raw juice entered at one end of the pan and was gentle pushed along, back and forth, from section to section with a wooden "pusher" the width of the groove. By the time the juice reached the opposite end of the cooker, most of its water content had evaporated, and a syrup fit for a king was drained off into a gallon bucket. A gallon of sorghum sold for fifty cents.

As the liquid moved from one end of the pan to the other, impurities rose to the top and were skimmed off and poured into a "skimming" hole that had been dug in the ground near the cooker. These holes were carefully camouflaged and many an unsuspecting greenhorn stepped into the hot goo and spent the next few hours trying to clean his leg, shoe, sock and britches leg of the green slime. The victim often never knew the setup was planned. I was too young to do the heavy work, but kept the crew supplied with cool water from the well. My reward was plenty of the sweet yellow foam that even the grownups enjoyed as a treat.

Closer to School

After we moved to the Graveyard Place, I had only a third of the distance to walk to school as I did from Grandpappy's place at the head of the hollow. School started in early August and ran for eight months. It started early so the children could be out of school in spring in time to help with the crops. After the first of August, most of the work was done except for tending the tobacco and harvesting. One day, probably in October, it rained and turned off cold while we were at school and caught most of the children barefooted. On my way home Mama met me with a new pair of hightop leather shoes and a pair of new socks. I sat down and she helped me put them on and they sure did feel good on my feet. I waded every little creek and puddle the rest of the way home. After they dried Papa put a coat of Neatsfoot oil on to keep them soft and water-proof. It was my first pair of hightop shoes, but I got new ones every year as long as we lived on the farm.

In addition to the hightop shoes, Papa and I had rubber boots that came up almost to the knees and were used for working or hunting when it was muddy or there were creeks to wade. They had no laces to loosen or adjust, and although they slipped on easily, if the feet were sweaty, sometimes they were difficult to get off. Papa made a "boot jack", a V cut into the end of a board that we could use to make the task easier.

"Mad" Dogs

My dog Ceef had grown into a beautiful shepherd in 1920 but was no good as a hunting dog. Having grown up with Grandmammy and my aunts, he was content to stay around the house with Mama. He was very protective and one day when a strange dog showed up, there was a fight and Ceef drove the stranger away. Next morning as I was on my way to school, I met the strange dog, and at a distance could tell he was foaming at the mouth, indicating he had rabies. I stepped out into the woods and the dog went by, snapping at the air and acting as if he were blind. Taking a shortcut back to the house, I told Papa what had happened and he took his gun, found the mad dog and killed him. Papa decided that Ceef should be penned up until it was certain whether or not he had contracted the disease.

Ceef was unhappy at being cooped up and begged to be set free, and I was tempted to turn him out but was afraid Papa would give me a whipping. A few days later when I went out one morning to take him some water, Ceef was not friendly. He snarled at me, showing his teeth, and there was saliva dripping from his mouth. Knowing that he had rabies, I went to Papa and told him. Again he got his gun and I started to cry and ran off up the road so that I would not hear the shot that would take Ceef's life. I did hear the shot and cried off and on all day. A few days later one of Sam Lancaster's milk cows came down with the disease and had to be killed. There was fear that the entire family might get rabies because they had been using milk from the cow. Once a person was infected, there was no cure and the infected person was doomed to die a horrible death. Fortunately, none of the family ever contracted the disease.

Our Neighbor, Sam Lancaster

Sam Lancaster just did not fit into the community but was tolerated and nearly everybody liked him. He never went to church, and possessed the most complete vocabulary of profanity of anyone for miles around. His wife, "Miss Wrett", and two boys, Carlos and Louie, ignored his antics and cussing, but to many people, it was either disgusting or amusing. One evening about bedtime Papa was outside and he could hear Sam cussing more and louder than usual, and he was even threatening to kill the entire family so Papa decided he had better go down to the house and see what was going on. Papa said Sam was mad at Wrett and was walking back and forth in front of her, waving his arms and spurting out enough profanity to turn the air blue. Wrett was sitting in her chair patching some clothes and ignoring him. Papa came back home without being seen and from then on also ignored Sam's actions. It was several days before we learned what had brought on the torrent of cussing and then we understood his frustration. Miss Wrett had been doing some spring cleaning and had moved some furniture without saying anything to Sam about it. Sam's bed had always been just inside the door to the bedroom so that when he went to bed, all he had to do was walk through the door and sit down on the side of the bed. That night when Sam went to bed, he sat down where the bed was supposed to be and found himself sprawled on the floor.

A story was told about Sam's cussing that I cannot vouch for, but it sounds like him. He took a wagon-load of watermelons to Fort Henry one Saturday and as the mules pulled up a steep bank at a store, the end gate on his wagon broke loose and the melons rolled out of the wagon bed, bursting open as they hit the ground. Some of the local whittlers who knew Sam were sitting on the store porch nearby and sensing a forth-coming burst of choice profanity, folded their knives and walked over to the wagon. Sam got down off the wagon, scotched the wheels, unhooked the inside traces, and walked to the back and surveyed the damage. He looked at the burst melons, then at the anxious men, and back to the melons. Finally he faced them and said "Gentlemen, I jest ain't worthy of the occasion" and walked away.

Lightning Does Strike Twice

About fifteen feet from one end of our house was the largest white oak tree I have ever seen. The first spring we lived there, lightning struck the huge tree on the side next to the house and we felt the house shake and it seemed to move on its foundation. When we could go outside, there was bark from the oak spattered all over the end of the house that looked as if it had been chewed up and spit against the logs. The old tree survived the strike, and when Papa said he had heard that lightning never struck the same place twice, we felt safe. Papa was mistaken because the next spring lightning struck the other side of the oak and the leaves began to wilt and die, and we knew it would have to be cut down.

A crosscut saw is nine feet long, but the huge white oak was almost twelve feet in diameter and the only way it could be cut down was to saw from three sides. Papa spent almost a day cutting a notch on the opposite side from the house so it would fall away from the building. If it fell the other direction, it would crush the house into the ground. While chopping the notch, he found several nails, some that had been driven in to hold wire many years before and they dulled the ax and saw. Someone helped with the sawing, and they worked a day or more, cutting from the side next to the house. Several wedges were driven in behind the saw to keep the tree from closing the gap the saw had made. With the wind in the right direction, the final cut was made and the old monarch fell to the ground from where it had started many hundreds of years before as an acorn. The largest limb of the giant oak measured almost six feet in diameter and the stump was big enough for Papa to build a chicken house on it. The log lay on the ground for several years before it was burned or rotted away.

Mama Gets Mad

Mama was one of the kindest persons I have ever known and was a deeply religious woman. Her faith was pure and simple, the kind that during a drought if a meeting was called at church to come and pray for rain, she would probably be the only one to take an umbrella. But I guess everyone has to backslide at least once, and when Mama took her slide into the world, she went whole-hog.

Bill Herndon was well known for his skill at breaking-in mules and Papa had two that sure needed to be broke. Kate and Nell were full of life, and sometimes it was difficult to work with them. Something had to be done so Papa asked Bill to do the job and he gladly agreed. The mules were hitched to the wagon down at the barn near the Boyd House, a pole inserted through the spokes of the rear wheels so they could not turn and extra weight was added for good measure. Kate was always looking for an excuse to get scared and when she found it, would scare Nell and away they would go until they tired out. The sound of a rabbit in the leaves was enough to send them on a wild chase.

Bill was certain that it would tame them some if they were made to pull a loaded wagon until their tongues were hanging out, so they started up the hill toward our house. He gave them the whip and by the time they were by our house, he was still lashing out at them, making them pull faster, and there was no doubt that Kate and Nell were about ready to drop. When Mama saw what was going on, her religion was thrown to the wind, and I have never heard two men get a better tongue-lashing than Mama gave Bill and Papa. She ran toward the wagon, picking up rocks as big as a fist, and Bill, seeing the Devil in Mama's eyes, jumped off the wagon and headed across the field toward his place up in Owl Hollow. Papa quickly removed the wheel lock and took Kate and Nell back to the stables. There was never a word mentioned about the incident. After I was grown, I asked Mama about the time she lost her temper with Bill Herndon, and she gave me a look that almost sent me reeling to the floor and told me never to mention it to her again. It was then that I realized what Bill had seen in her eyes, and I honored her request.

Grandpappy Buys River Farm

In the early twenties Grandpappy and Grandmammy received Uncle Milford's insurance money and decided to look for another place to live that would be closer to Blue Spring Church. Albert Champion sold them a narrow strip of land that reached from in the foothills all the way to the river. Much of the river part was swampy but there was enough good land to grow corn for Blanche and Mike, a cow, and for making meal for

56

cornbread. There were three houses on the place, and Grandpappy and Grandmammy chose the best one for themselves. It had a large log room with a fireplace that had a stone chimney, a small room attached for company to sleep in, and a lean-to that served as a kitchen and dining room. There was an orchard and garden space for Grandmammy. The stables were better than the ones Blanch and Mike had been used to, and they all settled down for a new life. Mavis and Tince were glad to be in a neighborhood where there were neighbors in all directions.

There was a cistern for water, but it needed cleaning so Papa helped to put it in tip top shape in time to catch the winter rains. Grandpappy wanted a well and had tried to dig one in Owl Hollow but was never able to strike water. Now he was certain water could be found easily, and he began to "water witch" for it. He was well-known for his ability to find water and had located streams for other people. Using a fork cut from a peach tree, Grandpappy held the two ends in his hands with the other end pointed up, and walked slowly back and forth where he thought water might be underground. The spot chosen was at the foot of a small hill near the garden and about 200 feet from the house. I walked along beside him and watched in awe as the branch started to bend downward toward the ground without his hands moving. The bend was such that the bark on the limb split and soon the fork was pointing almost straight down. Grandpappy said there was a good stream about 20 feet below the ground and when the well was dug later on, he had missed it by two feet. They struck water at 18 feet. I will leave it up to the experts to explain how the peach tree branch bent to more than a 45-degree angle. All I know is what I saw

.

Caught My First Fish

Shortly after Grandpappy and Grandmammy moved to the river farm, he took me fishing down on Panther Creek. He showed me how to look for a place to dig worms where the soil was rich and moist, and we soon had all the bait we needed. Then he cut a cane about ten feet long, trimmed it, and cut off some of the small end. He rigged up a fishing line, tied it to the small end of the cane pole, and we walked down to a fishing hole at the head of Mill Pond bottom. The water was shallow on our side of the creek and tapered off to deeper water on the far side. After showing me how to drop my bait into the deeper water and how to jerk on the pole if a fish took the worm, he sat down on the gravel bank behind me. At least one fish must have been hungry because in no time something was tugging at my line. In my excitement I pulled the little sunfish out of the water so fast that the line got tangled in a willow tree several feet up and Grandpappy had to climb the tree to untangle it. I spent the rest of the time admiring and playing with my prize until we went home. It was the first fish I ever caught.

I went fishing alone several times and took Grandmammy an assortment of sunfish, and she would clean and cook them for me and fuss because there was not enough to "feed a cat". Grandpappy must have thought I was ready for bigger fish, and one day said we were going to do some river fishing. We went by Albert Champion's stables where there were several fishbait trees and collected a bucket of catalpa worms and leaves for them to feed on until we were ready to use them. He took me to a place below Crutcher's Landing where the head of Panther Creek Island forced the water to the bank causing a big eddy. The government light that served to guide boats through the narrow channel was just above us.

There must have been a lot of hungry fish lurking in the eddy for Grandpappy was kept busy taking fish off my line and re-baiting it. They were not little sunfish like I had caught in the creek but were good eating-size catfish. Never since that day have I caught so many fish in such a short time. There would have been a lot more if my line had not slipped off the end of my pole and we had to quit and go home. Losing the line was a mystery for a long time until I became suspicious that Grandpappy had something to do with the "accident". When confronted, he just grinned and said we had all the fish he could carry up the bank anyway.

While we were at the river I recall asking him how far it was to the other side at that point and he said that he didn't know but would show me how to measure it. Looking across the river, he bowed his head until the line of sight and the brim of his hat touched the far bank. He turned his head slowly, keeping it as level as he could, until his line of sight touched the river bank on our side. He marked the spot in his mind and by stepping off the distance, he had a good estimate of the width of the river. It was not an exact science but if you wanted to swim across, it was better than just guessing.

Told We Must Move Again

In the Fall of 1921 Mr. Gorham told Papa we would have to move to another house, called The Point, at the upper end of the farm. The house had not been lived in for several years and was run down, and Papa had about five months to get the place livable. The tenants who had lived there before were sharecroppers who used the farm's livestock and .equipment and had no need for a pond or stables. The first thing was to dig a pond for the livestock which included two mules, a cow, a few hogs and Mama's chickens. It was also important to clean out the cistern and see that a good roof was on the building. Getting the pond and cistern ready in the Fall was more important because they could fill with winter rains that would stay cooler through the summer. The only outbuildings were a corn crib and a chicken house but there were no stables for Kate and Nell. There was also a lot of fencing to be done or repaired before livestock could be moved to The Point.

Papa borrowed a pond scoop and started work on the pond early in the Fall. He decided on a location that was about 200 feet below the house and would be about 50 feet from the stables. He drew plans for the pond, stables and feed lots, and had them on paper and in his mind before starting on the project. A pond scoop is a man-killer. It is made from heavy steel sheeting and is about three feet wide, three feet long, and a foot deep. Handles extend from the sides to the back so a man could guide it while scraping up a load of dirt. Lifting up the handles upended the scoop, spilling the dirt to form a bank to hold the water. A team of mules pulled it through the dirt, picking up about a cubic foot on each pass. I was just big enough to help by driving Kate and Nell while Papa handled the scoop. There are still signs of the pond that was dug in 1921.

Papa was good at drawing plans for anything he wanted to build, including the stables. He knew exactly how many logs and the size, the number of feet of tie lumber, rafters, and shingles he would need. The plans called for two ten-by-ten log rooms for Kate and Nell with an eight foot enclosed space in between to store harness, some fodder, hay, corn, and a few small items such as axle grease, plow points, and a few wrenches, but the building would have to wait until we moved to The Point in the Spring

59

The Simpsons Return

Landy and Mae Simpson and their eight children had moved south to Mississippi a few years before, and now they were returning to the land between the rivers. They had lived at the Graveyard Place and were good tenants, using the farm's mules and equipment and they needed to live near the farm supplies. Mae was a first cousin to both Papa and Mama, and had known each other all their lives. Because Papa had his own team and equipment, he would have to move to The Point as the upper place was known. The Simpsons were to arrive on the *Paducah* as she came down-river from Alabama. On the Thursday they were to arrive, Papa hitched Kate and Nell to the wagon, and all three of us drove to Boswell Landing to be on hand when the boat arrived. We waited all day but the boat never came and that was unusual because the *Paducah* was almost always on schedule. Papa decided to wait that night rather than drive the long trip back home and maybe have to turn around and come back to the river.

As evening approached, nearby families joined us, bringing food, and .the night soon turned unto a party. Someone brought a toe-sack filled with peanuts, and I ate so many that I got sick and vomited. Papa cut a clearing in a nearby canebrake big enough for me to lie down and he used the canes to make a bed for me. I went to sleep and didn't wake up until next morning. At sunup the boat had not come and everyone hitched up their teams and went home. Papa had work to do in the field and Mama had things to do in the house. I was to listened for the *Paducah's* whistle.

Friday night Papa and Mama were tired from losing so much sleep, and we went to bed early. Sometime around midnight, either Papa or Mama was awake and heard the boat's whistle blowing somewhere up the river, and there was a mad rush to get back to Boswell Landing. I was a sound sleeper at that age, and Mama said later that they tried to wake me, but there was no response. They put a shirt and overalls on me, carried me to the wagon, and we were almost to Boswell Landing before I woke up. The boat must have been a long way up the river or made some long stops because we were at the landing when it arrived. After watching Landy, Mae, and eight children, plus their belongings, come off the boat, Papa wondered if there was anyone left on board except the pilot. Mae and the two youngest boys and a few belongings were loaded on the wagon, and the rest of us walked the couple of miles home.

Moved to "The Point"

After living in a three-room house with ten other people besides Papa and Mama, it seemed like living in an empty house when we moved to The Point. At the Graveyard Place we had neighbors on both sides who were within hollering distance, but now I could get out and yell with all my lungs and there would be nobody to hear me. In front of the house, across the road were woods, filled with squirrels, that stretched for miles, and in back were fields and dry creeks where rabbits loved to hide from foxes, hawks, and owls. Between the two, we would have plenty of fresh wild meat. I was nine now and big for my age. There were even times when I was thinking about having my own rifle and going hunting by myself, but right now there was much to be done at our new house, and I would have to help Papa with the work.

Papa took me to the woods with him where he cut down a huge red oak to make shingles for the house and stables. Only a few feet of the base of the tree could be used for the shingles and the rest would be cut up into wood for the fireplace. The three or four twenty-inch sections were split into pie-shaped sections about six inches wide at the outside. A few inches of the heart was split out and used for firewood. Papa used a froe to rive the shingles, and he let me help so I could say that I had used a froe. He knew that the day of riving shingles was about to come to an end.

Papa had cut logs for the stables back in the winter, and they were now seasoned and ready to use. He had brought three or four wagon-loads of tie lumber from a sawmill, and it too was seasoned and ready to use. Everything was ready for a stable-raising, and then we could bring Kate and Nell home. They had been kept in the stables at the Boyd House, and was a lot of extra walking to keep them there. A day was set in the Spring of 1922 for a stable-raising and word was passed around.

On the day of the stable-raising, neighbors began to arrive about daylight and work was started. The women helped Mama prepare a big dinner for everyone and that was all the pay expected for the day's work. I remember being surprised at the progress of the building and by noon it was taking shape. I began to understand that Papa's drawings were actually turning into a buildings. A big dinner slowed down the work, but the stables were ready to be used by nightfall, except finishing the roof. Papa went down to the Boyd House and brought Kate and Nell home.

The mules were confined to a small feedlot in front of the stables so Papa started stringing wire and fencing in several acres of The Point. This gave Kate and Nell room to run more and there was more grass for them to graze on. Red, our cow, shared the new pasture with the mules and seemed happy to have company.

Old Red

Red was, without a doubt, the worst milk cow in the entire county. She was a good-looking critter and if she had been in beef country, would have been converted to hamburgers many years before her demise came naturally. She didn't give much milk and was the only cow I ever heard of that gave naturally skimmed milk, or what we called "blue john". It took almost a week's supply of her blue john to produce a pound of butter. Mama would empty each days milk into a crock and after it had clab- berd, "churned" it. In winter the churn sat near the fireplace so the heat would clabber the milk, and then a "dasher" was used to convert the mixture into butter and buttermilk.. In the spring when there was plenty of new grass, Red's milk supply increased and sometimes it would take on the flavor of wild onions or ragweeds which she seemed to delight in eating. It was just another one of her ways of being ornery. Luckily for the family, I did not care for any kind of fats, including butter, but we still had to buy some from Mrs. Ella Wofford. It was a drain on our budget to pay the ten cents a pound she charged. Miss Ella, as we called her, used a butter mold that not only measured out a pound but made it look pretty.

Mama was the only one who could milk Red. She didn't like Papa and had an ongoing hatred for me. Once when Mama was in a hurry to go some place, she asked me to do the milking, and I made an honest effort to help out, but after an hour there was not enough milk in the bucket to hide the bottom. I did the feeding of Red sometimes and for a fleeting moment we got along fine, but my friendship with Red was not dependable. When Red was out in the pasture, she knew to the minute every evening when I would come looking for her to drive her home. If she was in the pasture by the house, she made it a point to be as far away from the house as she could get. When she was in Hickory Hollow, after the corn was gathered, .she would be as far up the hollow as she could go. Papa put a bell on Red, and if there was little or no wind, I could hear the faint tinkling of the bell, especially if the flies were bothering her. Many years later I wrote a little poem about Red:

Old Red

She was the worst I've ever seen,
Contrary, stubborn, really mean
And ornery. There is no doubt
That she could lead me in and out
Of briars and weeds and even thorns.
You'd think she needed to have horns
To make her look her evil part.
But then those big brown eyes would dart
From here to there and back again
And make my heart so full of shame,
That I would try to be her friend,
Knowing that it soon would end,
Just as soon as she was fed......
That ornery cow we called Old Red.

Turning Plow and Coonfoot Harrow

Plenty of Work and Play

I had found a patch of dewberries near the middle of the pasture that were beginning to ripen and a few days later picked enough for Mama to make a cobbler. Dewberries look and taste much like blackberries except that they are sweeter and ripen a week or two earlier. The vines run along the ground instead of standing upright. A dewberry cobbler early in the spring is one of the great rewards of living in the country.

I never knew Papa to move to a new place but that one of the first things he did was to build a porch swing and a martin box. The swing was a work of art because he was an excellent carpenter, and he made the swing strong enough to hold two "fat people". At night there was nothing more relaxing in warm weather than swinging back and forth on the front porch and listen to the rhythm of the squeaking chains that supported the swing, and the haunting sounds of a whip-poor-will somewhere out in the woods. If you were lucky, you might hear the hoot of an owl or the bark of a fox. It was Nature at work and I had a front row seat.

There was plenty of work for everybody to make the place the way Papa and Mama wanted it, and now that I was nine and big for my age, I was given jobs that would ordinarily be done by a grown man. It was one of those jobs in the Spring of 1922 that changed me from a boy to a young man. There were two jobs one spring day that Papa wanted done. One was cutting and burning cornstalks and the other was plowing with Kate and Nell, and he gave me my choice. Although cutting cornstalks was a boy's job, I am sure that Papa knew which one I would choose and he was right -- I wanted to plow.

Plowing Looked Easy

I had never plowed but had watched Papa many times and it looked easy, there was something about being in command of a team of mules that was more appealing than cutting cornstalks with a hoe. He hitched the mules to the No. 9 Vulcan plow and dragged it over to a small patch of ground, made the first round, and turned it over to me. It had looked so easy when Papa plowed, but I soon learned that a plow had a mind of its own. There were times when it had rather be skimming along on top of the ground or running sideways than plowing a furrow like it was supposed to do. When it did decide to go under ground, it made a bee-line for some hidden root or rock that stopped Kate and Nell in their tracks and almost jerked my arms out of their sockets. That patch of ground was scarred rather than plowed. Once or twice Papa had to come to my rescue and pull the plow from under a big root. He was not a person to brag on me when I did a good job. Not that he wasn't proud of me, but it was expected of me to do a good job and that was all there was to it. Why should he reward me for doing what I was supposed to do?

Spring was a busy time for farmers, even little ones, with plowing and planting to be done, and as soon as the danger of frost was over, there was no time to waste. Papa had a simple schedule -- be in the field when the sun came up and stay there until it went down, with an hour off to eat dinner, a meal city folk call lunch. After sundown the mules had to be unhitched and taken to the stables where the harness was removed and they were allowed a few minutes to get a drink of water and roll in the dust. It is an experience, taking the plow harness off a sweaty mule, that city people have missed. After their romp, the mules were put in their stalls where corn and hay had been brought in for them. Mama had already milked and fed Red and the hogs, and she had put supper on the table for us. Much of the time supper was the highlight of the day, but once in awhile, I would be too tired to eat more than some milk and cornbread and would be off to bed, and no one needed to sing me to sleep. After what seemed to be about fifteen minutes of sleep, Mama was calling me to get up for breakfast. Papa had already fed Kate and Nell and was ready for another day while I had to be guided to the table, food put on my plate, and kept awake until Papa yelled for me to get going.

Farm work was hard, especially in the Spring, but there was always some time for fun. When the ground was too wet to work or those rare times when there was nothing to do, I went fishing, hunting, or just killing time somewhere in the hills. I have always suspected that Papa spent a lot of time just looking for work for me to do, especially when I was sure the fish were biting. He enjoyed farming those first years until there were a couple of crop failures due to dry weather, and then he became discouraged and would talk about when he worked for the streetcar or railroad companies. He got a regular paycheck regardless of the weather and there was action in the city that he missed. Farmers are at the mercy of the weather and every year is a gamble but they are rewarded with an independence that is treasured by most of them.

Kate and Nell get New Shoes

Soon after we moved to The Point, Papa turned over to me the job of taking Kate and Nell to the blacksmith, Mr. Will Rushing, to be shod. Mr. Rushing lived over on Panther Creek, and I enjoyed wading in the clear water while he was putting new shoes on the mules. I also enjoyed smelling the coal smoke from the forge and sometimes he would let me pump the bellows that turned the red coals of fire to white. I looked on in wonder as Mr. Rushing could get Kate and Nell to lift their hoofs for him. He held the hoof between his knees while he shaved off the extra growth that had accumulated since the last time they were shod. He used a drawing knife to remove the major portion of the hoof, and then a rasp file for the final trim. The shoe was heated and cleats were turned down for traction and then fitted to the hoof. Nails were driven through the shoe into the hoof to keep them in place. When he drove the nails in, I was sure they were going to penetrate the flesh, but they always came out at the proper place. The sharp point was clipped off and the end turned down to prevent the shoe from becoming loose.

In extremely dry weather sometimes one of the steel tires on a wagon wheel would loosen due to the wheel's shrinking. This was another job for Mr. Rushing, and I would take the mules and wagon to him. He would cut out a small portion of the tire and then welded the ends together again making the tire a bit smaller. After heating, the entire steel tire to make it expand, it was slipped over the rim of the wheel and then dipped in cold water, making it as tight as when it was new. In the spring we took our plow points to Mr. Rushing to be sharpened by heating and hammering them to a sharp point. While the metal was a cherry red he dipped it in cool water, causing the metal to harden but not hard enough to be brittle. I decided that I would be a blacksmith so that I could smell the coal smoke and live on a creek.

We Lived Well

We didn't make a lot of money, but we didn't meed much. Necessary things like sugar, coffee, and flour were bought from Miller Brothers General Store at Fort Henry or Ben Wofford's General Store over on Panther Creek. Papa set a limit of $100 to be spent on store-bought groceries from one tobacco crop to the next. When the crop was sold, he went to the store and paid the bill for the year and could get angry if it was much over his set amount. Mama's flock of Rhode Island Red chickens helped out with buying items such as store-bought tobacco, snuff, salt, black pepper, bluing, or a bottle of vanilla extract. These were usually bought from the huckster truck from Miller Brothers that came by our house each Friday.

Mama's flock of Rhode Island Red chickens were her pride and joy, and sometimes she ordered a dozen pure-bred stock eggs and would put them under a "setting" hen to hatch. When hatching time arrived, she watched over them day and night until they all were hatched. Mama culled the puny chickens from the flock and traded them, along with the week's production of eggs to the huckster truck. Her chickens also served as an efficient garbage disposal that has not be equaled. In front of the kitchen stove was a loose board about six by twelve inches, and when there were scraps left over from a meal, they were dropped through the floor and the chickens ate them. Those chickens knew when meal-time came and gathered under the house for Mama to dispose of her garbage.

Fast food in my time was how quickly Mama could put a meal on the table, especially breakfast. She once said that from the time she lit the fire in her stove until she had hot biscuits on the table was about 20 to 25 minutes. When we were working hard from sunup till sundown, my favorite breakfast was sorghum molasses and hot biscuits. Sometimes I might stir some butter or hot bacon fryings into the sorghum, but only if the work in the field was more difficult than usual. Papa liked fried bacon but did not want it crisp, just hot, Mama said. If we had ham, I did enjoy the lean meat a lot. At dinner (our noon meal) it was all vegetables cooked with pork fat and a big pone of cornbread. What was left of the cornbread was eaten at supper with sweet or buttermilk. In winter Mama would sometimes make flapjacks and we all had a feast. There is nothing better for supper in winter than pancakes covered with sorghum molasses.

Christmas in Owl Hollow

Christmas was not a big holiday with us, and there was no religious attachment at all. It was a time to give presents, and maybe have a special big dinner and if the weather was suitable, go hunting. Other than a new pair of overalls and some socks, my Christmas was getting some oranges, a couple of coconuts, a box of raisins, and a lot of various sizes of firecrackers. It was the only time of the year that I had either oranges or a coconuts and they were something special. Every part of the orange was eaten except the seed. The peel, after it is dried, makes some good chewing and the flavor would last for hours.

Opening a coconut was something that required a certain amount of patience and skill. Taking the small blade of a pocket knife, a hole was cut in one of the "eyes" and the milk drained out into a glass. I was allowed to drink the milk, and it was a delicious treat. Holding the empty coconut in one hand and a hammer in the other, it was turned and tapped gently for up to ten or fifteen minutes, to loosen the meat from the shell. Then a few hard taps cracked the coconut, and the meat came loose and was ready to eat. The second nut was later treated in the same way as the first one, but Mama grated the meat and made a coconut cake that I will never forget. The milk was used to moisten the cake.

The firecrackers were my real interest and I was out before daylight shooting them. There were small ones that could be held in the hand when exploded, and others that could remove a finger if they exploded in the hand. Then there were three, I never knew why just three, that were almost as powerful as a stick of dynamite. I would place each of them under a rock or inside a tin can, light it and run off several feet and watch it send the can almost out of sight. I had my own rockets in the twenties.

Ben Wofford Opens Store

Until Ben Wofford opened his store over on Panther Creek, we had to go all the way to Fort Henry if we needed something from the store even if it was just a box of matches. One of the rooms of his house was used at first, but later he built a store out in front of the house. It was more convenient than Miller Brothers, and Ben also had two pretty girls, Sadie and Bessie who made the store more attractive to me. One time when I was at the store Miss Ella, Ben's wife, told Sadie to take me upstairs where they had stored apples and to give me some to take home. The apples were piled in a corner and sure made the room smell good.

Ben was also good to the young boys in the neighborhood and each Saturday afternoon in summer, had a baseball game in one of his pastures. Papa thought it more important that I should work than play ball, but my last summer on the farm, he did let me off from work on Saturday afternoons. Whoever owned a baseball was usually the pitcher, and the ball was used long after the cover had been worn or pulled off. Once Ben took us across the river where we played a bunch of boys in Kentucky.

Decoration Day at Dover

When Uncle Milford's remains were brought back from France, they were buried in the National Cemetery at Dover. The funeral was one of the greatest sights I had ever seen, and every year after that, the family went to Dover on the 30th of May. The coffin was escorted by a lot of Army soldiers and as the service neared the end, taps were played by someone from a location we could not see. Guns fired at some time during the funeral, and there was a big flag draped over the coffin. Sometime during the service, two soldiers removed the flag, folded it neatly, and gave it to Grandmammy. Uncle Milford was home to stay.

May 30th was always a big day in Dover during the twenties, and the family went to the event every year for many years. There were military bands and famous speakers, usually a Congressman or Senator from Washington would be there. One person I recall being there on the 30th of May each year was Mrs. Casey Jones, widow of the famous railroad engineer from Jackson, Tennessee. I don't recall whether or not she had relatives buried there.

Going to Dover on Decoration Day, I suppose, sort of replaced going to the annual Fourth of July picnic at Tharpe. Somebody would give me a quarter to spend, and it was converted into two "Dopes", our name for Coco Cola, and three ice cream cones. Drinking that "Dope" and feeling the effects of the carbonated gas in my nose when I belched, made me feel ten feet tall. When it came time to eat, everybody gathered in the basement of the J. B. Walters General Store where the women spread a picnic lunch of hoop cheese, peanut butter, bologna, light bread, and crackers. Cold drinks were passed out to anyone who wanted one.

Mama would take home a loaf of light bread, a box of crackers, a box of corn flakes, peanut butter, and a jar of yellow mustard. These goodies were rationed out for several weeks and enjoyed to the limit by me. The corn flakes were the best-tasting food I had ever eaten, and I wished we could have them three times a day all year. I loved peanut butter, and the way it would stick to the roof of my mouth, kept a good taste going for a long time. Mama knew that the crackers were enjoyed by everyone so much that one year she tried to make some. Well, Mama was a good cook, but those crackers were nothing like the ones we bought at the store. The mustard was the last to go for it took only a little on some bread to go a long way, but I sure did hate to see it go.

The first two or three years we went to Dover on May 30th, we went by wagon. I don't recall whose wagon and team it was but am sure it was not Grandpappy's team, Blanch and Mike. In later years, arrangements were made with Frank or Rob Scarborough to take the women in a car. The rest of us started walking and when the women were unloaded in Dover, the car came back and met us and carried us the remainder of the trip. Sometimes we would be almost to Bear Creek before the car met us. Once when I was fourteen or fifteen, Ray Lyon and I decided to go and we walked all the way to Dover and back, but the 20 mile walk was not a problem for us.

The Soldier and His Dog

There was a young man who had lived down the river from Danville who was killed in France and was buried in the family graveyard. Papa and I visited the grave one day because we had heard an unusual story about the soldier and his dog. When the remains were returned from overseas, the coffin was taken to his parents' home before the funeral was held. The soldier's dog came into the room, sniffed around the coffin, whined, and laid down beside it. When the day came for the funeral, the coffin was carried up a hill to the graveyard and the dog stayed along beside it and could not be coaxed away. After the grave-side services and after the grave was filled in, the dog still refused to leave the site. Food and water were taken to the dog every day, and when bad weather came, a small house was built for him. Some mornings the remains of animals, that had ventured too close to the grave would be found, but none were ever eaten. The dog spent the rest of his life of several years lying by the grave of his master, and when he died, the dog was buried beside the fallen soldier.

Hog-Killing Time

Papa usually killed three or four hogs in the Fall and that would last us until the next hog killing a year away. The number killed depended on the size of the animals. He favored smaller hogs with more lean meat over the large fat ones that turned into a lot of lard. Some farmers waited for extremely cold weather, but Papa wanted it to be cold early in the morning but warming up during the day. He believed that if the meat froze before the salt had penetrated to the bone and joints, it would spoil later on.

Hog-killing was like a barn-raising or tobacco-cutting, and neighbors came to help. For their pay they would take a portion of the fresh meat home with them. These parts were usually a backbone, liver, ribs, or any part that was better if eaten while fresh. When a neighbor killed his hogs, we helped him and brought home some fresh meat. It was sort of a gala season when the crops were in. There was plenty of food stored for the winter, including hundreds of jars filled with fruits and vegetables, and the land would lay at rest until next spring.

There was no weather department to tell us what the weather was supposed to be tomorrow so Papa, like other farmers, developed an extra sense that was as accurate as today over a short period. There would be a day in late fall when all signs pointed to a chilly day tomorrow, and we started making preparations to kill hogs. Papa knew there would be a heavy frost and word was passed along about our plans. By the time daylight arrived, we had a big vat of boiling water and soon neighbors began to show up. Until I was eleven or twelve years old, Papa did the shooting of the hogs, but turned the job over to me when he thought my shooting was good enough.

A 22 caliber rifle was used and the bullet had to penetrate the brain so the animal would die instantly. If it missed the target, the hog would be crippled, and nobody wanted to get in a pen with a wounded hog. If the shot was fatal, the animal fell to the ground without making a sound and could be bled, insuring clean meat. In the early twenties it was thought that a knife blade had to penetrate the heart to make the animal bleed and often the shoulder meat was damaged. Later, someone discovered that the jugular vein was only an inch deep and that was as far as the blade needed to go.

After the hog was dead, it was taken to the vat, and boiling water was poured over it until the hair could be scraped from the skin. The lower part of the hind legs were slit and a hickory stick, about 20 inches long and sharpened at both ends, was inserted into the tendons to hold the hog, head down, from a large pole. The stick was called a gambling stick, perhaps because a person gambled his life while hanging a 400-pound hog by these sticks. If one end slipped out, it could become a deadly missile. There was always one man who was considered best at removing the intestines, heart, lungs, liver and stomach. After they were removed, they were placed in a wash tub. Later the women removed the eatable parts and stripped the fat off the entrails. There was talk about chitlings that were made from the entrails but I never knew of anyone in our area who ate them. As soon as one hog was scraped, another one would be shot, bled, and brought in, and the process was repeated until all the hogs were hung and gutted. All this may sound gruesome today, but in the early twenties, it was a way of life. Today the slaughter-houses, which are well-equipped, do the job more efficiently.

By the time the last hog was cleaned, it was time for dinner, our noon meal. After dinner everyone sat around visiting or loafing while the meat cooled and became stiff, making it more easily cut up into parts. Later the carcass was taken down and placed on a table where it was cut into bacon, hams, shoulders, heads, backbones, and ribs. Papa always did the final trimming to our hams and shoulders because he liked them lean. The extra fat was used to make lard. After the meat was cut up and trimmed, it was laid on the front porch to cool until next morning to be certain all animal heat was gone out of it. If the weather was cold enough to freeze the meat, a tarpaulin was spread over it because frozen meat won't take salt and it will spoil.

Hog-killing was a busy time for several days after the animals were killed. After the meat had cooled on the porch it was carefully packed in a box, (a permanent fixture on the front porch), and each layer was covered with salt. This was repeated until all the meat was covered. Several days later the meat was taken from the salting box, the salt cleaned off and the meat was hung in the smokehouse. Under Papa's sharp eye, it was my job to keep a low smouldering fire going day and night, using a mixture of seasoned and green hickory wood. After about three months of slow smoking, the meat was brown and cured and ready to eat. Home-smoked pork is some of the most delicious meat ever made and if smoked right, will keep for years without spoiling.

Mama spent a lot of hours trimming the last fleck of fat from the fresh meat and putting it in her big iron kettle that she used for boiling clothes. As the fat boiled, it was my job to keep stirring it with a large wooden paddle until the chunks of fat had been rendered into liquid lard. After boiling for awhile over a hot fire, the pot was full of liquified fat and a couple of gallons of cracklings. She poured the liquid fat into gallon buckets and they were stored in the smokehouse until needed. The cracklings were added to cornbread, known as crackling bread, a favorite of Papa's. I didn't care for it because it was too greasy, and I never cared for greasy foods.

During the days following the hog-killing, Mama used the hearts, lungs, liver, and sweetbreads, adding salt, pepper, and a lot of sage, to make a stew that a king would have given *all* his kingdom for just one big bowl. There were also brains and eggs for breakfast, one of the few times we had eggs, and one of the few times I was glad to get out of bed and come to the table. Then later she made souse from the head, snout, and feet and after soaking in vinegar for a day, it was delicious.

After the meat was salted away, Papa took it upon himself to make the sausage. He insisted nobody else put in enough pepper and sage. He was not a stingy man, especially when it came to putting pepper and sage in the sausage. Sometimes it was so hot that Mama could hardly eat it and then it was just right for Papa and mc. It was another of my jobs to turn the crank on the sausage grinder while he fed pieces of pork into it, some lean and some fat, mixed just right to make a perfect mixture. Some pepper and sage was mixed in as the meat was ground and then more was added in the washtub until it was exactly as he wanted it. Mama made cloth sacks and the sausage was stuffed into them and stored. She said with all that pepper, salt, and sage, the meat could go for months without spoiling.

I suppose every family had its own method of determining what part of the cured meat to eat first. At our house the first to be eaten was the bacon, or middling as some called it, and Papa sometimes called it "sow's bosom" and that always made Mama blush. Mama wanted to smoke some of the sausage and save it until Spring but was outvoted by Papa and me. We figured that if you have a good thing, take advantage of it, and let next year take care of itself. Once in awhile we would cut a ham or shoulder after the first slab of bacon was finished, but they both seemed to want to save the best until the last. I had to wait for the hams.

One Fall, Lohman Nance, who killed 12 to 15 hogs for himself and his farm tenants, decided to round up some wild hogs, fatten and kill them for meat. He built a strong pen way up in Stilly Hollow, complete with deadfall, and baited it. A few days later he found he had trapped four good sized hogs. I always wished I had been there because they said it was a pretty tough job persuading those pigs to lay down and be tied up for the trip home. Lohman gave them all the feed they could eat, but they refused to gain weight or get fat. He killed them anyway and later wished he had never trapped them because the meat was not good.

My First Gun

I believe it was in the Fall of 1922 when Papa and Mama bought me my first gun. It was a single shot Stevens 22-caliber rifle, and I cannot recall ever getting anything that gave me as big a thrill as the gun gave me. It was included in Mama's winter order from Sears and Roebuck and it usually took two weeks for the merchandise to arrive, but after a week I started meeting our mail carrier every day. I just knew the order had gotten lost, and the two weeks seemed to crawl by a month at a time. One day the package did arrive, riding on the horse behind Arb Rutland, and I hurried up the hollow to our house. I can't remember anything that was in the package except a greasy little rifle that was not even put together.

Papa took over the job of cleaning the gun and attaching the barrel to the stock. When everything was to his satisfaction, he took me out in front of the house and set up a target against a clay bank about fifty feet away. He let me shoot it the first time, an honor I never forgot. I missed the target. Papa took the rifle, sighted, and fired. The bullet was about two inches to the left of dead center and about an inch low. He made some adjustments on the sights and fired again, and the bullet was half an inch high. More adjusting and the next shot hit dead center, and he handed the gun to me. My shot was low and he told me that I pulled the

74

trigger with my hand instead of my finger. He told me to shoot from my shoulder and to never rest the barrel on a log or some other object except when target shooting because when you are hunting, you don't have time to look for some object to use for a gun rest. I had been given instructions on how to use firearms, but Papa warned me again, never point a gun at something unless you intended to kill it. Uncle Frank Champion told me that any part of a gun was dangerous. 'Said his Papa beat the heck out of him once with a ramrod. I never knew there were so many dos and don'ts about hunting with a gun until I had my own.

During the winter months when our supply of fresh pork was gone, when it was in season, wild meat was a big part of our diet. Papa was strict about not shooting game when it was out of season, but there were some who had little regard for the laws. One man in our neighborhood who killed meat any time he wanted to, was warned that it was against the law, but said that he wouldn't have a gun that couldn't shoot through the law.

Rabbits were a favorite wild meat at our house in winter, when they were fat and healthy. In summer they were likely to have "wolves", a grub of some sort, that infested the shoulder area. In winter the meat was delicious and made the best gravy I have ever tasted. Squirrels were also good eating, but they were smaller and harder to find. A young one could be fried, but the old ones were used for making dumplings, and they were even better than chicken and dumplings. There was an area across the road and beyond the Boyd Pond where red, or fox squirrels, could be found but they were often tougher than the greys. Occasionally I would bring in a big fat possum and Papa would fasten him up in a chicken coop to feed for a couple of weeks. He said a possum would eat anything and he wanted it to be cleaned out before he ate it. A possum, baked with quartered sweet potatoes was good eating and tasted a lot like pork.

Mama's favorite wild meat was squirrel and often, around mid afternoon when they were in season, she would ask me to go out and kill a couple for supper. She liked the meat on the head and cheeks and didn't want it damaged by a bullet. I was taught to shoot squirrels through the neck when possible, and if I brought one in that was shot elsewhere, she wanted to know if I had shot it while it was jumping or running. She also preferred young ones for they were better for frying, but it is impossible to tell a young from an old one when it is high up in a tree. It did teach me to try and not spoil the meat whenever I could help it.

In the early twenties there were three different kind of rabbits to be found in our area. Out in the hills were the small brown ones that we simply called hill rabbits. They were not as meaty as the others but were the tastiest of the three. In and around the creeks and fields were the regular old grey, or cottontail, the most available when needed for food. If Mama wanted fried rabbit and gravy for supper, I could have one killed and cleaned in less than an hour. The swamp rabbit could be found only down near the Tennessee River, and around the creek and sloughs. They were much bigger than either the hill or field rabbits, but the meat was coarser and not as tasty. One swamp rabbit would provide as much meat as two regular ones.

Mama Wants a Turkey for Thanksgiving

Although most of my hunting was for rabbits and squirrels. there were other types of game that was available for the killing. Like the time Mama decided she wanted to have turkey for Thanksgiving. There were no tame turkeys to buy, and we could not have afforded one if there had been. What Mama had in mind was a wild turkey. I had seen wild turkeys many times and knew about where they could be found but had no reason to kill one. I told Mama that I knew where an old Tom hung out all by himself, and she said that sounded alright to her.

Two days before Thanksgiving I took my Stevens rifle and headed for a spot out in the White Hills where there were a lot of mountain oak acorns and I had seen the Tom there two or three times. He was a loner, for reasons I never knew, but later suspected that he was just too old and feeble to keep up with the rest of the bunch. I had seen where he roosted and believed he would not be too far away, for turkeys are predictable. I found him feeding and hid along the path he was taking until he came near enough for me to shoot him. I always tried to kill game instantly because I did not like to see an animal suffer. That old Tom was a heavy bird and Papa guessed him to weigh between 30 and 40 pounds. He had been around a long time and there was plenty of food for him to grow on. Mama had to use her big iron kettle she used for washing clothes to scald him and soon learned that he was a tough old bird because after scalding he was reluctant to give up his feathers and, also, the meat was a little on the dark side. It was much darker than some of the old roosters she had killed at one time or another but Mama was not one to give up easily, and she cut the bird into pieces so he would fit into her biggest cooking pot. After cooking all day and until bedtime, the meat was too tough to stick a fork in and she gave up till next morning. Starting early she cooked all day but never could get it tender. That was the last time Mama ever asked me to kill a turkey for her.

Safer to Hunt Alone

Papa and I rarely went hunting together, and I am sure he had good reasons. Shortly after I got my rifle, he took me hunting with him out around the Boyd Pond. He had an eye like a hawk when it came to spotting a squirrel hiding in a tree. I have seen him suddenly stop and hold his hand behind him, a signal to stand still, slowly raise his gun and fire. Always a squirrel fell to the ground that I didn't even know was in the neighborhood. I was never good at spotting squirrels. We were walking along an old abandoned road, side by side, and I was messing around with the hammer and trigger of my gun which was a "no no" in hunting. Suddenly a bullet whizzed by in front of him, and he acted as if I had never heard a word he had told me about safety.

The incident may have planted a seed of fear, but it was another incident sometime later that sealed my fate for hunting with Papa. He had spotted a squirrel ahead, put his hand down, raised his gun, and fired. It was the only time I ever knew him to miss one. The squirrel got a little nervous and decided it was not a safe place to hang around anymore and took off jumping from tree to tree. For some unknown reason I raised my rifle and fired at the critter while he was in the air between trees and he fell to the ground with a bullet through his heart. Although Papa knew he had just witnessed the biggest accident of his hunting career, his pride was hurt, and he was very quite the rest of the hunt. From then on we went hunting separately except those times when there were several in the party. I suppose he thought there was safety in numbers. As far as I know, that was the only time I got careless with a gun and later Papa was proud of my shooting. He always said that guns were not dangerous but never trust the person holding it.

Papa owned the best 22-rifle in the neighborhood and it was his pride and joy. It was an octagon barrel Remington pump with a magazine that held 17 shorts and about 14 long-rifle shells. He was better at shooting from the shoulder than I was, but I could beat him when resting the barrel on an object. Sometimes I wondered if, deep in his heart, he wanted me to be a better shot than he was, but I never was. He would not allow me to shoot a shotgun until I was 14 years old because he said it would affect my accuracy with a rifle. He said the expected rebound, or kick as we called it, of a shotgun might cause me to pull off the target.

Tince and Me go Hunting

Soon after Grandpappy and Grandmammy and my two aunts moved from Owl Hollow to the river farm, I took my rifle and went to visit them. I knew Grandmammy was ready for some fresh meat, and I wanted to try my luck at hunting swamp rabbits. Tince wanted to go with me, and we headed down the north side of Panther Creek, but the only game we saw was a field rabbit and I shot it. When we got to where Campbell Slough entered the creek, we turned north and followed the swamp. I had promised Tince, when she decided to go with me, we would take turns shooting, and I would go first so she could get an idea how it was done.

Walking along the edge of the swamp I spotted the biggest swamp rabbit I had ever seen. He looked as big as a dog and in the excitement forgot it was her turn to shoot, and I killed it myself. Later I spotted another and the same thing happened. I just could not give Tince a chance to shoot a rabbit. There is a feeling when you are looking at a rabbit down the sights of a rifle barrel that cannot be described.

We hunted for another hour and finding nothing, I began to feel guilty about doing all the shooting and not letting her try her luck. We were on our way home when I saw a squirrel's nest high in a hickorynut tree and more to ease my conscience than anything else, handed Tince the rifle and suggested she shoot into the nest and maybe she would kill a squirrel. To my surprise and relief, at the crack of the gun a squirrel tumbled out, shot through the head. I had shot into dozens of nests and had never so much as roused a squirrel and never did in many tries later. Grandmammy cleaned the rabbits and squirrel, and there was plenty of fresh meat on the table for several days.

Grandpappy's Rafting

When he was a younger man, Grandpappy loved rafting timber down the Cumberland and Tennessee Rivers. It gave him time on his beloved rivers and also a touch of the humdrum city life when he reached Paducah. Timber was big business in the area, and there were several sawmills and hundreds of tie hackers that brought much needed cash to the farmers. Many of the trees were too large for the local sawmills to cut up into crossties or lumber and they had to be floated down the river to Paducah where there were huge mills with band saws that could handle them with ease. The big timber grew in the bottom lands and could be cut in summer or winter and floated out to the river when the spring floods came. If they could not be floated, they were dragged out by using a "log dragger". A raft might cover several acres of logs, held together with "dogs", two spikes connected together with a short piece of chain. Each spike was driven into a log and they were held together by the chain.

A lean-to was built for cooking and if the weather was bad, it was used for sleeping. The raft was rectangular in shape and a large oar was built at each end to help keep the raft lengthwise with the river channel. The oars also helped to steer clear of the many packets that plied the river. Steamboat pilots were not too kindly toward these floating obstacles and often had an exchange of conversation that one would not hear in church on Sunday morning. The huge logs could be devastating to the wooden hulls of the boats and always posed a danger, especially in fog or stormy weather. When the river was full in the spring, the raft moved along at a fast pace, and the trip from Fort Henry to Paducah could be made in a couple of days, but the crew was kept busy day and night.

Before Papa and Mama married, he was the cook on some of the trips and use to tell stories of events that happened along the way. One was about a crew member who was inclined to hit the bottle a little too hard and sometimes would oversleep. Once when the man was completely out, Papa killed a wild duck to cook for supper, but before he could get around to cleaning the bird, the drunk aroused and insisted he was going to cook the duck in his own fashion. Rather than start an argument, Papa gave the drunken crewman the duck, who cut it open, removed the insides, washed it good, and added salt and pepper. He then took a rowboat and went to the river bank and returned with a large batch of river mud. With the feathers still on, the duck was packed tightly inside a large ball of mud and placed on the open fire. The crewman returned to his sleep. Several hours later he awoke, remembered the bird, and rolled the baked ball away from the fire to cool. After it had cooled awhile, he broke it open and every feather came off with the mud. Papa said it was the best wild duck he had ever tasted.

Grandpappy was not an outstanding farmer, mainly because he was more interested in rafting than farming. He would plow the fields and get them ready for planting, but from there on my aunts did most of the field work. They grew just enough corn to feed Blanch and Mike, a cow and a couple of pigs, and have enough left over to take to the grist mill to grind into meal to make cornbread. Except for one year, as I remember, flour was bought ready-to-use from the store because Grandmammy liked the white flour better than the brown that was made from the homegrown wheat. Grandpappy "cradled" the wheat when he grew it and took it to Tharpe to be ground into flour. For some extra cash, a patch of tobacco was set out and there were small patches of peanuts, popcorn, sweet and Irish potatoes and broomcorn. The garden provided all the vegetables that were needed for eating fresh, canning, or drying. The orchard furnished apples, peaches, plums, and pears to be canned or dried. Wild nuts, such as black walnuts, butternuts, hazlenuts or scalybark hickorynuts were collected and stored for winter use. Sitting in front of an open fireplace, eating from a dishpan filled with cracked nuts on a cold winter night is an event that must be experienced to know what it is like to be near Heaven. Canned berries and muscadines added to the winter diet, and with food like that, no store-bought vitamins were needed.

Hayrake of the 20s pulled by two mules

Entertainment and Games

When you are an only child and your nearest playmates are more than half a mile away, and there are no telephones, you have a choice -- learn to entertain yourself or be bored to death. I would be eleven years old before Douglas, my brother, would come along, and although he was a welcomed addition to the family, our age difference made us live in different worlds. He had five years on the farm before we moved to Dover, a town about ten miles away, but that short span still influences his life and he is an avid gardner.

Before we moved from Paducah, Papa and Mama bought me a wagon. Not a small toy, but one large enough to be pulled by a goat, which I never had. The wagon had shafts for a goat, and they had planned to get one for me, then changed their minds after we moved to Owl Hollow. It also had a tongue that was more suitable for me to use when pulling the wagon. The wheels and framework were identical to the big one that Papa bought later, even to the painting, but on a much smaller scale. It was used for play and doing chores when heavy objects had to be moved, like bringing in wood for the fireplace or Mama's cookstove.

Railroads and Trucks

Another toy that gave me a lot of pleasure was a wind-up train. When wound tightly, the spring would propel the engine, coal car, and a boxcar around a small track for about half a minute. Watching the train run around in the small circle became boring, and I wanted more track on which to build my railroad empire. I learned that a man at Fort Henry had picked up some old telegraph wire, many years before, that had been left by the Union Army when they left for Fort Donelson during the Civil War. It was larger than bailing wire and just the right size for making a track,and the fellow gave me all I wanted, which must have been several hundred feet. I whittled hundreds of tiny crossties about two inches long and one-eighth-inch square. To attach the wire to the ties, I used carpet tacks and a lot of patience.

There was an area across the road from the house that was protected on one side by a high clay bank, and on the other side by woods. This is where I wanted to build my empire. A large animal could easily wreck my railroad with a misplaced foot and the high bank would offer some protection. The project lasted for over a year, working when time and weather permitted. The track was laid on level places, across small ditches and at one place went under a fallen log. Trestles, tunnels, and road-crossings were worked into the project, and stations were placed at points where the engine's spring ran down. Most of the time the train stopped where it was supposed to but sometimes it would overrun or fall short of the station. No one paid any attention to what I was doing because I was always playing out in the woods at something or another. One day Papa discovered my project and was so impressed that he even showed it to some visitors and that made me feel real proud. He wasn't one to brag on me, but sometimes he did things that were real nice. He said too much bragging on a child could ruin him.

When Dumas Miller started coming by our place in his huckster truck, I had to have a truck and began to plan it in my mind. Mama did a lot of sewing, and her thread came on wooden spools of various sizes. The two ends of a large spool made two wheels when cut from the middle section. A smaller spool made a good steering wheel, and the body and axles were just a matter of whittling and sawing pieces of wood to the right size. Small pieces of boards, some as thin as cardboard, could be found among the scraps at the sawmill and they were free. The front axle was fastened in the center so it would swivel and was turned by a string wound around the steering wheel. The bed behind the open cab, made from boards, completed the toy truck. Taking the idea from my railroad, I built roads for the truck in another section of the woods between the hog pen and Mama's garden. "Concrete" bridges with wings, like the one just built across Panther Creek, were built to cross small gullies. The concrete was made from a mixture of lime, sand, and water and as recent as the sixties, some of the bridges still remained.

Toy Boat

Papa was an expert with carpenter's tools, and built a boat for me to play with on our pond. It had a pointed bow, and was about 18 inches long,and he probably built it out of pity, after seeing some of the boats his son had made. His boat had everything I could wish for except some means of power to drive it across the pond. I rigged sails, but my boat spent more time going sideways, and in the wrong direction, than going where I wanted it to go. I did make a paddle wheel that resembled the one on *The Paducah,* using one of Mama's empty spools for a hub, and mounted it on the stern but could not come up with something to power it. The graph-o-phone had not been used for a long time, and the spring motor in it would be the ideal source of power. One day when I was home alone, I took the motor out, and mounted it on my boat, using a piece of leather for a belt to drive the paddle wheel. After several adjustments, and tries, it worked very well, and one winding sent the boat all the way to the far end of the pond. When Papa saw my boat and motor I got a mild scolding but didn't get a whipping.

The Sling

A "sling" could furnish a lot of entertainment just trying to figure out a way to make it a more accurate weapon. It would have been a deadly weapon if the aim had any accuracy, but the old saying about not being able to hit the side of a barn was surely the result of someone using a sling. David slew Goliath, according to the story in the Bible, with a sling, and it must have been the luckiest shot he ever made. I was able to sling a rock several hundred yards, but it was anybody's guess as to where or what it would hit. They were simple to make, which is probably why one was ever made in the first place. All you need are two strong strings about three feet long and a piece of soft leather from an old discarded shoe. Cut the leather into an oval shape about three inches long and cut holes in each end. Tie one end of the strings in the holes of the leather. Tie the other end of one of the strings around the thumb of your throwing arm and hold the other one firmly between the thumb and forefinger. Place a rock, about one inch in diameter in the leather pouch and swing it round and round until you reach your top speed, and release the string between the thumb and finger when you think the target is in line. This is only a country project because in a crowded city the destruction could be a disaster.

The "Flip"

The sling-shot or "flip", as we called it, was a refined model of the sling. Its accuracy was more dependable and it was capable of killing small game as far as fifty feet distance. The fork of a dogwood bush served as a stock, and instead of using strings, two strips of rubber from a discarded inner tube were used. One end of each of the rubber strips was fastened to each side of the fork and the other end was fastened to the leather pouch. By placing a small stone in the leather pouch, holding the stock firmly in one hand and the leather piece between the thumb and forefinger of the other hand, and pulling back on the rubber strips, the rock could be fairly accurate for a short distance.

Pop Guns

Probably the most popular of the "guns" was the popgun because they were easy to make, and dogwood berries, used for ammunition, were plentiful from summer right on through the winter months. All that was needed to make a popgun was a sharp knife, a section of bamboo, and a straight piece of wood from a limb of a dogwood. The hollow in the bamboo must be slightly smaller than the dogwood berry so it would fit tightly in the chamber. One berry was pushed through the bamboo, using the piece of dogwood, to within an eighth-inch of the other end. A second berry was pushed through quickly, building up pressure and forcing the first one out, and replacing it in the bamboo. The accuracy was not dependable, but if hit on bare skin, might sting a little. There were many variations and the popgun, and this was a popular recess pastime when school was in session.

When I was about ten years old, Papa made a bow and arrow for me. He fashioned the bow from a seasoned piece of sassafras and spent many hours shaping it to his satisfaction. Arrows were made from the "shoots", or new growth of sourwood trees that grew long and slender. I never mastered the bow and arrow, probably because the arrows were too difficult to make and too easy to lose.

A COUNTRY BOY *From Owl Hollow*

Country boys sometimes can have weird ways of entertaining themselves, or they may sound weird to most people. Insects, as well as animals were a source of entertainment for me, and sometimes could be painful if I got careless. Hornet's nest were always intriguing and I wanted to learn how they built them and spent a lot of time trying to learn their secret. Papa had warned me to keep my distance from hornets because he had a bad experience with them once. He told about a hornet's nest in an apple tree in the orchard, and when it came time for the fruit to ripen, the hornets threatened anyone who came near them. Papa took some rocks, and standing at what he considered a safe distance, starting throwing them at the hornet's nest. He saw one hornet come out of the nest and it came at him like a bullet, stinging Papa on the forehead. Either the impact or the surprise knocked him to the ground as if he had been shot, and he had a healthy regard for the insects from then on. I found many hornet's nest but only one was located in a place where I could observe them without the risk of being stung. It was on a limb overhanging a creek, and a big bend in the creek just above the nest allowed me to get within twenty feet without being seen by the hornets. I spent hours watching, but was never able to see what they were bringing into their nest. After the nests were deserted in winter, I would sometimes bring one home and study it.

Yellow jackets are almost as painful as hornets and they have their nests in the ground instead of being where they can be seen. Several times I have been stung by them just because I walked too close to their nest and didn't know it was there. One summer there was a yellow jacket's nest across the road from our house and a little too close for comfort. I had heard that by taking a bottle and forcing the neck into the hole where the insects went in and out, that they would fill the bottle and could be destroyed. One night after the yellow jackets were all in the nest, I went out and placed a big bottle in the entrance and next morning it was filled with hundreds of angry bees. I was not brave enough to just walk up to the bottle and remove it, and quickly put a stopper in to seal the yellow jacket's fate. There were also a lot of them flying around the outside of the bottle just looking for something to sting. Papa had said that once the yellow jackets were captured, they could be drowned, but he didn't explain how to get them to the water so I just let the bottle stay, and by the next day they had made another entrance and the bottle was empty. I let it stay and kept my distance from the nest the rest of the summer.

There was a large beetle almost two inches long that could be used as entertainment and also to scare the heck out of girls. I don't know the name of the creature but we called it the snapping bug. When captured and held between the fingers, the beetle would snap its neck, making a popping noise like someone snapping their fingers. They were harmless and could be a lot of fun, especially at school during recess.

Games We Played

One game we boys used to play was such a waste of trees that I look back on it with regret. One boy would select a sapling about 20 to 30 feet tall, depending on how brave the boy was, or how big a show-off he was. He would climb the sapling as far up as he could without bending it too much, and another boy, on the ground would chop it down. The faster one chopped, the faster the sapling fell with its load, but chopping it slowly would give an easy ride to the ground. The boys would change places and go through the same process again until as many as a dozen saplings were cut or until some other game took their interest. No one could imagine then that the day would come when people would actually conserve trees.

Another game played by the boys was called leap frog and could only be played at school because a number of boys were needed to make it interesting. One boy bent over and another would get a running start, place his hands on the other's hips or back, and jump over him as far as possible. Where he hit the ground, he also assumed the bent-over position, and the next boy had to make two jumps and so on until all were in a bent over position and then the last one raised up and started the process all over again. The lead boy at the time chose any direction he wanted, and it might be that he was at the edge of a deep water hole and that would usually end that game.

Stilt-walking was a favorite pastime and was also a good way to cross a creek in winter without getting your shoes wet. Stilts were easy to make for all that was needed were two small saplings each with a limb a couple of feet from the ground. Trim all but the one limb close to the trunk and leave the limb to be used about six inches long. The height from the ground depended on the depth of the water or how good you were at walking on stilts.

Reading books was way down on my list of things for entertainment until Gaylon Miller loaned me one that was written by Edgar Rice Burroughs. It was about a man called Tarzan, who lived in a jungle, and I read the book two or three times. Tarzan had been raised by apes and could swing from tree to tree, out-swim a crocodile, and when he yelled, the whole jungle stayed out of his way. He was just another animal in the jungle and asked no favors from any of the other animals.

There were two sweetgum trees that grew side by side on the bank of Hickory Hollow creek and they were out of sight of the house. If Tarzan could go from tree to tree, why couldn't I do the same? I did wonder if the trees in the jungle were as brash as a sweetgum but decided to try anyway. Climbing up 20 or 30 feet, I walked out on a limb that I knew was large enough to hold my weight and crossed over to the other tree where the limbs overlapped. It was a thrill, but I never did try to jump from one to the other like Tarzan, although it was given some thought.

The only card game Papa and Mama would let me play was Rook and we had to make our own cards. Every election year there were lots of candidates running for some sort of office, and each left us a card, with his name and the office he was seeking on it. Children would beg cards from them because all the candidate cards were the same size, but different colors. A family with a lot of kids, like the Simpsons, were sometimes shunned by the office seekers or they pretended they only had a few cards left. We had to draw the faces on the blank side of the card, and there were some pretty odd-looking Rook cards in the neighborhood.

The older folks had their own forms of entertainment like playing checkers or pitching horseshoes. There was only one horse in the neighborhood that was kept shod so we had to use mule shoes which were smaller and more difficult to make a ringer. Both of these games were played by both men and women and young and old but was more popular with the older generation.

Papa, the Barber

On Saturday afternoons, if it was not necessary to work in the fields, we could always expect company because Papa was the unofficial barber for the neighborhood. The closest barber shop was over ten miles away in Dover, and they expected you to pay fifteen to twenty-five cents, depending on which of the two shops you visited. Papa never charged for a haircut and even threw in a shave on special occasions. It was the neighborly thing to do and besides, one got to visit a lot. One of our neighbors, Landy Simpson, would never get his hair cut in March because he believed if he did, he would not live until the next March. There were others who refused to get their hair cut on Friday and that suited Papa just fine. Papa cut my hair but said it was so fine that his clippers sometimes just pulled it out instead of cutting it.

One morning when Papa and Mama had gone somewhere, Bill Crutcher came by and wanted a shave. He said he had a date with some girl and didn't have time to go home and shave and decided to ask Papa to shave him. As Papa was not there, he insisted that I do the job, and even though I had never shaved a person in my life, including myself, that made no difference to Bill. I got Papa's straight razor and shaving mug and made a lather with cold water. It would take too long to heat water on Mama's wood burning stove, and Bill was in a hurry. Bill sat down in a chair and reared back in a sort of barber chair position while I lathered his face. Holding the razor as I had seen Papa do many times, I started down one side of his face and immediately knew something was wrong. Everywhere a whisker had been, there was a tiny drop of blood oozing out of the skin. Apparently Papa knew something about shaving a fellow that I had yet to learn because when he shaved, there rarely was a drop of blood. Without a mirror to see what was happening, Bill insisted I continue the bloody work. When I finished, and he looked in the mirror, he almost fainted. Between the two of us we patched his face as best we could with some stuff Papa used when he cut himself, to make it stop bleeding. A little of the stuff is alright, but when we finished, Bill was afraid he was going to lose the skin on his face. He decided it would be better if he didn't meet his date and went on home, and it was a long time before Bill could shave again.

Flu and Other Illness

Illness in the early part of the century was a lot different from today, and it is difficult to describe . Up until the late twenties, there were people who became ill and died without a doctor ever seeing them. The modern generation will find it hard to believe that such a thing could have happened. There were actually people who died at a ripe old age, who may never have seen a doctor in their lifetime. There had been more country doctors in the days before it became too expensive and time-consuming to become a doctor, and although they were not well-trained, they were better than no doctor at all. It was truly a time of survival of the fittest for my first 16 years.

The flu epidemic of 1918 passed me by but caught up with me a few years later. I was visiting Grandpappy and Grandmammy one Saturday, and there were others there, including the preacher, who was to hold a service that night. All at once, it seemed, I went from feeling good to being very sick and I didn't want to be around so many people feeling the way I did, so I decided to go up the hill to where Gladys and Bill Kennerly lived. That hill never seemed to be as steep or as high as it did that Saturday afternoon, and I was afraid I was going to pass out before reaching the house. Gladys put her hand on my forehead and told Bill that I was burning up with fever and that she was going to put me in their bed in the living room. The next thing I remember was opening my eyes two or three days later and seeing Papa and Mama standing over me, and they were crying. They told me later that doctor Ryan had been there and had told them that if I didn't break out of the coma soon, that I wouldn't make it. There is no doubt that Gladys and her family saved my life.

About two years later I came down with the flu again, but this time I was home where Papa and Mama could take care of me and it was more mild than before. Just as I was getting over it, both Papa and Mama came down with the flu and were more sick than I had been. I had to wait on them, bringing food and medicine, for they were too sick to take care of themselves. Medication for the flu was plenty of cough syrup that Mama made and always kept on hand. It was a mixture of honey and the boiled-down sap from wild cherry bark, and it did the job well. Before they were able to be up, except in the house, our supply of cough syrup gave out. There was plenty of the wild cherry bark mixture, but there was no honey in the house for making a new batch.

There was a beehive near the house, but to rob it now would probably mean the bees would die before spring, and we decided against it. The next nearest honey supply was a bee tree on the ridge near the Boyd Pond, and it was decided to rob it for the honey. After putting on plenty of warm clothing, I took a water bucket and ax and headed up the hill in front of our house. Although I was getting over the flu, I was still weak and it was difficult to climb the hill. The bee tree was a large postoak near the road and took me a long time to chop it down. There was no need for protection from the bees because it was too cold for them to put up a fight. I didn't feel too sorry for these bees anyway, for they were the little black ones that fought to the finish when the weather was warm. After cutting into the area where the honey was located, I filled the water bucket with honey comb and closed the opening to keep the coons out until we could come back later for the rest of the honey. I never went back, but Papa checked on the swarm next spring and said they were doing fine, and ready to defend what honey was left. Mama made a new supply of cough syrup and we survived the ordeal.

There were other illnesses in the early twenties, but it was believed that most could be cured with a big dose of calomel, castor oil, black draught, or turpentine. After being treated with these remedies, you had to be awfully sick before you complained again. Papa took it upon himself to do the doctoring in our house and always had a cure for any ailment. He was sure that a young boy got wormy just like dogs and cows, and his favorite medication for the suspected worms was a concoction called vermifuge, a thick white liquid with the foulest taste of anything I have ever known. There is no way to describe the taste except, maybe to say that castor oil was like lemonade, compared to vermifuge. Surely by now it has been outlawed as cruel and unusual punishment. It seems that I am the only human who ever swallowed the stuff because I have never met another person who has taken it. One day when Papa and Mama were gone, I took what was left in the bottle about a hundred yards out in a sage grass field and buried it in the bottom of a ditch. No one ever asked me about the missing bottle of vermifuge, and if they had, there is little doubt that I would have lied about its disappearance.

Papa's Spring Cleaning

Papa never let a spring go by without a thorough cleansing of the insides, whether or not he might suspect worms were present. As he came through Dover on his way back from selling the tobacco crop in Clarksville, Papa stopped by Dr. Crow's office and bought a supply of calomel. Before it was time to start some real spring work, he doled out the calomel, and we knew winter was over. After taking three of those capsules, I spent more time out in the woods than in the house. We had no outhouse, so the woods across the road in front of the house became a favorite place to sit and let Nature take its course. I was too busy with my own problems to know what was happening to Papa or Mama, but I am sure they were not spending a lot of time in the house either. The calomel was actually a poison, and could not be left inside the body, so a big dose of black draught was used to flush out the calomel -- and it was back to the woods. After a few days, life returned to normal, and I didn't have to worry about another cleaning job until the next spring.

Papa read an article in the Atlanta newspaper that said a lot of people did not get enough iron in their system and this could cause them to be sluggish. I was always on the sluggish side of the energy level, and he thought maybe some iron was just the thing to pep me up. Everybody knows that iron dissolves in vinegar, and if you drink the vinegar that has dissolved iron, it should go right into the system. After all, it is impossible to chew up a nail, so why not let the vinegar do it for you. He took one of Mama's quart fruit jars, dropped in a handfull of clean nails and filled the jar with vinegar and sat it on a shelf to age awhile. Several days later I was given a spoonful of the stuff, and it didn't taste bad at all, which was a disappointment to Papa, because to him any medicine that didn't taste bad was no good. The worse the taste, the better the medicine. Each day I was given my spoon, filled with iron and vinegar, and after awhile, the concoction began to taste awful, and then Papa knew his iron medicine was working. It got so bad that I could not get the stuff down, and Mama tasted it one day and threw the mixture out. Papa must have decided that I didn't need iron; and that I was just plain lazy.

One of Papa's remedies was a good one that I have used in recent years with good success, but I doubt that doctors would prescribe it. Anytime one of us was cut by a knife or ax, Papa soaked the wound with coal oil. Once my chopping ax glanced off a piece of hardwood and cut deep into my ankle. He took a rag, poured coal oil on it, and placed it over the wound with a piece of string. It did not burn or get sore and healed quickly, and this happened many times with the same results. There was always a supply of coal oil, or kerosene, as city folks call it, because it was used in our lamps for lighting.

Papa would take a piece of cornbread to the field with him because he was a victim of what we called the "weak trembles". This condition could come on at any time while working and was almost the same as fainting. He had learned somewhere that when he felt the fainting coming on, if he ate something the feeling would go away, and he would feel strong again. Later it was learned that the "weak trembles" was actually a diet deficiency which was not uncommon at the time.

Mason's Clinic

There was a clinic in Murray (run by two doctors, the Mason Brothers) that was becoming famous, and even treated people from faraway places. One of them was an outstanding specialist in diagnosing illnesses and the other one was a good surgeon. A few people from our area had gone there, but usually too late to be helped.

I heard Papa tell about a Mr. Patterson, who lived across the river in Calloway County that had a severe heart condition. Papa had met him while fishing down on the river and had heard the story from Mr. Patterson himself. After Dr. Mason had examined him, he was told that they believed some kind of growth was crowding his heart, and unless it was removed, he didn't have long to live. The odds that an operation could help him were uncertain, but there was a chance it would be successful, and this was a choice Mr. Patterson would have to make. He decided to take the chance. The doctors explained that it was an experiment, but they believed it would work. They also told him that because they were not sure what effect painkillers might have, they would not use any when they operated, and the pain would be severe. Mr.

Patterson told Papa the pain was awful as they cut and sawed their way into the heart cavity. They did find a growth around the heart, and while the surgeon removed it, the other doctor held the heart in his hand. He said that lying there, watching his heart beat, and wondering if it would stop, was an experience he didn't want to go through again.

Country Doctors

Dr. Crow had his office in Dover, but it was difficult to find him there, because he was out in the county most of the time, seeing patients, and doleing out pills where needed. House calls were 50 cents, and if pills were needed, there was an additional charge of 10 cents. The doctor's pay was often a chicken, a slab of bacon, or half bushel of corn-meal. Sometimes he only received a promise, but I never knew of a country doctor refusing to go see a patient because of money. Once when Dr. Crow was in our area, someone told him about Mary Hensley giving birth to a baby the day before. Clem and Mary lived out on the ridge beyond the Boyd Pond, and was a difficult place to reach, but the doctor went by to check on her. Mary was up and doing the laundry and was doing very well.

Homeplace of Dr. Bufford (Died 1915). Owners: Duncan and Carol Kennerly

Dr. Ryan lived just up the river on Lost Creek, and although he was an excellent doctor, he was a farmer at heart. He had an outstanding record of saving patients with typhoid fever, and it was said that he lost only one patient with the fever in more than 20 years. That was once when a mother gave her daughter some raw tomatoes against Dr. Ryan's orders. In many ways the doctor was ahead of his time in his skill of treating the sick. Like other doctors, his pay was uncertain, but he always went if he thought he was needed, whether there was pay or not. It was Dr. Ryan who saved my life when a nail went all the way through my foot when I was about seven years old.

Pack Peddler Cures Cancer

I remembered a story I had heard at an early age about a pack peddler curing a cancer on the lip of Mr. Tom Crutcher. A few years ago, I asked his son, Buster, who was Aunt Tince's husband, about it, and he told it as I had remembered it. Mr. Crutcher had been afflicted with cancer of the lip for some time and it had gotten to the point where it was painful and noticeable. He had gone to doctors in Dover and Murray, but treatments had not been effective.

A pack peddler was spending the night at the Crutcher home, which was the practice in the early part of the century. He noticed the cancer and asked some questions about the history of it, and then told Mr. Crutcher that he thought he could cure it. He added that Mr. Crutcher would have to suffer terrible pain for about twenty-four hours, and there was no guarantee, but he knew of people who had been cured. Mr. Crutcher was desperate and agreed to try whatever the pack peddler had to offer. Next morning the peddler went out to the fields and woods, and after some time, returned with an assortment of plants, roots, and leaves. Putting it all in a pot, he let it simmer until the liquid had thickened and was dark brown in color. He smeared a generous portion on a cloth and covered the affected area, secured it with a cord, and went on his way. Buster said his father walked the floor for twenty-four hours, crying, yelling, and suffering so much that he threatened to remove the cloth, but didn't. After the twenty-four hours were up, to the minute, the cloth was removed, and sticking to it was what looked like flesh about the size of a marble, with fleshy strands attached, looking somewhat like a spider. The cancer never returned and Mr. Crutcher lived to be 87 years old.

Visiting Neighbors at Night

Because there were no telephones, radios, or television, people visited a lot, especially at night, during the winter months. A family might walk as far as two miles, visit until bedtime, and then walk back home. Those visits were an important part of community life, and I enjoyed going visiting with Papa and Mama. There was something about being out in the dark, carrying a lantern if it was a dark night, that thrilled me. I loved the night sounds and tried to figure out what animals were running through the leaves. Papa was a popular visitor for he subscribed to the Sunday Atlanta newspaper and was up with what was going on in the outside world. He read every word in the paper and then passed it on to neighbors, and it would end up as wallpaper on somebody's wall to keep out the cold. I loved the colored comics, or "funny papers", as we called them. My favorite was the Katzenjammer Kids, but I also enjoyed Happy Hooligan, Mutt & Jeff, Bringing Up Father, and many others. There were stories about places that I wanted to see some day.

A weekly newspaper was published at Dover and most people subscribed to it and those that didn't, read a neighbor's paper. It gave all the county news and told who had been in Dover and sometimes one of our neighbors would get his name in the paper. When it was "court week" in Dover, the paper told all about the trials and who was sent to jail and for how long. I don't recall anyone from our area that was ever sent to jail or the penitentary in Nashville.

There was a weekly newspaper called GRIT that was published somewhere up in Pennsylvania that several local people read, but it was more news of general interest, or a continued story, rather than a newspaper. Louie Hosford was the paper's carrier, and had to walk about ten miles to deliver a dozen copies. Louie collected 5 cents for each paper and had to send a portion of it to GRIT and kept the rest for himself.

Papa always liked to play pranks on people, and one dark night when we went to visit Landy and Mae Simpson and their eight kids, he had me blow out the lantern light some distance before we reached their house. We stopped at the front gate, as was the custom, and Papa changed his voice when he yelled out a loud "Hello" that brought Landy to the front porch. Still using his new voice, Papa asked if he could spend the night, a common request from a stranger in those days. Landy was polite but explained that he had a lot of children and there was no extra room in the house. Papa insisted that there must be room for one more person and said something to the effect he didn't believe Landy, and was coming in to see for himself. You just didn't talk to people like that, especially in their own home, and when Landy called for one of the kids to bring him his shotgun, Papa started laughing and made himself known. Landy let him know that he did not think it was all that funny, and he was a little cool the rest of the night

A few nights later, while we were sitting around the fireplace at home, somebody yelled a big "Hello" from our front gate in a voice that was not recognized, and when Papa went to the front porch, the voice asked if he could spend the night. Of course Papa knew right away that it was Landy, trying to get back at him, and he answered in his best polite voice that he would be more than welcomed to spend the night and to come right on in. Papa almost passed out, when out of the blackness came the biggest, roughest-looking stranger he had ever seen. It turned out that the fellow was real pleasant and we enjoyed having him. Papa did warn Mama and me next day of what might happen to us if we ever breathed a word to anyone about what happened that night.

The Latch String

If a neighbor invited you to visit he might say "The latch string is out", meaning that you were welcome to visit at any time. Few people had locks on their doors, but inside was a latch in a groove that kept the door closed. Just above the latch was a small hole through the door and a string that was tied to the latch, could be pulled through and the latch lifted from the outside. At night the string was pulled inside, and the door could not be opened from the outside. Papa used a latch system on the tobacco barn to discourage anyone from stealing his tobacco, but this one worked on a different principle. The latch was fastened to a secret board, and if you knew which board to push up, you could raise the latch and open the door.

Hunting Bee Trees

Honey was a regular part of our diet, and Papa had a beehive out under a big postoak, but he seldom took the honey from it. Each spring he would lift it, and if it was heavy with honey, he would take some, but most of the time the bees had used it themselves. He said that if the bees had too much honey when spring came, they would be lazy and might not make more honey and could starve. If the hive was light, it meant they had to go to work and replenish their supply. Our main source of honey came from bee trees, which were plentiful out in the woods, and it was free for the taking. Papa would rob the bees in early spring, giving the swarm all summer to find a new home and supply it with bread and honey for the next winter. The only exception was when we ran low and had to replace our supply during the winter months.

There were different ways to hunt for bee trees, but the favorite was to locate where the bees were watering, especially in dry weather, then watch as the bees took off toward their home. If the bee tree was nearby, the bee would fly directly from the water to the tree, but if it was a long distance away, the bee would circle, climbing higher and higher, before heading toward home. I have found them as close as a hundred yards and as far as a mile away from their watering place. After the direction is determined, a mental marker, such as a tall tree, was used to mark the course. Following the course, each tree that might have a hollow trunk or limb is checked to see if bees are going in and out of the foliage. If they are, then with closer inspection, one could locate the exact spot where they were entering the tree. The biggest drawback to hunting bees is that it must be done in spring or summer when there is lots of foliage to hide them.

Finding a bee tree was much like hunting for squirrels, and Papa and I enjoyed it as much as hunting for game. We were still just as competitive and often hunted them together, and I guess he thought it was safer than when I was carrying a gun. He was better than I was and found more trees because he had a sharper eye and could see them better, just like he could beat me finding squirrels. Before Papa's eyes began to fail him, or his arms began to get shorter as he preferred to call it, he had the sharpest eyes I have ever known, except for Wheeler Love. Both of us refused to hunt with Wheeler for he could spot a squirrel or bee tree before we were even near it.

Once the tree was discovered, the trunk would be examined closely from the ground to about eight feet up. If it had been discovered by someone before, there would be a faint "X" carved into the bark. You had to look carefully because sometimes the X was difficult to see. This was because there were people who, if they came across a tree with a X, would cut it and take the honey, the same as they would poach game. A dim X attracted less attention. If no mark was found, then you made your own X, and all honest people would respect it. It was an unwritten code of the land and you were expected to honor it.

All wild bees were not alike. There were the large yellow ones that Papa called Italian bees, and they were not as aggressive as the smaller black bees. Those little black bees would fight and sting to the last one and would even chase you through the underbrush. I believe they were what are called killer bees today. The best honey was made from clover and wildflowers, including the sourwood tree. There was a big area of mountain laurel out near the Love Place, and honey made from the laurel could be poison to some people, including me. Mama would boil the honey that came from that area and skim off the impurities that rose to the top. It didn't seem to bother Papa or Mama, but we did hear that a Mr. Riggins over on Bear Creek died from eating the honey. Of course, it could have been a ruptured appendix; no one ever knew for sure.

Hunting Ginseng

Country people seem to enjoy hunting for almost anything, whether it is for food, or money, or just the fun of hunting something. Ginseng is an elusive plant that grows only in certain favored locations and the roots, when dried, would bring us a dollar an ounce. It thrives on north hillsides where hardwood trees grow. A first-year plant has one stem and adds a stem for each of four years. The four-year olds were the ones with the largest roots, but they were more difficult to find.

Family Entertainment

It didn't take a lot of money to be entertained back in the twenties. During the winter months, a musical would be held somewhere in the neighborhood almost every Saturday night. Most of the time it was at Landy Simpson's house because they had the only organ for miles around, and the only one who could play it was his daughter, Nellie. Somehow the news would get around that there was to be a musical, and there would be a house full of people and a crowd out in the yard. Landy and Uncle Dave Champion were the fiddle players and Papa picked the banjo, and the music might go on until midnight. They were all good musicians on tunes like "Eighth of January", "Turkey in the Straw", "Old Joe Clark" and all the fiddle tunes that were popular at the time. Landy was my favorite because he could play tunes that I liked better than the hoedown type. One of my favorites was "Over the Waves", a soft and beautiful melody. Papa was extra good on the banjo and played every chance he got, even at home alone sometimes when the mood hit him. Uncle Dave was popular because he could act the fool while he played and could make everybody laugh. Nellie could make that old organ sway, and it was always a pleasure to hear her play.

The Showboat

Once or twice a year the showboat *Cotton Blossom* stopped at Fort Henry Landing for two or three nights of entertainment. Families for miles around came and spent up to 25 cents each to see the three-act plays. I never saw one of the shows because most of the church members believed it to be the work of the Devil, and besides, it was throwing money away, which made it a double sin. When the *Cotton Blossom* passed Pine Bluff, as it came up the Tennessee River, they would begin to play the steam calliope that could be heard at least five miles, depending on the weather. If I wasn't working in the field, I would run the couple of miles to the Government Light just to watch the boat go by and see the clouds of steam escaping from the calliope's pipes. Sometimes some of the crew members or performers would wave, and that made me feel ten feet tall.

At Fort Henry the showboat put on a different show each night, and those who could afford it went to all performances.

One time a fellow came to Blue Spring and put on a movie at the school house, the first that many of the local people had ever seen. There was no electricity, but he was prepared for such handicaps, because the projector was operated by hand and the light was furnished by a carbide lamp. All the movies were the Wild West type, and an advantage to cranking the projector by hand was that he could make those horses run as fast as he wanted them to run, or have them run in slow motion. He had a full house of about fifty people each night and most of them were church-goers. The price was 10 cents and the show lasted about two hours. It was the first movie that Papa, Mama and I had seen since leaving Paducah.

Box Suppers

Probably the most popular entertainment of the year was the local Box Supper that was held to raise money for some worthy cause such as school improvements. Each girl, usually of courting age, packed a box with her best cooking, and it was auctioned off to the highest bidder. This gave the lucky buyer the opportunity to share the lunch with the girl who had packed it. There was a rule that the girl and her box should be kept a secret until the box was sold, but secrets are hard to keep, especially if the box belonged to a popular lass. The auction really got going if there were two or more boys wanting to share a lunch with the same girl. Sometimes a box sold for as much as three dollars, while another with an unknown owner might fetch as little as a quarter.

Shivarees

When a couple got married, there was sure to be a shivaree within a few days and this was one of the hazards of getting married. The neighborhood bachelors would get together and choose a date that was a well-kept secret from the newlyweds. Then one night, without warning, guns began to fire, bells started to ring, dishpans were pounded like drums, and there was yelling like a bunch of Indians were attacking. The new husband was obliged to outwit the attackers, and if the house was not well-protected on all sides, he might slip away into the dark and not return until the group had gone home. Most of the time, however, the new husband was captured and a dunking in the creek or pond would result unless acceptable treats were served to everybody.

The first time I was present at a shivaree, I was not aware of what was going on. I was sleeping in the loft at Grandpappy's when Herman and Mavis were shivareed, and I was told about it the next morning. They said there were all kinds of noises, including guns, dishpans, and hollering and somebody even came up in the loft and turned me over in bed while looking for Herman, who had managed to escape the fellows.

When Mr. Moody Mathis got married the second time, I was in the crowd that shivareed him, but more as an onlooker rather than taking an active part. Mr. Moody was a big man and decided to have some fun with the fellows and dared them to throw him in the pond. A dare was something you didn't take lightly, and several of them grabbed Mr. Moody and there was a real tussle before he was put in the pond, taking three or four with him. After the pond dipping and the noise died down, refreshments were served, and the newlyweds could relax and go on with their normal way of living.

During the summer months, sometimes I would go to Ila Sills' house on Sunday afternoon, and a group of boys would play marbles until dark. There was a level spot in his back yard where no grass grew, and it made an ideal spot for the game. Each boy had a prized taw and would fight to keep it, and anyone who would steal another's taw was considered lower than a chicken thief. I was never good at marbles like some of the boys who could bust a taw at ten feet or more. Any marble you hit fair and square, except the taw, was yours to keep and it didn't take long for me to loose my marbles (a familiar expression), and I was out of the game until I could swap something of value for more. A trade might include a popgun, slingshot, and once I traded a penny for a number of marbles.

Candy-pulling was a favorite entertainment, especially with couples with courting on their minds. A gallon or more of sorghum molasses was boiled down until it was extra thick, and as it cooled, it would be pulled until it was white. Then, using scissors, it was ready to cut into small bites, that when hardened, could break a healthy tooth. It was something two people could do, and gave the courting couples a chance to touch hands without eyebrows being raised.

While the older ones pulled candy, the younger ones showed more interested in making popcorn balls to eat, than touching someone's hand. While the molasses was hot, it was mixed with a handful of popcorn and worked into a ball as the syrup hardened. The results was a ball of sweet popcorn that was a real treat, and sometimes a messy one that could cause some sticky hands.

Going Modern

Every time Panther Creek flooded, or the backwater from the Tennessee River came up to the road that forded the creek, all traffic was stopped except people walking who could cross on a swinging bridge. I don't know when the swinging bridge was built, but it was a while before we moved from Paducah. Each end of the bridge was fastened to a large tree with two steel cables about two feet apart, and a wooden floor,

Swinging bridge near Blue Spring. *Stand:* Gertie and Mable Hosford, Edith Sills, Gaynell Simpson, Tince Lyon, Kinnie Hosford. *Seated:* Clyde Lyon, Ila Sills, Kirby Hosford, Lois Sills, Hazel and Opel Hosford, Nellie and Kennedy Mathis. (Early 20s)

Photo sent to me by Elizabeth Hosford

fastened to the cables, served as a walkway.   Steps at each end gave access to the bridge, and it was so cumbersome climbing up the steps that many of the older women refused to use it.   Boys enjoyed getting on the bridge and starting a swinging motion that sometimes resulted in one falling into the creek below. Grownups didn't appreciate it if the bridge was rocked while they were crossing.

In the early -- or mid-twenties the county decided to build a steel bridge across Panther Creek just below the ford.   Watching the workers build forms for the concrete helped me later when I built a road for my toy truck. The heavy pieces of steel were hauled in, one piece at a time, on wagons with extra-wide steel tires and pulled by the biggest mules I had ever seen. A new road was being cut along the hillside just above the spring and an expert at using dynamite was sent from Dover to do the blasting. After each blast, a crew of several men, using picks and shovels, removed the dirt and chunks of rock until an area wide enough for a wagon and team was cut out of dirt and limestone rocks. The road and bridge did make it possible to cross Panther Creek until water flooded the road leading from the bridge to the hill on the other side.

Grandpappy, the Ferryman

Nearly every spring the Tennessee River flooded over her banks and sometimes the backwater would go up Panther Creek as far as the Will Rushing place. Grandpappy said the snow melting in the East Tennessee mountains caused a lot of the flooding. When the water rose high enough to cut off traffic at Blue Spring, the next road crossing was at the Rushing place and made the short walk to church a long trek that could take an hour or more. Grandpappy took it upon himself to ferry people across, using a jon boat that he called a "skiff". He loved people and this gave him an excuse to meet and talk with them.

Ferrying was not always an easy job. When the river flooded early in the spring, the weather might be cold and blustery, and there are few places colder than on the water in cold weather. Grandpappy never refused to set people across regardless of the weather, and I have been with him when his hands would be so cold he could hardly hold the paddle, yet I never saw him wear gloves. Instead of rowing with two oars from the middle of the boat, he sat in the back and paddled with one oar, switching from side to side to keep the boat on a straight course. He taught me how to paddle, and keep the boat going straight without switching sides with the oars.

The Radio Arrives

About the biggest thing that happened in the early to mid-twenties was when Gaylon Miller, who lived at Fort Henry, bought a radio. We had read about radios in the Atlanta newspaper, but most people were dubious about the contraption because they could not believe somebody in Chicago could yell loud enough to be heard on a machine at Fort Henry. Not only were people skeptical, but some of the more religious of the neighborhood wondered if it might not be the work of the Devil and hoped the thing would go away soon. Gaylon was one of the Miller Brothers who ran the store, and he had more money than most of the people. He even had bought a car and was one of two families who drove cars to the Blue Spring church. Papa was ahead of his time and was always looking for improvements, whether it was equipment or fertilizer, and went to Gaylon's one night to see the gadget for himself. He came home amazed and said he actually heard people talking from all the way up to Chicago and as far south as Shreveport. He said he heard people in New York and Cincinnati and predicted that one day radios would be in most homes and people would be listening to people talk and play music from dozens of cities from all over the country.

It took Papa over a year to talk Grandpappy and Grandmammy into buying a radio. There were improvements being made, and you could buy one that had a big speaker so that everybody in the room could listen to it. Gaylon's radio had head-sets and only three people could listen in at one time, leaving several to wonder what was going on. When Grandpappy heard that there was a station in Nashville that had country music on it, including some good fiddling, he started to get interested.

I can't recall where Grandpappy bought the radio, but more than likely it was ordered from Sears & Roebuck or Montgomery Ward, and Papa was elated for he loved country music. When it arrived, they sent for Papa to set the thing up and get it operating. Papa said he had never seen such a mess of wires, batteries, and boxes of gadgets that had no name. The instructions said that a 100-foot wire had to be strung, the higher the better, and another wire attached to it that lead to the radio. A big tree out by the woodpile served as the base to one end of the wire that was called an aerial, and the other end was fastened to a tree at the edge of the woods toward where Gladys and Willie lived. Papa said there were big red letters warning that the wire to the radio should be disconnected if there was a thunderstorm around. Papa said that he didn't want to even be in the neighborhood if lightning struck that wire, and especially didn't want to be in the same room with the radio.

The big wooden box included four dry cell batteries of various sizes and a note giving further information that a regular car battery would have to be purchased and hooked up before the radio would operate. Somebody went to Fort Henry and made arrangements for the Dover mail carrier to pick up the battery. A few days later the radio was working very well except when there was a thunderstorm, even many miles away, and then it squawked like a scared chicken. At night over half a dozen stations could be heard, but the most popular ones were Chicago and Nashville.

Saturday nights a crowd could be expected, some from three or four miles away, to listen to the fiddle program from Nashville. Another favorite was a fifteen-minute program from Chicago called "Sam n' Henry"; but the name was changed later to "Amos n' Andy" and it ran for many years. One time when Grandmammy was in the kitchen someone tuned in to a lady singing opera, and Grandmammy came running, thinking there was a murder in progress. There was a station in Shreveport, Louisiana that was owned and operated by a man who ran a clinic that promised to cure everything from tick bites to hydrophobia. The fellow talked continually all day long every day and somebody wrote him a letter that implied in pretty strong language that he was no more than a quack doctor and could not cure anything except a bulging pocketbook. He read the letter on the air and then told the writer off and invited him to come to Shreveport and kiss his ass, and added that if he wasn't home, he would leave the ass tied in his back yard. Some people thought it was funny, but Grandpappy and Grandmammy never forgave him for talking nasty on their radio.

The Automobile

In the early and mid-twenties drummers (traveling salesmen) began to use the road from Tharpe to Fort Henry, selling their wares, and the road came by our house. Once when Mama and a couple of the Simpson girls and I were picking blackberries at the Boyd Pond, we heard a car off at a distance that was coming our way. We knew it could only be a drummer, and the women didn't want some stranger to see the outfits they were dressed in to pick berries. If I had been alone, I would have stood by the road and maybe he would have asked me to ride with him. Everyone wanted to see the car, and decided we would hide in the woods where the driver could not see us, but we would be able to see him and his car. We hid behind a large fallen log, and as the car approached, it was decided that we were too low for a good view and would have to stand up. We were higher than we thought and just as the car passed, we were in full view and were seen by the driver and he waved at us. It was an embarrassing moment for Mama and the girls.

Clem And The Drummers

Clem and Mary Hensley lived out on the ridge beyond the Boyd Pond on the Tharpe to Fort Henry road. Their house was at the top of a hill when coming from Tharpe, and in hot weather, drummers and their cars would be hot and dusty by the time they reached Clem's place and sometimes would stop for a drink of water. After their cistern went dry, the nearest supply of water was Summer's Spring, half a mile away, and water was brought from the spring and stored in jugs. One drummer who stopped for water got quit a surprise. Clem also kept other liquids in jugs and by mistake, handed the thirsty man a jug of new whiskey that took the fellow's breath away, and it took him a long time to start breathing again. Clem said he never saw the fellow again. This is supposed to be a true story.

Another story, not supposed to be true, but which caused a lot of laughs at the time, concerned a drummer and his car. It was the first car that came by Clem's place and the first one he had ever seen. He saw the machine slowly coming up the hill toward his house, and the headlights made it look like some huge animal and the motor sounded like animal growls to him. He gave the contraption a blast from his shotgun, and it stopped and the driver took off across a field. Mary heard the shot and came out to see what was going on, and Clem told her what had happened. When she asked if he had killed the thing Clem said he didn't know if he killed it or not, but that he made it turn a man loose.

Religion, a Way of Life

There are some things that can be compared to the twenties, and there are many that can be contrasted. In the twenties the people between the rivers believed there was a Heaven and a Hell and all souls were going to spend eternity in one or the other. Heaven had streets paved with gold and Hell was a place of eternal burning of brimstone, or sulphur. I remembered smelling some sulphur smoke once when Grandmanny was sulphuring apples and sure didn't want to spend eternity smelling sulphur smoke. Religion was a serious business and nothing was allowed to get in the way of saving souls. There were some who had little or no religion, but they were few and mostly ignored. I heard a preacher remark once that if you wanted to find a honest to goodness God-fearing man, just go up one of the hollows and you would find him. He could have added that God was about the only thing such a man feared. Church was not only good for the soul but it also was often the only time when people got together to swap news of the neighborhood. There were three churches in our area, Blue Spring Church of Christ at Blue Spring; Horton's Chapel Methodist Church near the head of Panther Creek, and Saint Mary's Methodist Church near Fort Henry. The closest Baptist Church was down on Byrd's Creek, and it was near another Church of Christ. In the early twenties there were religious debates between the Baptist and Church of Christ, but like most debates, each side always thought they won.

Short Skirts and Bobbed Hair

It was in the early twenties that women around Blue Spring started to bob their hair, and as far as the preachers were concerned, it about put them in a social class with prostitutes. Dress hems, which had been down around the ankles for a hundred years, started to creep up toward the knees, and eyebrows creeped up along with them. Those two "sins" were the topic of many sermons and the wrath of many preachers was vented from the pulpit. One preacher, I can't recall his name, preached as if he believed that every woman who bobbed her hair or wore dresses up toward the knees was doomed to go straight to Hell if she didn't mend her ways. One sermon I recall was on a hot September night and there were cardboard and palm leaf fans in action all over the place. The preacher was dressed in a white shirt, coat, and tie, which was the custom, and he could be picked out in a crowd because all the other men wore overalls.

The sermon was the usual kind, if you don't do this or that, your chances of reaching the Promised Land were just about zero. With arms flailing the air as he paced back and forth across the pulpit, sweat soon began to flow freely down his face, and there was too much for a handkerchief to handle. He stopped suddenly, took off his coat and laid it on a bench behind him, and then continued his fight with the Devil. A little later he stopped again and removed his necktie, and laid it down with the coat, and the sermon went on. Half an hour later, about the time his voice was getting raspy, with the sweat still pouring down his face, he stopped and started to unbutton his shirt amid startled groans from the crowd. While everybody waited for his next move, the preacher continued in a hushed voice, "Don't you ladies worry as I'm not going to take off any more clothes, but I will say this -- I could take off my pants and still have on more than some of you ladies". By the next night hemlines had dropped several inches and nothing else was said about wearing apparel. The preacher knew psychology and used it to the fullest. That was a part of religion that everyone expected in the early twenties. It was a time when people depended on the local weekly newspaper for their politics, the preacher for their religion, and God for the weather to make their crops.

Another sermon I recall hearing at Tharpe one night was by a preacher who also knew how to use psychology on the congregation. Before the start of his sermon, he announced that there were some boys present who liked to go in and out of the church during the sermon. He told them it was not necessary to go to all that trouble to be noticed, and if they would stand and give him their names, he would announce to the crowd that they were there so everyone could take a good look at them.

To those courting couples who must talk during the sermon, he said they were excused, because there was no doubt some other fellow was about to beat his time, and the preacher realized how important it was for the fellow to keep his girl. The preacher began his sermon, and there was not a single interruption throughout the evening.

Preachers in the twenties used more parables than they do today and some of them left a lasting impression with me. One was about a man who couldn't seem to get along with his neighbors, and decided to move across the river to what he believed would be a better neighborhood. While the ferryman was taking him, his family and their livestock to the other side, he asked the ferryman about what kind of people lived where the family was moving. The ferryman inquired of the fellow about the kind of people the family was leaving and he said that they were hard to get along with and were not to be trusted. The ferryman told him that he would find the same kind of people in the new neighborhood.

Grandmammy, Bro. Taylor and Grandpappy

Preachers Didn't Get Rich

My experience with preachers and churches was confined to the Blue Spring Church of Christ and whatever the others did was known to me only from other people who visited them. The Methodists held a revival every year at Horton's Chapel, and I always wanted to go but never had the opportunity. Those who were there told about Mrs. Emma Rushing shouting, and it sounded like something interesting to hear because I knew she was a very religious woman. Churches had preaching only one Sunday a month, and ours was on the first Sunday. Brother Allison, who lived at Bumpus Mills on the other side of the Cumberland River at that time, was our once-a-month preacher for many years. He rode a horse and his pay was whatever collection was taken up for him; and once he had to borrow a quarter to get back across the river, yet he never missed a Sunday when it was his time to preach. There was another preacher, Brother Coleman, from New Providence, who took Brother Allison's place for awhile. One thing the preacher could depend on, however, was a big dinner that always included the best a family had to offer.

There was one time a preacher, I believe it was Brother Coleman, who didn't think too well of my action one Saturday night, and Grandpappy agreed with him. The preacher had eaten supper at Grandpappy's house, and I was also there, probably because the presence of the preacher meant the presence of a lot of good food. It was dark by the time the three of us started to the church house, and I was walking several feet in front of them when I noticed a large crooked stick lying beside the road that looked much like a big snake. It's difficult to let an opportunity like that pass, so I hid in the bushes, holding one end of the crooked stick as it lay across the road. Just as Grandpappy and the preacher approached the stick, I moved it slightly, and those two jumped farther than I had ever seen anyone jump before, and it wasn't toward the stick. There was no way to go around because there was a fence on one side and thick bushes on the other. It was either remove the "snake" or walk through the undergrowth around, and it seemed they had no intention of stepping into the bushes. Grandpappy felt it his duty to protect the preacher and started looking for big rocks to throw, but every time he hit the stick, I wiggled it as if it was hurt. No telling how long that would have gone on if I hadn't got tickled.

110

Grandmammy's Soup

Once when Grandmammy had the preacher for dinner, she made a big pot of her famous soup that everybody loved, but she never put enough salt and pepper in it for the rest of us. This Sunday Mama and a couple of my aunts were there, and knowing that extra salt and pepper were needed, each secretly added the extra seasoning. At the table it was customary for the preacher to give thanks and then everyone would wait for him to take the first bite of the food. He knew Grandmammy made the best soup anywhere and lifted a big spoonful to his mouth and froze. His cheeks and eyes bulged and he started to turn red. He left the table and made a beeline for the back door and ran out into the yard. Before he returned to the table, Grandmammy took a sizable taste of the soup to see if something was wrong and she also headed for the back door. Four people had salted and peppered the soup.

Out-of-State Visitors

A year or two after we moved to The Point, Fred Lyon and his family drove all the way from Paducah to visit us. Their children, Orvil and Johnnie and another girl, were a few years older than me but had never seen the country as it was around Owl Hollow. Johnnie saw a field from our kitchen window, some distance away where bales of hay were scattered about, and she thought they were hogs. The car they came in was a Hupmobile, a better-than-average car of the day. One of the features I recall was the wide running boards that were at least a foot across. On the floor just in front of the driver's seat, was a gadget that looked like a big button that could be operated with the heel of a shoe. When the gadget was pushed down the motor was quiet but when pulled up, that engine could be heard a mile away.

Papa asked me to go down on the creek and try to catch some bass for supper. Later when I returned with several nice fish, Fred wanted me to take him fishing. Papa knew that I had my own way of catching bass in an emergency and told Fred that I was very secretive about where the best fishing holes were, and the matter was dropped. Everybody knows that good fishing spots are guarded just like good hunting grounds are a secret.

Champ Sanders

My favorite out-of-state visitor was a cousin of Papa's, Champ Sanders, who lived in the Ozark Mountains of Arkansas. Champ was a big fellow and one of those people who always had fun wherever he went, and it was contagious. He brought a fishing rod and reel and a homemade artificial lure with him, the first one I had ever seen. When he learned that I was familiar with Panther Creek, he appointed me as his official guide, and it was a honor to go fishing with a fellow who used a rod and reel. We went down on the lower part of the creek to a hole where I had seen a big bass swallow a young muskrat as it swam across the water. I was hoping that the big one would latch on to Champ's artificial bait. He caught a couple of nice ones, but the big one was left still lurking somewhere down in that hole of water because he was too smart to be fooled, and that is probably why he grew to be so big.

After he had fished awhile, Champ handed the rod to me and gave me a few instructions about how to use it. I listened, although I had been watching his every movement, and felt that I knew all there was to know about casting. I made a cast that resulted in what was undoubtedly the biggest backlash that had ever been seen up until that time. He just laughed and said that it happened to everybody sooner or later and not to get discouraged. He spent half an hour getting the line straightened out and insisted I try again, but suggested I try for a shorter cast. He showed me how to use my thumb as a brake and how to guide the line back and forth on the reel between my fingers so as not to pile it in one place. I cautiously cast again and that time it worked. He let me take the outfit to the creek by myself, and somehow I did manage to catch a bass, a thrill I'll never forget.

Champ and his wife spent two or three weeks with us and told a lot of interesting tales about the Ozarks. He worked for the railroad and got free transportation like Papa did when he worked for the Illinois Central in Paducah.. When they left to return to Arkansas, we took them to the station at Danville, a few miles up the river where the railroad crossed the Tennessee River, and they boarded the train for Memphis. Just before he got on the train, Champ handed me the rod and reel and cautioned me to take good care of it until he came back for a visit. He said he was planning to buy a new one to use at home, anyway. It was one of the greatest gifts I had ever received and kept it for many years.

Papa Tells Me to Shave

By the time I was 12 years old there was enough fuzz on my face to line a bird's nest, and Papa and Mama kept after me to shave. I remembered what I did to Bill Crutcher when I tried to shave him and was considering just letting my whiskers grow forever or until they could be cut with Papa's clippers. I recalled the blood oozing from Bill's face when I shaved him with Papa's straight razor. The problem had not been Papa's razor, because he had one of the best in the country, but the thing that was lacking was experience. Even with all his experience, Papa kept a stick of some kind of medication to use when he cut himself.

One Sunday morning when Papa got through shaving, he called me into the kitchen and told me I had gone long enough without shaving and this was the day to start. He had just finished and there was not one place bleeding on his face and that was encouraging. While he talked, he was stropping the razor so that it would be keen, and to test it would jerk a hair from his head, hold it between his fingers, and if the razor cut it cleanly, it was ready to use but if it split the hair, it was back to the strop. I had watched many times as he had stropped and tested the blade, but it was always for him; now I was to be the victim. I knew that one day he would accidently cut the piece of leather into two parts and then I could use it for making slingshots, but it never happened.

Papa took some extra time showing me how I should hold the razor and that it should lie almost flat on the face, and not at an angle like I was plowing a furrow. He whipped up a lather with his shaving brush and mug and handed the soap-laden brush to me and left me to my fate. I lathered my face and held the razor blade next to the skin by my right ear and pulled, and lo and behold, the fuzz was gone and my ear was still intact. With the added courage I continued and tried the other side of my face and began the life-long job of keeping my whiskers short. I was now a grownup!

Farming

In spring and summer the people between the rivers worked hard and were able to eke out a living by growing tobacco for a cash crop and some corn and hay to feed the livestock. Each family had a big garden for growing vegetables to be eaten fresh and canned or dried for winter use. Mama canned lots of tomatoes, green beans, beets, peas, and corn. She kept a two-year supply of canned food on hand just in case there was a bad year when there would be little to can. We also grew popcorn, peanuts, sweet and Irish potatoes, watermelons and cantaloupes. There are not many events that can equal going to the melon patch and pulling a big, ripe watermelon, taking it to a clean gravel creek bed and dropping it on the rocks. The heart of the melon, the sweetest part, separates from the seedy part, and holding it with dirty hands, you eat until you are full. Or you might choose a Rocky Ford cantaloupe and cut it open with a pocket knife and eat it fresh off the vine. I can't help feeling sorry for all the city folks today who have become accustomed to eating fruits and melons that are pulled green and never experience the delicious taste of those naturally ripened.

Tobacco being the cash crop, got the most attention and was sometimes a year-round job, depending on the weather conditions. A tobacco plant starts out from one of the smallest seeds in the plant kingdom. Preparing the bed for tobacco plants differs in different areas, depending on the amount of trees that are available. Around Owl Hollow there was far more timber than farm land, and we went to the woods to burn our plant beds. In February Papa started looking for the right location, a gently sloping hillside with rich top soil and plenty of trees to cut, and pile for burning. Before the first tree was cut he laid out a space about 8 feet wide and up to 50 feet long. No one paid any attention as to whose land the plant bed was on, and it had been the way of life since the area was settled over a hundred years before.

With a nine-foot crosscut saw and double-bit axes, we began to clear the area, cutting the wood into eight-foot lengths and piling it on the place Papa had marked off. The lighter brush was piled on the bottom with the heavier pieces on top to weight it down so it would burn cleaner. Dried leaves were raked up for several feet around the pile to be used to ignite the brush. The cleaned area also served as a buffer to keep the fire from spreading into the surrounding woods.

Papa liked for the brush to settle for at least a week before it was burned. When the weather was just right, he wrapped some old rags around a couple of green sticks, soaked them in coal oil, and set them on fire. Each of us took a torch and starting from the lower end, one on each side, and went along the edge of the bed, setting the leaves on fire. Starting the fire was sort of a celebration after the many days of hard work chopping, sawing, and piling the brush and logs. The fire would burn for hours, and someone we had to stay with it at all times to keep the unburned wood pushed back into the fire. A few days later, saplings about six inches in diameter which had been saved, were laid around the outside of the plant bed. Next the soil was dug up and pulverized until it was like dust. Using about a gallon of ashes from the burned bed, Papa mixed the tobacco seed with the ashes and scattered the mixture over the entire plant bed. Along one side of the bed, Mama sowed some lettuce seed to have before her garden started to produce. To protect the seed and small plants from frost, tobacco canvas was stretched tightly over the entire area, and the rest was left to Nature.

While we were waiting on the plants to grow, we were busy cutting and burning cornstalks or clearing out fence rows to get ready for plowing. I enjoyed plowing when the ground was just right, and turning over the soil in early spring, and smelling the fresh earth, is something only a farmer or gardener can understand. Papa liked to plow where the tobacco was to grow, have it harrowed and boated, and let it settle awhile before laying off the rows and making the hills. If the weather was normal, the plowing and other preparations worked out fine, but a wet or dry spell could force us to do a lot of work in a short time.

After the danger of frost had passed Papa used the number 9 Vulcan plow to make rows each way, and where they intersected, a handful of fertilizer was tossed in and a hill was made over it. By the time the hills were made, the tobacco plants had grown big enough to set out and we had to wait for a rain before going further. When the rain came, it was a scramble to get the plants set out while the ground was wet. Everyone pulled plants and tied them in bundles of fifty and when a day's supply was pulled, it was to the field. One person, usually a youngster, dropped a plant on each hill, and another person, using a tobacco peg, punched a hole in the center of the hill, dropped in the plant, and pressed the soil tightly around the roots. With all the stooping, there were many sore backs by the time night came, and sometimes it was difficult to stand up straight.

Papa said that one of the things that made him so tired, especially in the spring, before the body got toughened up, was that he worked hard all day and then dreamed of working all night. Mama said that he kept her awake much of the night, yelling at Kate and Nell, or grumbling about too many rocks in the field. Papa did a lot of dreaming, but outdid himself one night when he dreamed that he was walking along a road, and got sleepy. He dreamed that he laid down under a tree and went to sleep, and had a dream in that sleep -- guess you would call it a double header.

Hoeing and Suckering Tobacco

When the tobacco plants began to grow, Papa thought it was of the utmost importance to remove, with a hoe, every sprig of grass that tried to grow near a plant. The removal of weeds and grass between the plants was done with a double-shovel plow or a coon's-foot harrow. We grew a variety of tobacco known as Kelly, that was a dark-fired variety used mostly for making snuff, chewing-tobacco or cigar wrappers. The Kelly tobacco had to be topped at about eight to ten leaves to the stalk and allowed to spread out over the ground. After topping, suckers started growing where the leaf joined the main stalk, and they had to be removed by hand, starting at the top and working down. Three sets of suckers had to be removed before they gave up. It was necessary to keep them removed so the growth would go into the leaf instead of into the sucker.

To sucker a tobacco plant, it was necessary to stand over it, and use both hands to work your way to the bottom. The broad leaves made it impossible to see what was underneath, and on rare occasions, when the hands reached the bottom, they might come to rest on a clammy snake of some sort. People talk about the fast-draws of the western cowboy, but they could never equal the fast draw when a hand touched a snake under a tobacco plant. It was a dark and cool place for snakes to escape the hot sun or the rain. At noon and supper time our hands were covered with tobacco gum, a black substance that clung to the skin. The best way to remove it was by using homemade lye soap, but one had to be careful, or some of the skin might rub off along with the tar.

In September the tobacco began to ripen. The leaves started to crinkle and lose their glossy green color, and Papa would pass the word around that he was going to cut his tobacco on a certain day; and early that morning several neighbors would show up ready to work. Farmers swapped work, and no money was involved, but a big dinner was expected for their labors. A good tobacco cutter had his own knife and nobody would dare ask to borrow it. It was a special knife with a long handle; the lower edge of the blade was used to split the stalk almost to the bottom, and the upper side of the blade was used to sever the stalk. The plant was turned upside down, to wilt before being strung on a tobacco stick. The sticks, each holding several plants, were hauled to the barn and passed up the tiers by men working one above another. The sticks had to be placed so air could pass between them to keep the tobacco from spoiling.

Tobacco barn. *Right:* Landy Simpson and Uncle Dave acting the fool.

Fireing Tobacco

The plants hung in the barn with all the doors open until the leaves turned a golden yellow. Papa was fussy as to the right shade of yellow, and when it was to his liking, all the doors were closed and a small smoking fire was started. The heat was increased until it was warm throughout the barn and keeping it at the right temperature was a 24-hour-a-day job. The fire continued until the tobacco was a brown color and was completely cured. There were many nights when I would go over to Lohman Nance's barn where several men would gather and tell stories, some too dirty to put down here. Sometimes they passed around a bottle, but because of my age, never offered me a drink. There was much to learn from these grownups, especially Kennedy Gorham, who had gone to school at the University of Tennessee in Knoxville. His stories were always interesting and sometimes racy. When a bottle was passed around, Kennedy just smelled it and passed it on. That taught me that I didn't have to drink whiskey to be accepted.

After firing, the tobacco became dry and so brittle that it could not be handled because it crumbled at the slightest touch. Later a warm wet spell of weather would bring the tobacco "in order", pliable, so it could be stripped from the stalk and tied into "hands", and put in a large bulk to

Grandpappy, Uncle Walter Lyon, me, and Kate and Nell hauling tobacco

ripen. Some years Papa would be ready to start another plant bed before the last crop was ready for market. While stripping, several pounds of the best tobacco were laid aside for personal use. Papa smoked a pipe most of the time and would mix dried rose petals from last summer with the strong tobacco to give it a milder flavor. Uncle Frank Champion, who was blind, always helped us strip tobacco and would pick some of the leaves, by smelling them, and make several twists to last him until the next crop. He made a twist for each month.

Sell Tobacco in Clarksville

When the tobacco was ready, Papa loaded it on the wagon and early the next morning, Kate and Nell were dressed in their best harness, and before daylight Papa was on the way to Clarksville, about 40 miles away. I enjoyed hearing him talk about places he went through like Bear Springs, Indian Mound, Oakwood, Woodlawn or New Providence. Selling the tobacco crop was a great event for me, because Papa always brought me a nice present. Once it was a Ingrasol pocket watch, another time it was a small chopping ax, and once my first pair of long pants. Papa, like so many fathers, did not realize that his little boy was almost as big as he was, and still growing. Up until then I had worn what they called Buster Browns, a knee-length outfit that made my big feet look even bigger than they were. I was so proud of my new pants that I could hardly wait until Sunday to show them off. They were at least two sizes too small, but I managed to get into them and was off to church. All went well and I was the envy of every boy there until I got into a scuffle with Ily Sills and a shoe came untied. When I bent over to tie the shoe, there was a sound of cloth ripping and a hole, big enough to run a fist through, appeared right where I sat down. Until church was over, I spent my time trying to stay on the outer edge of the crowd and facing them at all times.

Other Crops

Papa was a good farmer and was always competitive in anything he tried to grow. That applied not only to the two main crops of tobacco and corn, but also to other things as well, including watermelons, cantaloupes, peanuts, popcorn, or sweet potatoes. He grew the best melons in the neighborhood and was always glad to share them with others. When there were lots of watermelons, Papa would take a wagon load down to Blue Spring on Saturday and dump them in the cool water. There was a deep hole just below where the spring came out of the bluff but which was too shallow at the lower end for the melons to float away. Anyone who happened along was welcome to eat one or take one home. This practice started one Saturday when he took a wagon load of melons to Tharpe and tried to sell the whole load for a dollar, but no one wanted them. When he came home, he took them down to the spring and dumped them into the water for anyone who wanted them.

Peanuts was one of my favorite things to grow, and we planted enough to enjoy throughout the winter months. When they began to sprout and come through the ground, it was my job to be at the patch before daylight to keep the quail and crows away. Like beans, the peanut pushed up through the soil and became a delicacy for the birds. Papa said that was the only time they could get me up before daylight without threats. After the peanuts matured the whole plants were pulled and stacked with the nuts inside the stack to protect them from the birds. After drying for several days, the nuts were stripped off and the vines fed to the mules and Red.

Farming Was Hard Work

To say that farm work was fun all the time would be as misleading as saying that any other hard work is fun all the time. One advantage of farming is that there is always a light at the end of the tunnel, which can be in the form of a rainy day, when it is too wet to work, or the Fall and Winter days when there is time to hunt, fish or do anything that might strike your fancy. As long as there was fun on down the road, there was the hope that fueled happiness.

Spending every daylight hour on the south end of a north-bound mule, holding on to two plow handles between rows of corn or tobacco on a hot day is not fun. I was always one that sweat a lot, and many times I have seen the drops of sweat dripping from my overalls and my clothes were as wet as if I had been in the creek. Taking the harness off a sweaty mule at the end of the day was no fun either, but there was always the light at the other end of the tunnel that made work easier. Thinning corn with a hoe or scraping crabgrass from around the tobacco plants could start you sweating and keep it flowing all day. Many times I have been plowing with a mule and double-shovel plow, while over in the field next to me would be someone plowing with a riding cultivator. I could never understand why Papa didn't buy one and make plowing fun instead of work.

One of the first jobs of farm work given to me was looking for worms on the tobacco plants. A six or seven-year-old is ideal for the job because he is right down there even with the worms. The tobacco worm is a green little monster that is easy to handle when found in its early life, but a full-grown one can bite. Some people call them horn worms because of a "horn" that extends from it. I never understood why it is was called a horn worm because it was on the opposite end of where horns grow on cows, goats or sheep. There was no spray to kill worms until sometime after we moved to The Point, when a poison powder called Paris Green, was blown onto the plants to kill the worms. Papa did all the spraying, and I have seen him come home for dinner or supper covered with the poison but not knowing that it was dangerous, Papa survived.

Harvest Time

In the Fall we were kept busy storing food to be used during the Winter. The day before a frost, which Papa could tell by the clouds, he

Seed drill belonged to Uncle Herman Crutcher, now owned by son, Alvin Earl

would have me cut the sweet potato vines off at the ground. He said that if the frost killed the vines while still attached to the potatoes, they would not keep as well and also the flavor was affected. A few days later we dug the potatoes, rubbed the dirt off, and after drying out in the sun a day or two, they were stored in a box inside the kitchen. Frost didn't hurt turnips and they were left in the ground until colder weather and then were dug and stored in a "hill", a trench where they were protected with a lot of straw and dirt; we had fresh turnips all winter.

Broomcorn was just that -- it was used for making brooms. When the tassels matured, they were cut and allowed to dry completely. The tassel was made up of long straws that were not only used for making brooms but as a toothpicks or pipe stem cleaners. If a toothpick was needed, you simply went to Mama's broom, yanked out a straw, and it did the job. Not knowing that such an act could be unhealthy, we had no problems.

Will Welker, who lived out on the ridge toward Dover, was the only person in the area who had a machine that made brooms. We took our straw to him and he made it into brooms, keeping a portion for his pay. Papa said the Mr. Welker's house was built on the divide between the Tennessee and Cumberland Rivers and the water from one side went to one river and from the other side went to the other.

Visiting Relatives

I did a lot of visiting relatives while growing up, perhaps because I was an only child until I was eleven, or maybe because Papa had a way of finding things for me to do when I was at home. Grandpappy and Grand-mammy's house was a second home, and I spent a lot of time with them. It was also handy to the creek and river. At home, Mama rarely cooked eggs because she used them to trade for groceries, but Grandmammy would cook them any time I wanted them. One Easter morning she cooked six for me before I had my fill. There was an upstairs where I loved to sleep and not be disturbed in the mornings. There Are two things I have done against my will every day of my life, one is to go to bed at night and the other is to get up in the morning. The loft, as Grandmammy called it, inspired a little poem that I wrote many years later:

Grandma's Feather Bed

Did you ever try to sleep,
But rolled and tossed all night?
Or lay there slowly counting sheep,
And mad enough to fight.
Just how they made those beds with lumps
I'll probably never know,
And while I lie among the bumps
I dream of long ago,
When Grandma had a bed upstairs,
A place she called the loft,
And I would climb those steps in pairs
To reach that bed so soft.
Where I could always lie and dream,
A pillow 'neath my head,
When nights were short, or so they seemed
On Grandma's feather bed.
The loft was noted for a sound
That nowhere else has been,
The raindrops as they gently pound
Down on a roof of tin.
Then came the humid summer nights,
The worst you ever saw,
But Grandma had a cure for plights,
A bedtick filled with straw.
Or if the straw was short demand
Corn shucks were used instead,
And if you even moved a hand
It made a noisy bed.
Now when it comes my time to die,
When all is done and said,
I'm sure my wish will be that I
Had Grandma's feather bed.

I helped Grandpappy cut and haul wood for the fireplace, and it was about the only time Blanch and Mike were hitched to the wagon in winter. He never cut and hauled more than one load at a time. Papa, on the other hand, cut and hauled in the winter supply in September and got it over with.   The only time I ever saw Grandpappy lose his temper was while we were out in the woods to get a load of firewood. After the wood was cut and loaded, we climbed on the wagon; Grandpappy gave the signal for Blanch and Mike to pull and Blanch obeyed at once, but Mike just stood there with his ears laid back. Grandpappy repeated the command several times with the same results and finally muttered something, which I did not understand. He got down off the wagon and cut a long switch that was larger than a man's thumb, and climbed back on the wagon and again gave the pull command. Mike didn't move a muscle, and Grandpappy drew that big switch back over his shoulder and let Mike have it right down his spine. Mike was as surprised as I was at Grandpappy's action and took off like a scared rabbit.

Grandpappy and Grandmammy had an orchard that included two apple trees, a winesap, and a rustycoat, that I watched so I would be around when the apples were ripe. The winesap was the best eating apple I have ever tasted, but for some reason the tree bore fruit only every other year. I never understood this and nobody ever explained it to me. The rustycoat had a full crop every year, but the apples were hard as rocks and not as tasty as the winesap. Grandmammy said they made excellent frying apples and were good for drying or sulphuring. There were several peach trees of questionable ancestry, and the fruit was small but delicious if you could find one before some fat worm had gorged himself on it. Grandmammy was an expert at pealing peaches, avoiding the worms and the bad parts.

Grandmammy liked to have me around when she was drying fruit. She would hand me a clean bed sheet to take up on the porch roof where there was plenty of sun, and then I scattered the pieces of fruit over it. Using a long limb of a branch with lots of leaves on it, I kept the flies, yellow jackets and wasps away from the fresh fruit.   Naturally I would snitch a piece of the fruit for myself occasionally, being careful not to let Grandmammy catch me in the act because if she did catch me, she would fuss and say there wasn't going to be anything left when I got through eating the drying fruit.

I also helped her sulphur apples, a process I have not seen in use since.   She used a five-gallon crock and put a metal container in the bottom to hold coals of fire, sprinkled with sulphur.   She put freshly-sliced apples in a cloth bag, and hung it in the crock so the fumes came up through it for several hours. Although the apples turned yellow, they stayed fresh for months, and she made delicious apple pies with them.

Making kraut was another event I helped with. She used the crock, filling it with finely-cut cabbage and lots of salt. A piece of wood was placed on the kraut, weighed down with a heavy rock that she kept in the smokehouse just for this purpose. After awhile, some awful-looking stuff rose to the top and was ignored for several days while the mixture fermented. Then came a day when the stuff was skimmed off, and the weight and wood were removed, leaving the best kraut I have ever had. I always got a big plate of the fresh kraut for helping her.

Shortly after moving to the river farm, Grandmammy decided she wanted a magnolia tree in the front yard. She ordered one and when it arrived, I helped her set it out about ten feet in front of the door so she could look at it while sitting on the front porch. We spent most of a day digging a big hole, mixing in manure from the stables, and plenty of rich soil from down on the creek. It grew and did well for a few years, but the winter of 1925 was very cold and the tree was killed to the ground. We all thought it was killed for good, but later in the Spring, a sprig of new growth came out and made a lot of people happy. Grandmammy still had her magnolia tree, and it stands at the old home place and can be seen today.

The Government Light

Uncle Walter Lyon, Grandpappy's brother, lived for several years in the house on top of the hill from Grandpappy's house and had the job of lighting the Government navigation light near Boswell Landing, and sometimes I went along with him. It was a job that had to be done each evening just before sundown in all kinds of weather because the river boats depended on the light to guide them through the narrow channel. We walked the road that separated Grandpappy's and Tom Crutcher's farms to Campbell Slough, then turned right to where a jon boat was kept for crossing the slough. The light was a regular lantern, hanging from an arm that was attached to a large pole set in the ground about ten feet from the vertical river bank. A pulley system allowed the lantern to be lowered for servicing. Uncle Walter cleaned the chimney and wick and poured enough coal oil in the bowl to burn until daylight next morning. The supplies and instructions, as to the amount of oil needed to burn all night, were left by a Government boat about once a month. The boat might come along at any hour of the day or night and was seldom seen by Uncle Walter. His pay for making the trip of about two miles round trip was 25 cents a day, but a quarter bought a lot in those days.

Uncle Walter was a truthful man and deeply religious, not only on Sundays but every day of the week. He led prayer at church often and even then, I marveled at his sincerity. I tell this about him because of the stories he told me, and there is no doubt in my mind that they are true. Once while he was cleaning the lantern at the Government light, he looked down at the river below, and as far as he could see, there were thousands of fish of all varieties and sizes swimming along on top of the water. Another time, as he passed Crutcher's Landing, and tie yard, he noticed a huge catfish lying alongside of a jon boat. The fish was about the same length as the boat, and most of the boats were 12 feet long. He said it was a yellow catfish. One Fall evening while he was at the light, a flock of blackbirds passed just down the river from him. The flock was about a hundred yards wide and reached as far as he could see in both directions; he added that he was glad they didn't fly over him. The event that impressed him most, happened when he was a young man. He was out in the woods, down on his knees praying, and looking toward the sky. His eyes were closed, and when he opened them, there in the sky was a beautiful golden door. There was no doubt in Uncle Walter's mind that some day he would enter through that door.

Uncle Clayton and Aunt Ida

Uncle Clayton Barbee was Mama's brother and was a controversial person in the eyes of a lot of people. His wife, Aunt Ida, was one of the sweetest persons I have ever known and they were always close to each other. Before he was married, he owned a pretty horse, Mag, and a rubber-tired buggy, which was like owning a BMW today. Mag had some features the BMW doesn't have. Uncle Clayton would drive some girl home from church, or some other place at night, and when he was ready to return home, he curled up in the seat and went to sleep and awoke to find Mag standing at the lot gate.

126

A COUNTRY BOY *From Owl Hollow*

After Uncle Clayton and Aunt Ida were married, they moved to Murray Kentucky, and Mama decided to visit them. She wrote a letter asking that Uncle Clayton meet us at the Pine Bluff ferry on a certain day. We walked the several miles to the river and were ferried across in a motor-boat. Uncle Clayton was there, waiting for us in a Dodge Brothers automobile, and took us on to Murray. He worked as a mechanic in a garage located on the square, and I spent a lot of my time watching him working on motors.

Uncle Clayton liked his whiskey, but I never knew him to be drunk or even act as if he had been drinking. Once a week the milkman left bottles of milk, and although they all looked alike, one was filled with whiskey. Mama was against drinking but tolerated his toddy, and once while we were there, she agreed to let me take a sip to see what the Devil's brew tasted like. It was the first time I ever tasted whiskey. Uncle Clayton was an excellent cook and learned about a run-down restaurant that was for sale real cheap and bought it. He went into the kitchen and started cooking his best foods and within a few weeks had more customers than he could feed. He sold it for many times more than he had paid for it and moved to Bailey's Creek, not far from where we lived.

Uncle Clayton moved to Bailey's Creek for one purpose, and that was to make whiskey. He said he was going to make the best whiskey ever made in the area and that he would make it for five years and quit, regardless of the outcome. He hired an expert from Golden Pond, Kentucky, an area known far and wide for the good quality of its whiskey. He added a few of his own touches to the method, like storing his product under ground for a year in 55-gallon white oak barrels that he charred himself. His whiskey was made from pure corn mash with no additives. He used the money from the sale of his restaurant to live on the first year and it paid off.

I visited Uncle Clayton and Aunt Ida many times after they moved to Bailey's Creek because it was only about an hour's walk through the woods. The house they lived in was the same one where I had stood on the front porch in January of 1918, and watched as they carried Grandpa Barbee's coffin up the hill to the graveyard. Every time I visited them, they would cook some favorite dish of mine and that made me feel important. My favorite dish was a butterscotch pie that was thick and sweet with lots of white stuff on top. Where I sat at the table, I was next to a barrel of whiskey, and nearby were glasses and a dipper for anybody who happened to come by, and they were welcomed. I never tried it, but people said it was the best whiskey they had ever drunk, but Uncle Clayton never sold a drop to anyone who lived in the county and that was in his favor when he was brought to court in Nashville later.

Uncle Clayton never talked to me about where he sold his whiskey, and I didn't ask, but did know it was not sold locally. Once when I was visiting them, a big black automobile drove up and Uncle Clayton went out and talked to the driver. A few minutes later another big black car arrived and then another, until there were six of them lined up along the road in front of the house. Nobody said anything to me, and I stayed in the house and watched as men carried bucket after bucket of whiskey and poured it into the cars. I knew there was a big tank hidden somewhere in or under each car and that each car held a lot of whiskey. After they had loaded and gone, Uncle Clayton explained that the cars were from out of state, and were buying most of his output. Sometime later he told me that the cars belonged to Al Capone of Chicago. The Chicago gangster paid him several times more than the average gallon price for the right to all of his product. One of the drivers told Uncle Clayton that Capone got up to $200 a gallon in Chicago and St. Louis for the whiskey. Two other times, when I was visiting, the big black cars came and loaded and went on their way. It was an exciting event for me to witness.

Revenuers were kept pretty busy in the land between the rivers, and Uncle Clayton's operation was raided and he was arrested. They were Federal Agents, and he was indicted in Nashville by U.S. authorities. There was a story that went around after the trial that I cannot vouch for, but a lot of people believed it to be true. Uncle Clayton's lawyer, I believe his name was Brandon, who had practiced law in Dover at one time, defended him. The story goes that his lawyer asked the judge to sample some of the whiskey to see for himself that it was not the rot-gut kind that was so plentiful, but the judge refused. Several times the judge was asked to sample the booze and he finally agreed. A glass of the evidence was set before the judge and he took a small swig and then a swallow. After a pause he raised his gavel, pounded the stand, and said the case was dismissed. Looking at the arresting officers he told them to leave the defendant alone in the future and added that anybody who made whiskey that good should not be bothered and never to bring him into his court again. That was the only time Uncle Clayton was bothered by the law. As he had promised, he retired at the end of five years, a wealthy man for his time. He and Aunt Ida spent the winters in Florida, the first people I ever knew to go there for a vacation.

Aunt Gladys and Uncle Willie

I visited Aunt Gladys and Uncle Willie Kennerly many times, but the one I remember most was one time when Uncle Willie was operating the Fort Henry ferry. Their house was not more than a hundred yards from the river, and what could be better than living with the Tennessee almost at your doorsteps. On my way there I stopped at Ben Wofford's store and bought a dime's worth of stick candy from Miss Ella, Ben's wife, and it was probably one of the biggest ten-cent's-worth of candy she ever sold. It was early in the spring,and Panther Creek was higher than usual, and I walked across on a foot log. After crossing the creek the road followed a hollow toward Fort Henry and in the hollow I carved my initials and the date on a big beechnut tree. There were already names and dates cut into the tree by Yankee soldiers during the Civil War. By the time I got to Aunt Gladys' house, I was sick as a dog from eating too much candy, but it didn't take long for her to diagnose my illness, and the excess candy was removed from my insides with a big dose of castor oil. After that she cooked some eggs for me, and I was well on my way to recovery.

Uncle Willie had a way of making me feel important. He would talk to me as if I were an adult and discussed problems with me. Duncan and Hill, their two sons, were too young to help out at that time. The river was falling fast, and each morning the big ferry boat would be partly on dry land, and it took a lot of prying to get it back into the water. We decided to outsmart the river, and moved the boat several feet out into the water and tied it to a big tree. Next morning there was plenty of water under the boat, but it was about two feet below it. The chain was so tight that it could not be loosened and Uncle Willie had to cut it with a hack saw, and it sure made a big splash when it fell into the river. Aunt Gladys half-laughed and half-scolded us for not leaving slack in the chain.

I made several trips across the river and wished that Papa was running a ferry some place instead of farming. Uncle Willie became an expert at operating the ferry at night which was done only if there was an emergency, such as ferrying Dr. Blalock, or someone going to Mason's Clinic in Murray. He was well-read and very good with mathematics and by figuring the speed of the current and wind, he was able to strike the road on the opposite bank even on dark nights. Uncle Willie never gave up on a problem and believed that problems were there to be solved. I don't know how much schooling he had, but he could quote more bible verses than most preachers. He was also good in history and geography, not only the U.S., but also about foreign countries. Aunt Gladys and Uncle Willie had five children: Duncan, Hill, Ward, Cherry and Kathleen.

Aunt Mavis and Uncle Herman

Soon after Aunt Mavis and Uncle Herman married, they moved to a house near his father, Mr. Tom Crutcher. I visited them because I enjoyed being with them and also they lived within throwing distance of Panther Creek. Uncle Herman was a quiet, deliberate person, interested in settling down and farming and buying land, and he proved to be an excellent farmer and planner for the future. Their first baby was named Thomas, after both grandfathers, but was always called Gabby. I visited them often when Gabby was a baby and remember noticing the devotion both parents had for him.

When Gabby was two or three years old he contracted diphtheria and died. Because the disease was considered so contagious and deadly, I was not allowed to visit him or even attend the funeral. Without anyone knowing it, I walked down the creek near the graveyard and watched from a distance. I could hear Aunt Mavis crying, and it affected me very much because I knew they loved Gabby a lot. We never knew for sure how Gabby caught the disease because there had not been a single case of diphtheria in the neighborhood prior to his. It was decided at the time that he may have gotten it from a letter that Uncle Herman had handled while carrying the mail. There had been a letter from a family who had lost one of their children to the disease.

Later when other children had been born, and Uncle Herman had bought a farm with Panther Creek running right through the middle of it, I visited them a lot. I was always amazed at how he discussed the farm work with Aunt Mavis and the children because it was so different from my home. Papa was the one who made the decisions and I went along without complaining, and in our family it was best that way. I was never good at planning ahead because I was too interested in what was going on

130

at the present time.   Beside Gabby, Aunt Mavis and Uncle Herman had five children: Alvin Earl, Alton, Dixie, Sammie, and Rebecca, better known as "Cookie".

Aunt Tince and Uncle Buster

I visited Aunt Tince and Uncle Buster more often than the others because they lived closer to Grandpappy and Grandmammy.   I may have felt closer to Aunt Tince because we were nearer the same age, and had played together when we lived in Owl Hollow.   I had watched as they built a new house, not more than a hundred yards from Panther Creek, and about half a mile from the Tennessee River. I spent a night with them before the house was finished and slept in a room with plenty of access to the outdoors.   It was cold and Aunt Tince saw to it that I was well protected from the elements by covering me with three or four quilts, and I added to my comfort by pulling it all over my head, so that not even a warm breath of air could escape.   I don't know how many cats Aunt Tince had at the time, but before I could go to sleep, seven had found their way from the cold outside through an opening in the ceiling, and curled themselves on the cover to take advantage of the warm lump underneath it.   They were not aware the lump was a person.   I slept all night without moving, as was my habit, and next morning when I turned over, seven terrified cats tried to be first climbing the wall, and be first to the hole in the ceiling and out to freedom.

Uncle Buster was a farmer, mechanic, carpenter, blacksmith, and merchant and was pretty good at all of them except, maybe, the merchant. He was just too good-hearted and could never refuse anyone credit.   He was a good mechanic and installed a Model T Ford engine in a jon boat, and it ran like a scared rabbit.   He couldn't afford the price of a propeller and fashioned one himself from a piece of sheet-iron.   He named the boat the "Sea Hag", from a character in the *Popeye* comic strip at the time.

They owned a German Shepherd named Bosco, one of the smartest dogs I have ever seen.   Grandpappy and Grandmammy ate supper early and Bosco was there and fed a generous meal, then he rushed home to get a second one.   Sometimes the backwater would almost surround the house, leaving only one ridge of dry land on which you could reach the house.   Once I visited them when the water was high, and about fifty yards from the front porch.   Their two small sons, Tommy and Buford, were playing near the water. They would toss in a stick or rock and each time would get closer and closer to the water.   Bosco was lying nearby watching the action. Aunt Tince was sitting on the porch sewing and I ask if she wasn't afraid to let the kids play in the water so far away from her. She told me to sit down and watch.   When one of the boys ventured too close to the water, Bosco got up, took hold of their clothing, and pulled them back to safety. This happened several times while I watched in awe.

Aunt Tince could make the best thickening gravy and chocolate pie I had ever had.   She loved the gravy, and had it almost every morning for breakfast. Her pies were always thin and runny and often had to be eaten with a spoon, but the flavor was out of this world.   She had a wonderful sense of humor and everybody took advantage of it, especially Uncle Buster and Papa.   After Tommy and Buford, another child came along later and he was named Charles A.

Aunt Gertie and Uncle Mintor

Aunt Gertie, Mama's older sister, and Uncle Mintor lived at the head of Panther Creek.   There was a spring in their front yard that had a spring house built over it, with a pool of cool water inside where milk and butter were kept. To me it was the greatest thing anybody could hope for, but they just took it for granted.   There was lots of water around with plenty of minnows and frogs to keep a boy entertained for a year.   They had a daughter Pauline, and a son, Everett who were closer to my age than my other cousins.   Pauline was only six months younger than me.

Mama and I would visit them once or twice a year and this was something to look forward to.   I fished for the minnows, using anything handy for bait, because they would bite at almost anything.   I even caught them by using green blackberries, and I know fish don't care for berries that are ripe, much less green ones. Because of so much water, Aunt Gertie had a lot of geese and Mama planned one of her visits when the down was to be plucked from the birds, but that was one job I stayed away from because it was so messy.   I felt sorry for the geese because they sure didn't enjoy giving up all that warm coat. Mama would take some of the down home with her and used it to make quilts and pillows.

Dogs And Other Pets

Most boys who grow up in the country are attached to a dog most of their young lives, but that was not the case with me. I had dogs, but they were pets around the house, and seldom went with me farther than the fields when I was working. When I went hunting or fishing, I preferred to go alone because the presence of a dog drove the animals into hiding where they could not be seen. No animal was beyond my desire to try to make a pet out of it, and often they became pets that didn't set too well with Papa and Mama.

My first dog was a feist named Ikey. While we were living in Paducah, Mama and I were in Ikey Cohen's store one day when a lady came in with a basket full of the cutest puppies a boy ever saw. Mama agreed that I could have one, but that it would have to go to Owl Hollow the next time we visited there. Ikey was a lot of fun, but soon he was taken to Owl Hollow. I do not recall just how it happened but he became Grandmammy's pet, and we were never as close as a boy and his dog should be. My next dog was Ceef, the one given to me by Mr. Cephas Barnes in 1918, and he also became a resident of Owl Hollow. After we moved to The Point, somebody gave me a collie pup and she was named Brown, because of her color. Brown was never a hunting dog and if she did tree a squirrel, refused to bark to let me know where she was. Later she was given to a man who lived somewhere near Model.

There was one dog that I did became attached to, but it ended in tragedy while he was still a pup and I never owned another. Doug Barnes gave me the pup whose mother was a reddish color and a short-haired breed of questionable ancestry, but was known far and wide as the best coon and possum dog in the county. We named him Red, because of his color. Doug knew I hunted coons and possums and picked what he thought was the best of the litter for me. He picked up each of the puppies, roughed it up a little, and pushed it away from him. Most of them tucked their tails and ran for cover, but one of them got mad and came back at him ready for a fight. That was a good sign of a hunting dog, according to Doug, and indicated that the dog would not be intimated by a coon or bobcat.

When Red was three or four months old, I took him with me to the Humphreys Field, an old abandoned farm out in the hills where there were lots of big sassafras trees that Mama liked for stove wood. Red showed signs of being a good hunting dog as he worked both sides of the wagon looking for some animal he could chase. After cutting the load of sassafras, I headed for home, paying little attention to Red. When I got home, Red was not with me, but I wasn't too concerned, thinking he had found something interesting, and a good hunting dog never leaves a trail on his own. After an hour or so, I began to worry and went looking for him. About half a mile out on the ridge road, I found Red lying in the road, crushed by the wagon wheel. He had gotten too close and the wheel had run over him. To say I was broken-hearted would be putting it mildly, for I cried off and on for several days. Somewhere out on the ridge is a small grave and in it are the bones of the only dog I ever really loved. Others had hunting dogs and used them to an advantage, but I liked to hunt alone after Red died.

Dug Out Fox Den

One Spring I kept watching an old fox den on the creek back of our house because there were signs that it was being used to raise some young. There was fresh dirt and fox tracks around it, indicating it was being used, and the hair that rubbed off on the entrance showed that the foxes were red ones which usually had their dens out in the hills. I checked as often as I dared without disturbing them and causing them to move the cubs to another location. When I thought the cubs were about a month old, I took a pick and shovel and starting early one morning, began to dig out the den and get to the young foxes. It was easy digging and by noon had reached the nursery and three cute little balls of grey fuzz. Even red foxes are grey when they are young, but these were older than I had expected. I don't know where the parents were and never got a glimpse of them, but was pretty sure they were watching me all the time I was digging.

I took the cubs home and turned them loose in our front yard, which was enclosed with a paling fence to keep the chickens out. We fed them milk for awhile and when they were old enough to eat meat, we killed rabbits for them. They soon started to turn red and became very playful. When they were about four months old, I gave one to Lynn Love, a cousin, who spent a lot of time out in the woods hacking crossties. The fox followed him to the woods and became a good pet, but he had to be fastened up at night because of a habit of thinking all chickens were his for the catching. My two cubs were kept in the yard where they could not get to the chickens, but they never gave up trying. One day Sid Callicott, an avid fox hunter from Henry County, came by and offered me $25 for my two foxes and I sold them to him. He took them home and turned them loose, hoping to start foxes there, but he told me later that he never saw any sign of them again.

Fox Hunting

Mr. Callicott loved fox hunting and owned several good hounds. Once or twice each Fall he would bring his hounds to our place and we would go out in the hills where I knew the dogs would find a trail. Grey foxes stayed around the fields and if jumped, would run around in circles, not more than half a mile distance. The reds on the other hand might take the dogs on a chase of several miles, sometimes going beyond our hearing range. A trained fox hunter can tell you the exact position of each dog by the sound of his baying and whether or not he is leading the pack. Late Fall is the best time for fox hunting, after the leaves have fallen and about an hour after dark. Foxes don't stir early and must be given time to make a trail for the hounds to find. Locate a good spot on top of a hill and cover yourself with plenty of dry leaves if it is cold, and you can stay comfortable for hours. Never lay on your back because the cold ground will be too close to the lungs and you might catch pneumonia. Always sit up or lay on your side or stomach.

Mr. Callicott's fox hounds were well-trained and stayed near us until he gave them the order to hunt. Even when they were on a hot trail, when he sounded his fox horn, the dogs came back to him. I have known fox hounds to stay on the trail of a fox for three days and nights and have seen them so tired that both the dogs and fox were not moving much faster than a fast walk. I was told that once a fox gets hot from running, he will not go into a den because the sudden cooling would kill him.. At times the fox would take the hounds as far away as Bailey's Creek and out of hearing range for several minutes. I learned that foxes are smarter than we give them credit. One pair of red foxes that lived in Hickory Hollow would actually take turns leading the hounds. When one tired, it ran upon a fallen tree trunk and the other, probably its mate, continued the chase. The trick has fooled a lot of hunters into thinking their dogs were slow.

Charlie, the Crow

During the years we lived on the farm I had many pets, including rabbits, squirrels, foxes, crows, terrapins, lizards, dogs, and cats, but the ones I remember best were Charlie, my pet crow, and Blackfoot, a wild red fox. Charlie had a habit of making a lovable pest of himself and that was eventually his undoing. He had the run of the place, including the house, and could go in and out at will in warm weather through the open window. One day Mama was sitting by the window sewing and noticed that Charlie was very busy going in and out of the house. She watched and saw that he was taking something to her bed and pushing it under the edge of her pillow. She investigated and found that the crow was bringing in some greasy bacon skins she had thrown out in the yard for the chickens. Charlie was hiding them neatly behind her clean white pillow and he had to go. I gave him to a boy who lived near Mint Spring.

Once when I was playing out in the front yard, Mama could hear bursts of laughter and came out to see what was going on. I had caught a toad and a pine lizard and had them hitched to a small piece of wood like a team of mules. They were about as mismatched as Blanch and Mike, Grandpappy's team, and every time the lizard tried to escape in one direction, the toad jumped in the other direction, dragging the wood and lizard with him. Country kids do strange things to entertain themselves.

Blackfoot

When I was about ten, I had a pet that was, without a doubt, the outstanding one of my farm life. It was a red fox that I named Blackfoot because of the black hairs on his paws and lower legs. Blackfoot was kept a secret from Papa and Mama because at that time foxes, like hawks and owls, were shot on sight. The den was an old one that I had watched

136

for two or three years from a distance, and seen the cubs as they played. Usually there were two or more cubs, but this year there was only one.

The den was on a hillside just off Hickory Hollow, where a big tree had been uprooted by a storm many years before and had caused a large depression with the roots standing upright, guarding the den. It was from the depression that the foxes, many generations ago, had dug their den that could not be seen unless you were within a few feet of it. Once I had watched as a pair had moved their three young ones to another den about half a mile away. The old tree trunk lay out over the hillside, making an excellent place for one of the foxes to stand guard. The time I watched the moving, I had walked to within a few yards of the tree before the male fox came out to take his stand as watchman. He sensed that I was somewhere around, but as long as I stood still he could not spot me. After sniffing the air and looking in all directions, he barked, and immediately the female came out of the den carrying a cub and disappeared over the hill. Later I heard her bark from somewhere up on the hill and the male became restless and again started to sniff the air and looking around. After awhile he barked, and the female trotted back to the den and went inside. When the male barked again, after going through all the precautions, she came out carrying the second cub and went up the hill. The same action was repeated the third time, except when the female came out with the third cub, the male leaped down from the log and followed her to their new home. The male could count, and knew when all the cubs were safely out of the den.

One Spring I discovered that instead of the two or more cubs, there was only one and he didn't venture out as much as when there were more. Watching from a distance I noticed that the cub, when he did come outside, never seemed to have a desire to romp and play like most cubs usually do. For several days I went to the den and each time got a little closer before the cub went back into the den. One day I stayed at the edge of the depression and waited for the cub to come out to where he could see me. At first he was hesitant, but after three or four days of waiting at the edge, he came outside and made gestures that he wanted to play. I made a few small movements toward the cub and soon we were playing like a boy and puppy would play.

At first Blackfoot was just a ball of fuzzy grey energy, but it wasn't long before he started to develop into the most beautiful red fox I have ever seen. Maybe he was more healthy because he was the only cub and got all the food he needed to grow strong. For weeks I visited the den as often as I could, and he lost all fear of me and got to where he would run to meet me when he saw me coming toward him. The parents didn't seem to object, for I saw them a number of times watching us from a distance. There is no doubt that they had seen me many more times than I had seen them and had grown to accept me as a part of the family. One day when I went by to play with Blackfoot, he had gone. I had not been to the den for several days and there was no sign that they had been there recently. It was a sad time for I felt he would not come back and wondered if I would ever see him again.

That Fall I was in Hickory Hollow checking on muscadines and walking along a dry creek bed when a movement caught my eye farther up the branch. Something had leaped from the gravel creek bottom to the bank, but I did not see enough to know what it was. I didn't have my gun with me so I picked up a stick, just to make me feel a little safer. When I reached the place where I had seen movement, standing a few feet away watching me was Blackfoot, but he seemed reluctant to come closer. When I started talking to him, he began to wag that fluffy tail and came to me. He had become a wild creature, but there was something about me that must have brought back memories and soon we were friends again.

The following Spring, while following an animal trail near where I had last seen Blackfoot, I saw him coming down the path toward me and I froze. Instead of trotting the way foxes and dogs do, he was walking slowly with his head down as if in deep thought. About ten feet away he realized something was blocking his path, and he froze also, and we stood there eyeing each other. After a few seconds he must have recognized me, and as if to say 'Oh, it's only you", walked around me and on down the trail. He was not acting normal and I worried about him.

Late one afternoon that Fall I was sitting near a hickorynut tree in upper Hickory Hollow, waiting for squirrels to come to the tree to feed so I could kill them for supper. I watched as a squirrel came toward me, jumping from tree to tree, when suddenly there was Blackfoot following the same squirrel, just waiting for him to come down to the ground. He saw me about the same time and seemed happy to see me. I rubbed his belly and back of his ears and he soon trotted off. It was the last time I saw Blackfoot alive.

I was certain that Blackfoot had a mate, but she had managed to stay out of sight until one day when he was about three years old. I was walking up the hollow near the old den when I noticed a fox about fifty feet away from me. Normally a wild fox would have disappeared long before I came into sight, but this one was sitting and watching me. I stepped slowly toward the fox and when about thirty feet away, it turned and trotted a short distance and sat down and looked at me again. By now I was pretty sure this was Blackfoot's mate and that she wanted me to follow her. Each time I walked toward her she would start off up the hill, and I followed her for about half a mile across another hollow and up another hill where she stopped by the body of Blackfoot. I was stunned and as I approached, she trotted off about twenty feet and sat down, watching my every move as I examined Blackfoot. There was no sign that he had been in a fight nor any sign he had been shot. The body seemed to be in perfect condition, and I have never been able to understand what happened.

I had nothing with me to dig a grave, but there were plenty of rocks around. I placed Blackfoot's body at the foot of a big mountain oak and covered it with enough rocks that it could not be disturbed by other animals. Looking back, after I had walked away, his mate was sitting by the pile of rocks looking at me, and I could not help but wonder if she thought I could bring her mate back to life. I have never felt so helpless as I did then, and cried as I left her alone with Blackfoot. I visited the place a few times before we moved and each time I cried a little.

Grandpa Barbee

Judging from stories I heard over the years, Grandpa Barbee was a pillar of the community and highly respected for his honesty. If differences came up between neighbors, they went to him and each told his side of the story, and whatever Grandpa decided was accepted without question. There was only one exception, but it was settled by each giving in a little. Seldon McDougal and Moody Mathis could not agree on the location of the line between their property in the river bottom. Bottom land was rich and productive and a few feet might mean the difference in several bushels of corn. In this case the difference amounted to 20 feet, and when Grandpa saw there was no chance of either giving an inch, he suggested that the disputed space be set aside for a road so that mussel boat owners and others could use it as a road to reach the river at the mouth of Panther Creek. Both agreed and each put up a fence, leaving the 20 foot space for a public road. Until the land was flooded by the Kentucky Dam, the strip was known as "The Devil's Fence Row" and was used for many years.

Mama never talked much about her side of the family, but once in awhile she would tell of some event, and it was usually something amusing because she had a great sense of humor. She told a story about Grandma Barbee's plan to surprise Grandpa with a special dinner for his birthday. Grandma had never killed a chicken in her life, but was determined to have chicken on the table when Grandpa came in from the field. Neither had she ever fired a gun, but that didn't keep her from taking Grandpa's muzzle loader out to the back where the chickens were feeding along with some other animals. Grandma was a small women so she rested the heavy gun on a fence post, took aim at a chicken, and pulled the trigger. Muzzle loaders would sometimes have a "long fire" when it took a few seconds for the spark to follow the powder trail into the chamber and explode the powder. She held on, closing her eyes and waiting for the expected explosion. The feeding animals were moving around and Grandma probably moved the gun slightly during the "long fire" which resulted in the sudden death of three chickens and one sheep. She said Grandpa sure was surprised and went around giving out fresh meat to the neighbors.

Left: Grandpa Charlie Barbee. *Right:* Uncle Clayton, his horse and buggy

One time when Grandpa had been to Dover and was returning home late at night, his horse suddenly reared up, almost throwing him to the ground. When he finally got the horse settled down, he tried again, but the animal refused to go past the certain spot. He peered into the darkness ahead and saw a large white object move slowly toward them, and the horse, having better night vision, acted as if he was ready to go back to Dover. Again the object moved a little to one side as if it didn't know whether to run or attack. Grandpa was not a superstitious person and was determined to find out what the object was. Tying the horse to a tree, he walked toward his adversary. The object turned out to be a newspaper, probably discarded by a drummer, and the breeze was lifting it and moving it around. Mama used this story to point out that if Grandpa had not investigated, he might have always believed he had seen a ghost.

One of Grampa Barbee's neighbors owned a big sow that seemed to have a craving for everything Grandpa grew, and fences were no problem if that sow decided to go into his field. He had been known to load his old muzzle loader with blackeyed peas instead of the lead pellets and pepper the sow several times. She had become gun-shy and the sound of a gun sent her running franticly toward home. One day Grandpa shot a squirrel at the edge of his field and a few seconds later was almost run over by the sow. She had heard the gun but didn't know from which direction the sound came.

That Model T Ford

In 1926 or '27 Papa bought a Model T Ford touring car from Uncle Bill Kennerly who had been using it to carry the mail from Dover to Fort Henry. I have no idea how much he paid Uncle Willie for it, but it could not have been much, because we didn't have much money at that time. I was elated and wanted to learn everything I could about the car, and of course, wanted to drive it. It was up-to-date because it had a self-starter, but the battery was often too weak to turn the engine over fast enough to start it, and it had to be cranked by hand most of the time. The first thing you learn about a Model T Ford is how to hold the handle in your hand when you crank it, or you might end up minus a thumb or finger or maybe a broken wrist. Always keep the thumb alongside the fingers so if the engine "kicks" or backfires, the crank will slip out of your hand without taking a thumb, finger, hand, or bone with it.

Winter was a bad time for starting a car because that was before lightweight oils and you had to be prepared to jump out of the way if the engine did start. The stiff oils caused the transmission to send power to the rear wheels even if it was in neutral. One method that was used a lot was to jack up one rear wheel so the wheel would spin while the car would stand still.

The Model T engine was a simple piece of machinery compared to today's models, but driving one could be a little complicated, especially when all you had ever driven was a team of mules. There was no oil or water or fuel pumps of any kind. There were no gauges to warn or advise you, no tail lights to protect the rear, nor heater to keep you warm in cold weather. For some reason, known only to Mr. Ford, there was no door on the driver's side, and if someone was sitting in the passenger seat, the driver was obliged to climb over where a door should have been. With long legs like mine it wasn't unusual to find myself in an awkward position, with one leg over the steering wheel and the other somewhere outside, trying to get in. Once you were in, however, simplicity ended and complications set in.

Pedals, Levers and Confusion

On the floor lurked three pedals with a combination that would make opening a bank safe a simple task. On your left was a long lever that reached just high enough to catch your britches leg when trying to enter without a door. The lever was supposed to be an emergency hand brake, but I have never known one to last long enough for an emergency. When pulled back into pants-leg-catching position, the car was in neutral; pushed all the way forward, you were on your way, ready or not. It was tough to master the three pedals and hand brake, and added to the confusion were two levers on the steering wheel column, just below the steering wheel. These were to be operated with your hands, while at the same time two big feet were trying to sort out the pedals on the floorboard.

The lever on the right was used to feed the gas (instead of the foot pedal as used in today's cars) and the one on the left acted as a hand-operated timer that regulated the spark. With the spark lever all the way down when cranking the engine, it would start fine but rotated in the wrong direction and swung the crank with it. It could be a dangerous situation and a lot of wrists were bruised or broken, and a lot of cuss words were used to describe the Model T.

With three pedals and three levers to operate in addition to keeping an eye on the road, it was fortunate there were only a few cars on the road at that time. Once in the car, with the motor running, the first act was to pull the spark lever down to give more power. Then while pushing the left floor pedal half-way down, the emergency brake lever could be eased all the way forward. This was a delicate maneuver because if the floor pedal was too far up or down, the car started on its way. When the left pedal was pushed slowly all the way down, the car was in low gear, and you had to pull down on the gas lever to gain enough speed to release the pedal all the way back into high gear, meanwhile easing off on the gas so the car would not lunge forward. The amount of gas could be controlled and if you were lucky, things went smoothly until the first long hill, and that is where complications started all over again.

The floor pedal in the middle was for reverse and here again you had to be a genius to operate it. If it became necessary to go backwards, you pushed the left pedal half-way down and the middle pedal all the way down. If your foot slipped and both pedals were pushed all the way down, the car had a hankering to go in both directions at the same time. The pedal on the right was the brake. It was not all that important because if the brake wasn't working, you could slow down by pushing the left pedal all the way down, or push it half-way and then push the middle on all the way down. Once you learned the secrets of the car and had an IQ of 150 or above, you just might become a good Model T driver.

Not Convenient, That Ford

Henry Ford wasn't much interested in making his cars convenient or comfortable. When you had to put gas in the gas tank, the driver was not the only one who had to get out of the car. Anyone sitting in the front seat had to get out because the passenger was sitting over the gas tank, and the front seat had to be removed. There was no gas gauge and you had to try and out guess the car as to when you should add fuel, and it was not unusual to run out of gas. Because there was no fuel pump, the carburetor got its gas by gravity flow from the main tank, and if you drove up a long steep hill the it ran dry and you came to a sudden stop. You could then cut the front wheels, and let the car roll back until it was crosswise in the road, and wait until the carburetor refilled. If someone was with you, then you could scotch the rear wheels with a big rock or log, remove the front seat, and place a tire pump hose tightly over the ventilation hole in the gas cap and build up enough pressure to force the gas to the carburetor. The first method was more popular and most long hills had a wide spot at the proper place just for the purpose of letting your car refill its carburetor.

The Model T had four coils (located under the dash) to guarantee an ample supply of spark. Each coil was in a wooden box about the size of an old-fashion matchbox, and with the engine running, each one carried enough volts to knock the heck out of you. They were easy to remove if the car was to sit idle for a few days, or if the weather was damp. If they did get wet, you simply put them in the oven and dried them out. The Model T was much like a mule, stubborn and unpredictable from start to finish, yet reliable most of the time. You had to control your temper because a bad temper and a Model T combination meant certain disaster.

Grandmammy Gets Shocked!

The road crossed Panther Creek near Blue Spring, and it was the custom in warm weather, when fording the creek, to stop in the middle, take off your shoes, wade around to the front, and fill the radiator. Once while I was doing this chore with Grandmammy sitting in the back seat, she screamed, jumped out into the water, and waded to the bank. Somehow she had gotten a big electrical shock, but I have never figured out how it happened. Like I said before, the Model T was unpredictable. As far as I know, Grandmammy never set foot in that car again and referred to it as "that electric chair" and she insisted it was "hainted".

The Long Trip

In the Fall of 1927 Mama decided to visit her sister Gertie whom she had not seen for several years.   Aunt Gertie and Uncle Mintor and my two cousins, Pauline and Everett, had moved to Henry County several years before and we had not seen them since.   I was almost 15 years old and practically a veteran at driving our Model T Ford, and it was decided that I would drive Mama, and Papa would stay home and take care of the chores.   I was excited about the trip and anxious to see and drive on new roads, some of which were said to be paved.   When we left home, the roads were dry and the weather fine as we passed Fort Henry and Mint Springs and headed on to the Paris Landing ferry.

In the excitement the ferry had not been given much thought, but as we got closer, I started to recall the time I had spent with Uncle Willie at the Fort Henry ferry and the steep river banks.   There was no worry about getting on the ferryboat, but getting off on the other side was a different situation and could be trouble.   What if the engine died, and the brakes were not able to hold, and if they did, how would I get started again on the steep bank with a big river in back of me.   We arrived at the ferry which had a big dinner bell to ring to get the attention of the ferryman on the other side of the river.   I rang the bell and soon saw a man came down the bank on the far side to the ferryboat and headed across the Tennessee toward us. He landed and tied the boat securely and motioned me to drive onto the ferryboat.   This was it -- there was no turning back now.   Holding the left pedal all the way down with my left foot and holding my right foot on the brake pedal, we crawled onto the ferryboat.   After reaching the other side, the boat was tied up again, and the man came back to our car. He told me to give the car plenty of gas and not to slow down for anything until I was on top of the bank.   I took him at his word and almost squirted out of that ferryboat and up the bank as fast as I could go in low gear.

We drove to Paris; and it was the first time I had ever driven in a city where there were other cars, and it was scary.   To get to the road that we were to take out of Paris, we had to drive right through the middle of the city and even across some railroad tracks, and it was a relief when we reached a road that we had all to ourselves.   A few miles out in the country we passed Sid Callicott's house, with a big curved driveway in front of it, and on a road that was paved all the way to town. Mama said that to own a house like that you must have a lot of money. She wondered if Sid's wife, Betty, was at home. Miss Betty had been my first school teacher and gave me a whipping, and I had no hankering to visit her. A few miles farther on, we found Aunt Gertie's place which was a nice house, but not as good as where the Callicotts lived. Mama and Aunt Gertie had a lot of visiting to do and there was a lot of country my cousins wanted to show me.

I was amazed that there were no rocks of any size to be seen and wondered what they used in their slingshots. The ground was sandy and a lot more level than Stewart County and their main crop was sweet potatoes instead of tobacco. Grandpappy already knew about the sweet potatoes and had asked us to bring him a bushel. The potatoes were cheap that year and I remember we were charged fifteen cents for the bushel, and Mama bought a bushel for us also. There was a creek nearby (they called it a river) and we could wade it for miles in clear water with a soft sandy bottom. Another interesting place they took us was the clay mines. Under several feet of sand was a thick layer of clay that was free of grit and could be chewed like gum. They told us the clay was shipped all over the country and was used for making dishes and other things like that. They showed me an engine, the old one-lung type, that had been running continually for 25 years day and night, and was still going. It was just like the one Will Rushing used for his grist mill to grind corn.

The morning we were to start home it was turning cold and the roads, even in the sand, were beginning to freeze, causing the car to pull hard. Mama had brought along a blanket to cover us in case the weather turned cold and it felt good, except it was no good at keeping my feet warm. You can't drive a Model T with your feet wrapped up in a blanket. The road between Paris and the river had lots of ruts and with the mud freezing, it slowed us down to a slow pace. It was no problem going down the riverbank to the ferryboat because the freezing ruts acted as a brake, but the ferryman warned us there might be trouble going up the bank on the other side. I gave the Ford every bit of the throttle and all the spark it had, and we made it, but a couple of times the car almost stalled before we reached the top of the riverbank, We were almost frozen ourselves. Crossing the river with a brisk north wind kicking up whitecaps is just about the coldest place you can find. The spray from the whitecaps froze on the windshield, and with no wipers, I would have to get out and scrape off the ice. We made the rest of the trip without incident, and, except for the cold, everything went along nicely. Mama had managed to put enough cover over the sweet potatoes so that they were not affected by the cold. Papa had a roaring fire in the fireplace when we got home, and it sure did feel good to my nearly-frozen hands and feet.

Humorous Stories

The people who lived between the rivers were not educated as far as formal schooling was concerned, but their IQs were right up there with the best of them. Until Kennedy Gorham attended the University of Tennessee to learn how to farm, I can't recall anyone ever going to high school before 1929. They may have been behind in schooling, but most had a sense of humor to go along with their IQ and sometimes that can take you farther than a degree. The following are some stories that made the rounds in the twenties or before that are typical of their humor. Some of the tales had a touch of the truth that was the basis of many of them.

Jack Phillips could throw the fastest and crookedest baseball I have ever seen, even in the major leagues. He had almost perfect control and could hit the catcher's mitt every time. It was said that the catcher could close his eyes when Jack was pitching and never miss a ball. This much I can vouch for because, I have seen him throw a baseball many times, but I can't guarantee the following story about him.

A couple of fellows from over in Calloway County were in the Blue Spring area squirrel hunting, and after slogging around all day without killing one critter, they met Jack Phillips walking along the road with several squirrels and he wasn't carrying a gun. They were curious and asked where he had gotten so many without a gun, and Jack told him he had killed the squirrels with green walnuts. Their curiosity hit a peak and they wanted to know more, so Jack reached into his pocket, pulled out a walnut, and assured them that was what he had used to kill the squirrels. He realized they didn't believe him and invited them to come along and he would show them. Jack had a good eye and soon saw a squirrel in a tree above them, laid down his load, threw a walnut with his left hand and knocked the animal out deader'n a doornail. The men just stood there

147

stunned, and looking at the fallen game.   When they came back to normal, they congratulated Jack for his marksmanship and admitted they were amazed at the feat, especially because he threw left-handed.   Jack explained that he was not really left handed, but if he used his right arm, he tore up the squirrels too much.

A lot of steep hillsides were farmed in our area, but the steepest was on the road to Dover.   Someone on his way to town one day came upon a farmer, lying on the road and cussing up a storm.   When asked about the trouble, the farmer confessed that it was the third time he had fallen out of his field that day.

Someone told about a judge in Dover who was so crosseyed that when he was a young man, he was hired to dig a well, but dug it so crooked that he fell out of it. After he became a judge, there were three brothers brought before him accused of stealing some hogs. He had them lined up in front of the bench and asked the one on the left to state his name.   The brother in the middle answered that his name was John.   The judge turned to him and told him to be quiet until he was addressed whereupon the one on the right answered that he hadn't said anything.

A farmer was repairing a hay mower one day when a drummer, a city fellow, came by in a car.   The drummer had stopped to ask directions to Fort Henry, but this being the first car the farmer had ever seen, he asked what the contraption was that the drummer was riding in.   He told the farmer it was an automobile and asked the farmer what the piece of farm machinery was that he was working on.   The farmer told him it was an aught-to-mow-hay, but it didn't.

The first year that Sam Phippen didn't run for sheriff there were so many wanting the job that it became difficult to separate the good ones from the bad.   If my memory serves me right, there were about 18 candidates in the race.   One fellow got so carried away about getting votes that he forgot where the state line was and ended up in Kentucky near Golden Pond and got drunk. He got only six votes and he had a lot more relatives than that, and a few days after election he was arrested for carrying a pistol.   It was said the judge dismissed the case when the man explained that anyone with as few friends as he had should be allowed to carry a gun for protection.

When I was nine or ten years old, Papa took me with him to Murray. Much of what happened on the trip has escaped my memory, but a few events remain clear. Papa let me drive Kate and Nell except while going onto the ferryboat and in Murray where there were some cars that the mules liked to keep a good distance away from. Crossing the river was exciting because I always loved boats and the water. In the restaurant in Murray I embarrassed Papa when I ordered pork and beans instead of a steak like he did. We seldom had beef at home and Papa thought I should eat it whenever there was an opportunity. On our way back home that afternoon we stopped at a graveyard where Papa had seen something on another trip that he thought was amusing. A poem in the graveyard went like this:

Notice good people as you pass by
As you are now, so once was I.
As I am now, some day you'll be
Prepare today to follow me.
Underneath someone had crudely scribbled:
To follow you I'm not content
Unless I knew which way you went.

Grandpappy was a truthful man, and the only joke I ever heard him tell was one that he had heard many years before about a place in North Carolina that was known for its healthy climate and old people. He said a stranger was passing through the area and saw an old man, with a long white beard, sitting on the woodpile sobbing. Suspecting the old fellow had lost a relative or close friend, the stranger asked what was troubling him, and he said that his Pa had spanked him. This whetted the stranger's curiosity, and he went on to ask why his Pa had spanked him. "For sassing Grandpa", the old man replied.

Some people could take a simple story and turn it into a major event. That's what happened when a new school building up the river from Jack Gray's place was dedicated. That night there were hundreds of people from miles around who came to see the activities and to visit. The weather was warm and a lot of men, and all the boys, went barefooted which was not uncommon because shoes were expensive. One fellow stumped his toe where a sapling had been cut off just above the ground, and when he got to where there was some light he discovered the toenail was missing but could not find it in the dark. Next morning he went back to the building to try to locate the missing toenail and was surprised to find half a dozen toenails lying around the stump. The school was known as "Stumptoe School" from then on.

Phil Noland was an old bachelor who lived all his life with his brother John, near Tharpe. Phil was said to be a stingy man and once walked two miles back to the store to return a box of matches which should have had 500 matches but he only counted 499 when he got home. His one luxury was his French harp, which he would play at the slightest hint of a suggestion. One Spring day Phil was plowing in the river bottoms and when supper time came, he didn't show up, nor did his team of mules. Someone went to the field to check on him and found the team tied up, but there was no sign of Phil. The mules were taken home and put in their stables, and next morning Phil still had not shown up. It was a week later before he returned home and explained that a steamboat had come down the river and he had boarded it and gone to St. Louis to buy himself a new French harp. He said it must have been court week in St. Louis because there sure were a lot of people there.

Sometimes something happens to a person and he doesn't think it is funny, but others do. One cool Fall night I went over on Panther Creek to visit Aunt Mavis and Uncle Herman shortly after they were married. On my way home while going up the hollow from Ben Wofford's place, I spotted a big possum in the top of a hackberry tree, between me and the night sky, and I decided to climb up and get him. Hackberry trees don't have thorns but are covered with a knotty bark that can tear clothes and skin if you are not careful. I took plenty of time working my way up the tree, and when I was just below him, the possum started to buzz. I knew that possums didn't buzz and recognized it as a big hornets' nest and I came down that tree a lot faster than I went up. My shirt and overalls were torn and there was some blood, but you just don't hang around a hornets' nest, even at night.

Fishing

The major drawback to farming, as far as I was concerned, was that the farming and fishing seasons came at the same time. Papa always seemed to think that farming was more important, an idea that I never understood, and wondered where he got such a thought in the first place. There were days when it was too wet to work in the fields and that gave me a chance to go down on Panther Creek, or the Tennessee River for a day of fishing or just lying around. Sometimes Papa would go with me, and then fishing was almost a chore instead of fun because he went to catch a mess of fish and expected me to help. The best thing when I was alone was being on the creek bank where the whole world was mine, and I just wanted to stay there forever. Then darkness would set in and I got to thinking about the big cottonmouths that were hanging around and in no time, was ready to head for the hills.

Papa and I did go down on the creek fishing once when it was too dry to work in the field. The crops were wilting for want of rain, and he thought it was best to stay out of the field for awhile. We were down near the Rocky Ford and met a Mr. Lashley and his boy who lived up near Mint Spring. Mr. Lashley was known to be one of the best tobacco growers anywhere and soon he and Papa were talking about the weather. Mr. Lashley told Papa that in dry weather he plowed his tobacco as deep as he could and followed with a boat, smoothing the ground so it would hold the moisture better. Papa decided that was just what he should do, pulled in his fishing line, and told me to do the same. It's bad enough to have to leave on account of darkness, but to quit fishing because somebody said to plow deeper was beyond my understanding. A couple of hours later we were plowing and boating in the tobacco patch, and I never forgave Mr. Lashley for messing up my fishing trip.

The Big One Got Away

Most of the time when Papa and I fished together, we went to the river because he wanted the big ones to eat. Once we were fishing from the bank with cane poles, a few hundred yards below the Government Light, and I walked several feet out over the water on a fallen tree where the

151

water was deeper. Papa was down the river a few yards. The water and trees kinda made me sleepy, and I was almost dozing when my pole started going down toward the water like it had a chunk of lead on it. It wasn't a bite but a big hard pull, and I came to life just in time to keep from being pulled into the river. When Papa saw I had hung onto a big one, he threw his pole up on the bank and came running and yelling for me to play him. Papa didn't seem to understand that it was a matter of pulling the fish out, or him pulling me in, so I kept on fighting. When the fish was about half-way out of the water, he gave up but I kept on pulling until his weight broke my line and he dropped back into the river. Papa was sure upset with me. He said it was a big yellow catfish that would have weighed at least twenty five-pounds. The yellow catfish was some of the best eating of any fish in the river.

One reason it was so much fun to go fishing on the creek was because everything was convenient. On the bank of the creek at the head of Mill Pond bottom were some of the best worms that a fish ever ate. They were big red worms, but what set them apart from other worms was the way their smelled. Grandpappy had shown me the place the first time he ever took me fishing. They smelled just like Pepto-Bismol, and it was the only place I have ever found them. The fish seemed to like them better than other worms, especially the pan fish that I enjoyed catching. At the lower end of the bottom and on the other side of the creek, was a canebrake where bamboo grew fifteen to twenty feet high, and all you needed to get a first-class fishing pole was a sharp pocket knife, and I always had one with me. There were good fishing holes all the way to the river with names that usually indicated what kind of fish were caught there. Down near the river was one that was called the grinnel hole, a kind of mudfish that wasn't fit to eat but sure could put up a fight, and Papa liked to catch them even if we didn't eat them.

Once while I was fishing in a big hole just below Mill Pond bottom, a young muskrat came out from under some roots just below me, and started swimming across the hole. About half-way across there was a big swirl in the water and the animal was gone, and a big bass had muskrat for lunch. I spent many hours trying to snag that bass but never got a rise. He was too smart and I guess that is why he grew so big. Farther down was a hole where I caught a lot of pan fish, or perch as we called them. They were also called sunfish because they came in a variety of colors including red, green, blue, or yellow. They were good fighters for their size, and good eating if you could catch the larger ones. My favorite fishing hole was just above Rocky Ford, and I called it the surprise hole because one might catch any type of fish and sometimes a turtle. Many years later I wrote a little poem with that fishing hole in mind.

The Fishing Hole

Of all the places that I'd rather be,
I'd pick out a spot near an old maple tree,
Where the dark shade is cool when the sun is high,
A creek and a fishing hole running nearby.
The grass on the bank to be used as a bed,
A big mossy rock for resting my head.
A fishing pole stuck in the bank of the stream,
The ripple of water as it runs in between
The rocks at the end of a big fishing hole --
Won't ever get rich but I sure can grow old!

There were many small fishing holes all the way up Panther Creek and I fished every one of them at one time or another. While fishing on Ben Wofford's place in a hole not more than two feet deep, with some logs lodged on the swift side, I hung some kind of fish that broke my line before I knew what was going on. It was either a big bass or catfish but I doubt that a catfish would be that far up the creek. If we were really hungry for fish, I was not above "grabbing" a couple of big bass but never told anyone how I caught them. Slipping some gang hooks under the mouth of a bass was easy in the clear water and a sudden jerk resulted in bass for supper.

Fishing was a lot of fun, but there were problems if one became careless. Stinging nettles, a weed that grew along the lower part of Panther Creek, were painful if the bare skin came in contact with them and could hurt for an hour or more. After a few encounters you develop an instinct that helps to keep a safe distance from them. The cottonmouth snakes could also be a problem because they always stay around the water and don't like to be disturbed. They are aggressive and will lay in a path where you are walking, daring you to come near.

Storms in summer could be rough on a fisherman because there were no buildings nearby for protection. Once while I was fishing the creek just above Rocky Ford, I decided to walk over to the river and try my luck for something bigger. I had a pretty good string of pan fish and could use them for baiting a throw line. It was dark and cloudy with a constant drizzle but not bad enough to keep me from fishing. Just as I reached Campbell Slough, there was a sudden downpour with thunder and lightening, and the wind started bending the trees toward the ground. I had stayed under a big tree until the lightning started playing around, and then I ran out in a field and got behind a haystack for protection. The bolts of lightning were hitting the ground all around me, and I had never been more scared and wondered if there would be anything left if I were hit by one of the bolts. When the storm passed, I went to the tree that I had used for a shelter and a big limb was lying where I had been standing. I had dropped my string of fish and they had been washed into the slough. Cold, wet, and scared I headed for home without any sign I had been fishing. I believe there was a tornado that failed to touch down but was as close as I ever wanted to be to one.

Goggle-eyed Perch

The upper part of Panther Creek, above Blue Spring, was much different from the lower part. It was crystal clear with a clean gravel bottom with small fishing holes not more than a few feet deep and the fishing was different too. There were a few bass and goggle-eyed perch, that I learned later were called rock bass by sportsmen. The goggle-eyed-perch were elusive and no one seemed to know their habits or any special method of fishing for them. Occasionally I caught one and marveled at the red eyes and the powerful fight they could put up. One day while I was fishing near Mr. Frank Wofford's place, he saw me and came down to the creek to visit awhile. He noticed that I had caught a goggle-eyed-perch and wanted to know how I had caught it. After explaining that I had no special way of fishing for them, he said there were lots of them in the creek and would show me how to fish for them, but I must promise to keep it a secret; and I promised. He knew that I fished for food and not just for the sport of it and would not fish them completely out. He took my pole and in a few minutes had caught more goggle-eyed-perch than I had ever seen in all my life. I caught a few more and headed for home. I'll keep my promise to Mr. Wofford, although he has been gone for many years, because if everyone knew the secret, soon there would be none left.

Like hunting trips, I never took food or water with me when I went fishing. There was always some kind of food handy and it was fresh. There were berries, nuts, hall apples, roasting ears, and turtle eggs. Farmers had no objections to a person picking a couple of ears of corn, and they were easy to cook. Just build a fire, throw the corn on with the shuck still on it, and in about ten minutes the corn is ready to eat. I always took salt with me when I planned to eat out. Turtles dug out nests in the sand and gravel bars along the river and fresh ones were easy to spot. You could always find a can of some sort, even if you had to use the bait can, and when boiled, turtle eggs looked and tasted like the yolk of a hen egg. There was no white in the eggs. There was one pecan tree on the creek bank below Rocky Ford, and once in awhile I could find a pecan before a squirrel beat me to it. Few people knew about the tree, but every squirrel in that part of the country knew about it. Hickorynuts were plentiful in Fall and the scaly bark hickorynuts were delicious eating.

A Fishing Partner

Until I was about twelve years old, most of my fishing was done alone. Occasionally Papa and I would go together, but too often there seemed to be some work to do that was more important than fishing, something I could never understand. Later, my cousin, Ray Lyon, and I fished together whenever possible. Ray was older and stronger than me and he was easy going and loved fishing as much as I did. This opened a whole new world for me because Ray was an expert at handling a jon boat, and we could go up and down the river, across to Kentucky, or row over to Panther Creek Island. At the head of the island was a big gravel and sand bar and at low water much of it was exposed, and there was lots of shallow water to wade.

There was also an old boiler, about half-submerged, that we inspected over and over trying to figure out why it had blown up many years before.

Grandpappy said he had heard that the boiler exploded sometime around the turn of the century while a packet was trying to push through the swift water. The low water required a full head of steam and sometimes the old boilers just couldn't stand the pressure. He said that he was told the boiler went right through the boat and blew the pilot house away, killing the pilot. Several others were also killed, and the helpless boat floated back into deeper water and sank. In extremely low water there was only a narrow channel with water deep enough for a boat, and this was the swiftest spot between Paducah and Muscle Shoals. There have been times when I would be fishing under the Government Light when a towboat, pushing several barges, would come up the river and the barges would scrape the river-bank. I would have to climb up as far as I could and watch the barges pass just a few feet below me. Once a pilot talked to me while he was passing not more than 25 or 30 feet away.

Panther Creek Island

Panther Creek Island was a heaven during thunderstorms because there were buildings where one could get out of the wind and rain. Moody Mathis farmed the island in summer and needed stables and a lot for his mules. The team and farm equipment was brought over in a hand-rowed ferryboat and were left until the corn was laid by in the Summer. The stables were built to withstand the flooding and were the only buildings nearer than the foothills where Grandpappy lived. The shoot between the island and Kentucky was dry during low water but was swift and dangerous as the water rose. Six men drowned in the shoot several years before when the swift water overturned their boat. There was only one survivor, and he was the only one of the group that could not swim. He held on to the boat and was rescued farther down the river while those who tried to swim to the bank were swept under and drowned.

Ray and I caught some mighty fine catfish where the swift water hit the bank on the Kentucky side. Once while we were fishing from the bank, I hung one, that when I set the hook, just kept on going, giving me the chance of going with him or letting go of the pole. The water was too swift for me to try to wrestle a big catfish, and I always liked dry land, anyway. This fish was much larger than the one I had hung when Papa

156

and I were fishing and Papa guessed that one weighed at least twenty-five pounds.

At the lower end of the island, on the Kentucky bank, was the hull of an old barge that had been there for years and nobody seemed to know how it got there. The old barge made a good fishing spot because the fish enjoyed hiding under it, and when a bait drifted underneath, you usually got a bite or hung the line on some object that would not let go. Fishhooks were too expensive to lose under a barge so we did very little fishing there. On the Tennessee side of the river, across from the barge was Lyon Spring, a source of good cool water that bubbled out of an outcropping of limestone rock. The water was a welcomed change from the warm river water we usually drank but was only available in Summer when the river was low.

Trotline and Other Fishing

Trotlines might have as many as 100 fishhooks, and sometimes more, and this was a popular method of fishing in the rivers if you were out to catch a mess of fish. The main drawback was finding enough bait for that many hooks and still have a reserve to replace bait that was stolen by the fish. Sometimes we seined the creeks or sloughs for minnows and crawfish if the water was low enough. The easiest way to get bait in the Spring was from the "cooker" where they were cooking out the mussels. There was a man who cooked out the mussels on the river bank at Panther Creek, and the mussel boats brought their shells to be cooked out. He would give the meats to trotline fishermen or anyone else who wanted them. Most of the mussel meats were taken home and fed to the hogs and chickens. In exchange for the meats I sometimes helped the fellow examine the meats for pearls and slugs which was often the only reward he got for his labor. Occasionally a good pearl would be found that might bring a hundred dollars or more, depending on how perfect it was. Slugs were pearls that were misshapen and were sold by the ounce. When the boats came along to buy the mussel shells, there was usually someone on board who bought the pearls and slugs.

After finding a supply of bait, Papa and I would borrow a jon boat and tie one end of the trotline to a limb that was strong and hanging out over the water, and while I held the boat in the right position and moved slowly toward the channel, he baited the hooks and dropped them into the water. When the end of the trotline was reached, a heavy weight was tied to it and dropped into the river. The line should be "run" every two or three hours to take off any fish that might have been caught and to re-bait the hooks. If Papa wanted to catch drum, a scaly fish, he would have Mama make a batch of dough balls to use for bait and it was almost always effective.

Yellow Eels

Sometimes Papa went trotline fishing with some friend, leaving me behind to fret and pout, but there was one time I got even with him. While they were river fishing, I went down on Panther Creek to a fishing hole near Mill Pond bottom where I had seldom fished. The water was a little murky from recent hard rains and that was discouraging, but I seldom let anything stop me from fishing. I had a large supply of good-smelling worms and hoped that if the fish couldn't see the bait, maybe they would smell it. Soon after I threw my line into the water, something took it and acted as if it had no intention of leaving the water. It put up the biggest fight of anything I had ever hooked in the creek, and I was sure it had to be a big catfish. I gave just enough slack to keep it from breaking my line but kept it tight enough to keep it from disgorging the hook. Once it came close enough for me to see that whatever it was, it was yellow. I was certain it was a yellow catfish and wondered why in heck a big yellow was that far up Panther Creek. Leading the fish to shallow water was no easy task, but after awhile it began to tire, and let me pull it to the edge. It was not a catfish, but instead it was a big yellow eel; the first one I had ever seen. I had caught several of the black snaky-looking eels and had heard about the yellow ones and that they were an excellent eating fish. The color was a beautiful yellow when the eel was first pulled out of the water but dulled a little after being out in the air. That eel didn't give up, even after he was out on dry land and kept trying to go back toward the water. I had no desire to try to remove the hook and just tied the fish to a bush like you would a dog, and rigged up another line and started fishing again. A few minutes later the same thing happened; those two eels must have been twins. That was my last line so I tied a stringer to both of them and headed home.

158

Mama recognized my catch as being some of the best eating fish to come out of the water and said she had seen one when she was a little girl when Grandpa Barbee brought one home from fishing. We cleaned the two eels, and when Papa came home later empty-handed and full of excuses, Mama greeted him with a big platter of fried fish. He sure did dig into that platter and ate a lot before he knew the whole story of how they got there. Papa seldom bragged on me but he did this time because I had done what he was supposed to have done.

Blue Spring School

Blue Spring School got its name from a big spring a few hundred yards away that flowed about 500 gallons of water per minute. The school was a typical one room building, like most of them were at the time, and the one teacher taught all grades, first through the eighth. In the twenties another room was added, but we had two teachers for only a couple of years. One teacher, Mr. Louis Rumfelt, his wife, and baby lived in the extra room for the school year, carrying all their water all the way from the spring in buckets. There were as many as 60 pupils and only one teacher for many years. Many of the children just went to school until they were old enough to get married, and there were grown boys who never completed the eighth grade. One boy I recall, was grown and had gone to school all his boyhood life but never got past the second grade. Not that he was dumb, he just wasn't interested, and when he did quit and got married, he became a successful farmer.

Another boy, or rather a young man I recall, was the best and most natural baseball player I have ever seen. There is no doubt in my mind that he could have been another Babe Ruth if he had been discovered by the big leagues. His name was Curn Mathis and he was one of the nicest fellows I ever knew. He and Edith Sills married and raised twelve healthy children in a three room-house.

School teachers seldom returned to Blue Spring for a second year, especially if they were from places that were more modern, with things like bathtubs and toothbrushes. Those who were raised in the area like

Miss Betty Crutcher or Carmen Greenup were used to our way of life and were more satisfied to remain as our teachers. There was one exception, Miss Bonnie Hilliard, who was determined to civilize us, and right off started showing us how to clean our teeth by using the blackboard chalk.

Miss Bonnie did get off to a bad start the first morning of school when she sent Kirby Hosford and another boy to the spring for a bucket of water. Her second mistake was when she told them she was going to time them because she had no idea how far it was to the spring. Going to the spring for a bucket of water was a chore that everyone vied for because it got you out of the building for awhile. As soon as Kirby and the other boy were out of sight, the other boy waited while Kirby ran all the way to the spring and back and then the two of them walked in as if the water was just outside of the grounds. It doesn't take forty or fifty kids long to empty a bucket of water on a hot August morning, and a couple of girls were sent for another bucket. We watched as Miss Bonnie glanced at her clock and we could tell that she was beginning to get nervous as the time passed and the girls were not back. When they did finally return, she gave them a tongue-lashing like we had never heard and let all the pupils know that just because she was new, they were not to take advantage of her and trips to the spring had better be quicker in the future. When the next two couples took almost twice as long as it had taken Kirby and the other boy, Miss Bonnie began to smell a rat, and at noon recess went to the spring herself. Kirby and the other boy, I cannot recall his name, stayed buried in their books all afternoon and as far as I know were never punished.

Miss Bonnie Hilliard was probably one of the best teachers we had at Blue Spring because she not only put book learning in our heads, but also did a lot to bring us into a world that was new to us. It was not an easy job to change people of our community, and Miss Bonnie found plenty of resistance from the pupils and their parents. Fortunately she had a good sense of humor that doubtless pulled her through some difficult situations. She laughed a lot, but she could be firm when she needed to be. She would run and play with us at recess, but once inside the building she returned to Miss Bonnie, the school marm, and you were better off if you behaved yourself.

Christmas Play

The first year Miss Bonnie taught at our school she decided that what the community needed was for the school to put on a play. Many of the people considered watching or taking part in a show just about as sinful as making or selling whiskey, but somehow she got her way. Papa, Landy Simpson, and some other men hauled tie lumber from a sawmill and built a stage. At that time I was the tallest boy in school and Nellie Simpson was the largest girl, and we were selected to play the leading parts. I thought little about it until we started to rehearse our parts and discovered that I was supposed to kiss Nellie. Nellie was sort of a tomboy who was related to me and we played and climbed trees together, and she was the only one who could climb to the top of the tobacco barn faster than I could, but kissing her was something else, especially in front of a lot of people. I would be the laughing stock of every boy in the neighborhood and would never be able to live it down. Miss Bonnie finally agreed to dress up like a man and take the part herself and I would pull the curtains.

The play was scheduled to be put on during the Christmas holidays, and Miss Bonnie needed some evergreens to use for decorating the stage. The only evergreen that grew in the area at that time was cedar, and she asked Walton Simpson and me to go out and cut some and bring it to her. We knew where there was plenty of cedar near the school, and we cut several branches with our pocket knives and brought them to her. It was

Blue Spring School before the area was flooded. Caught fish from window

the only time I recall seeing Miss Bonnie angry, but when we gave her the cedar, she lit into us like an angry cat and told us to go right back out there and bring her some cedar. She said that when she wanted cedar, she meant lots of cedar, and not the piddling amount we had brought her. Miss Bonnie shouldn't have bawled us out like that, especially in front of the school. If there's one thing a country boy doesn't like, it is to be bawled out for something he thinks he is doing the best he can.

We left embarrassed and mad and determined to get even with Miss Bonnie in our own way. We went up the road about half a mile to where my uncle, Walter Lyon, lived and borrowed his chopping ax, went up on the hillside, and chopped down a cedar tree that was about six inches in diameter and about 20-feet tall, and dragged it all the way to the school house. Leaving the tree outside where Miss Bonnie couldn't see it, we went to the big double doors and asked if she wanted us to bring the cedar inside. She must have still been mad about something because she cut us off, and told us she wanted it inside, and where else would she want it? Walton and I got a good hold on the tree and started through the double doors and were half-way in before Miss Bonnie looked up and saw what was going on. She yelled for us to take that thing outside, but it was too late because the limbs were like the barbs on a fishhook and there was no way of reversing our plans. We had to keep going and went down one aisle and back up the other, giving just about every kid in school a thrashing with the limbs. Even Miss Bonnie had to get down under her desk to keep out of the way of the thrashing limbs. The cedar log, stripped of its branches, lay out in front of the school building as long as there was school there. The play was a huge success in spite of our efforts.

Fishing and Studying Don't Mix

Any time there was water around where a fish might be lurking, I fished, and that was what happened one Spring when Miss Bonnie was teaching our school. The school building sat on a hillside and the lower side was several feet above the ground. The backwater from the Tennessee River was higher than usual, and during recess, I spent my time fishing while the other kids played. When we came inside for study, my seat was by a window and just outside was two or three feet of water. I had my fishing line with the bait still on it, and it seemed a shame to waste it, so I threw the line over the window sill and tied the other end to my ankle.

At lunch time the kids threw scraps of food out the window, and it must have attracted fish because all of a sudden my ankle was being pulled up toward the window sill. The boys around me saw what was happening and started giggling, and teachers are trained to watch for giggling boys. Miss Bonnie was there in no time, grabbed my fishing line, and started pulling in my catch. I guess fish are slow thinkers because this one came along without resisting until it was right in front of her and must have decided that it had rather be back in the water than looking a startled teacher in the eye. That catfish gave one mighty flop, and Miss Bonnie was as wet as if she had been in the water with him. She dropped the fish on the floor and looked at me, started laughing and went back to her desk and laughed some more. That kind of reaction scared the heck out of me because I didn't know if I was in for a whipping or if the incident had driven her crazy. After what seemed to be an hour, she told me to get rid of the catfish because it was still flopping and making a thumping noise and the kids seemed to think it was funny. I took it out and tied it up until school was out and then took the fish home and Mama cooked it for supper. Papa guessed it to weigh about five pounds. I never understood why I was not punished until several years later when Miss Bonnie told me that she had intended to punish me, but realized what a ridiculous situation she was in and couldn't stop laughing long enough to give me the bawling out I deserved. She said that there were not many teachers who had experiences like that.

Even my best intentions sometimes got me into trouble. Like the time Miss Bonnie asked each pupil to bring some sort of insect or small animal to school the next day. I don't remember just what the occasion was, but I doubt that she ever repeated the assignment, On my way to school, where I crossed Pond Hollow, I passed a patch of hazelnut bushes that was a favorite feeding place for a kind of big wooly worm about five inches long, with a vicious look but which was really very gentle. It was yellow with black rings around the body and two spots that looked like eyes decorated the head. I had, on many occasions, picked one off the leaves and held it in my hands for awhile and it became gentle and would crawl up my arms.

On my way to school that morning I picked one of the worms off the bush where it was feeding, and by the time I arrived at school, it had become real gentle and was crawling all over my arm. Miss Bonnie was working with some papers at her desk when I walked up, and asked her to close her eyes and hold out her hand. I dropped my prize into her hand, and when she opened her eyes, she must have thought she was looking into the face of a Chinese dragon. The wooly worm started right up her arm toward her shoulder, and Miss Bonnie fainted and fell out of her chair. Some of the others revived her with some cool water while I took care of the worm. I never tried to surprise her again, for which I am sure she was grateful.

I was lucky to have several good teachers at Blue Spring, including Miss Betty Crutcher, Miss Cozy Lee Futrell, Mrs. McDougal, Mrs. Sally Martin, Mr. Louis Rumfelt and others I can't recall. Mr.Rumfelt was known for giving a lot of homework and when there were chores to do, it was dark before I would get to my school work. Once I had over 100 arithmetic problems to work, and Papa was a little upset that I had so much to do. Lighting was poor, and either my studying at night or some disease affected my eyes, and I had to drop out of school. Grandpappy took me to an eye doctor who came to Dover one day a month and had him examine my eyes and fit me with glasses. I wore glasses for several years, but when I tried to read my eyes would start watering, and I had to give it up. I was in the sixth grade, and my next school experience was when Prof. Ed Gorham permitted me to enter high school in Dover.

Old and new Blue Spring School about 1905. Picture sent by Frank Wofford.

About Snakes

There are a few incidents that some people will not believe, because they have not seen them with their own eyes. There is a world of difference between observing captured animals, and watching them in the wild as they live according to their natural ways. The following are some incidents that I saw in Nature with no interference by humans. To those who doubt, I have no quarrel, because I just might feel the same way if I had never seen these things with my own eyes. Mother Nature is a powerful force and given time, and left alone to act in her own way, can do the impossible. The most important thing about observing Nature in the rough is learning to "freeze" and stand motionless for a long period of time. Animals in Nature, as a rule, won't object to the presence of humans if they don't move, because more than likely they won't see you.

Diamondbacks Grew Big in the Hills

One day Papa and I were out in the hills, not far from the Boyd Pond, when we came upon a diamondback rattlesnake skin that had been shed a day or two before. Papa cut a small vine, laid it along the skin, and cut it off at the exact length. When we got home he measured the vine and it was just over ten feet and six inches long, and Papa estimated it had shrunk at least six inches, making the rattler over eleven feet long. When you realize there are such diamondbacks somewhere out in those hills over ten feet long, you have a tendency to watch where you are going.

Either that Summer or the next, I was walking along the road by the Boyd Pond and saw ahead of me, a diamondback crawling across the road. He was about the size of a stove pipe and, judging by the width of the wagon tracks, must have been close to twelve feet long. His head was bigger than a man's hand and his body so heavy that it flattened out on the bottom. He carried his rattlers pointing up and they were not as large as I expected in comparison to the size of the body. I watched from a safe distance as the snake crawled into some thick undergrowth and disappeared.

I recalled a story that I heard when I was younger about a big diamondback that "charmed" a small child and that the youngster was a mental case for several weeks afterward. I had not given the story much thought because I had doubts that it happened, but with this monster, I was taking no chances. There are too many people who take Nature for granted who often don't live long and then others wonder what happened. Experts say that a snake can't "charm" or hypnotize its prey, and I'm not going to argue with them, but some things I have seen in the wild keeps me wondering.

Can Snakes "Charm"?

Once when I was walking down the road to the garden, a bird's unusual behavior caught my attention. A small sparrow was doing a lot of strange things up in a wild cherry tree, flying and hopping from one branch to another. As I did when I saw any strange action by a wild animal, I stood still and watched as the bird continued to flutter and hop, descending with each changed of perch until it was on the lowest branch, seven or eight feet above the ground. From there the sparrow fluttered down to the ground as if it were sick. Because my attention was on the bird, I had not noticed a big chicken snake lying on the ground with its mouth wide open and not moving a muscle. The bird had fallen 3 or 4 feet from the snake's head, and acting as if it were drunk, it staggered into the open mouth and was slowly swallowed by the snake. I was so fascinated that I never tried to save the sparrow, although later I wished that I had.

A similar incident happened one time while I was visiting my cousins, Pauline and Everett Byrd, who lived at the head of Panther Creek. We noticed some strange actions by a frog and watched with horror as it "walked" right into the open mouth of a water moccasin. We hit the snake with a stick and it spit the frog out, but the frog went right back and offered himself for dinner. We chased the moccasin away and watched the frog as he acted like it was drunk, and within an hour it had died from some unknown cause.

Black racers are harmless but are big bullies, and can make you hurt yourself, as I learned by accident. I had been down in the pasture picking some dewberries for a cobbler when I noticed one of the biggest black snakes I had ever seen. He was only a few feet away and had his head raised high in the air watching me, as if curious about what I was doing. He was a little too close for comfort so I started to edge away, but as I moved, the racer moved toward me. Not knowing what he had in mind, I moved a little faster and so did the snake, and in no time at all I was running full speed. While glancing back, I ran into a wire fence, bounced back toward the racer, and when I changed directions, so did the snake. I chased that rascal all the way across the pasture and into a sage grass field and lost my fear of black racers.

Snakes can do strange things, and the strangest I have ever witnessed was an episode between a black racer and a copperhead. It was in Hickory Hollow just across the creek from Mama's garden when I noticed a black racer rolling over and over in a clump of pennyroyal, a herb we used to keep off ticks and chiggers. As I watched, the racer stopped rolling and started crawling slowly away from the pennyroyal toward a medium- size copperhead, a few feet away. The racer came in behind the copperhead and touched the tail with its nose and started to slide along the side toward the head. When the copperhead turned to strike, the racer retreated to the clump of pennyroyal and started to roll again. Again he went back to the copperhead and pressed his nose against its side, and this time moved closer to the head before the copperhead turned to strike. The racer repeated the movement several times, and each time came a little closer to the other snake's head. When the racer at last was allowed to reach the copperhead's head, he coiled himself around the copperhead quicker than you could bat your eye, and just as suddenly uncoiled and crawled slowly away. I waited, expecting the victim to move, but nothing happened. After a few minutes I picked up a stick and prodded the copperhead and discovered it was as dead as a doornail. I had killed many snakes, and they were always unwilling to die that easily, but the racer must have known a vital spot that I had never found.

Another experience I had with snakes was because I became careless while watching a squirrel in a tree instead of watching where I was putting my feet. I was on a ridge out in the White Hills, in an area where clumps of huckleberries grew. These bushes gathered leaves and rattlers liked to coil up in them. As I was walking backwards, watching the tree top for a squirrel, I heard the warning rattle of a rattlesnake and it sounded as if it was at my feet.. When you hear one of those critters right at your heels, your thinking goes dead and automatic reaction takes over. Suddenly I was flying through the air and when I hit the ground, there in another clump of huckleberries, was another rattler right under my feet, warning me to stay away. I was hopping around the huckleberry bushes like a kangaroo, and I didn't stay around to look for the squirrel. The way I was shaking, I couldn't have hit a cow.

Wild Hogs

Our wild hogs were not the kind found in some other parts of the country, but they could be just as dangerous. They had been domesticated at one time, but had escaped from being rounded up in the Fall and had taken up life in the hills. They had changed from the well-rounded bodies of the hogs we killed for meat to a lean-type porker that could get nasty at times, especially if there were young pigs they felt needed protection.

One Spring day I was in Stilly Hollow looking for hawk's nest, gazing up into the trees and not paying much attention to the ground when suddenly, about a hundred feet away, several wild hogs decided I was an unwelcomed guest and came at me with threatening grunts and squeals. There were plenty of trees nearby, and in a situation like this you don't look around -- for the best one because the best one is the one nearest you. I was never an outstanding tree climber, but I shinned up that one in record time. Hogs have a short memory and bad eye sight and soon lose interest if you are out of their reach, and they will go on about their business of hunting for food. Another time they might gnaw at the tree, but there's no need to worry because they don't have the type of teeth to gnaw down a sapling. These hogs acted unusual because they would wander off, have a change of mind, and come rushing back to the tree. Small trees don't have large comfortable limbs to sit on and after a while it gets uncomfortable up there. I must have hung on to that sapling for close to half an hour before those hogs wandered off far enough to where I felt safe enough to come down. I made sure they were gone before heading home in the opposite direction.

"No-Fence" Law

Until the late twenties, the county had what was called a "No Fence" law which allowed livestock to roam the country any place they chose. A farmer was required to fence the livestock out instead of keeping them inside a pasture. Papa was very much in favor of the law, and when there was a move to do away with it, he got hot under the collar and gave his opinions in several letters to the local newspaper. The issue really got hot and for a while it appeared that there was trouble brewing between neighbors. The letters to the newspaper started using a fictitious cow, "Old Pied", to drive home their point of view. The cow was all over the county, and one fellow wrote that she had been shot with blackeyed peas and that they had sprouted and were growing out of her back. In the end, the "No Fence" law was repealed, and farmers had a year to get their livestock out of the woods and fence in their own pastures.

A year or two before the law was repealed, Papa and I had put three strands of barbed wire around Hickory Hollow and were farming it. Papa was ahead of his time in many ways when it came to farming. He used fertilizer when others thought it was a waste of money and he proved them wrong. He had his eyes on the five small fields in Hickory Hollow and believed they would produce good crops because it had been "laying out" for many years. Mr. Gorham, the owner, told Papa he could farm it, but he would have to do the fencing.

There were remnants of a barbed wire fence from many years back, and we used every piece we could find. Most of the wire had been nailed to saplings and trees, instead of post and they had grown about six inches over the wire. If the wire could not be used in its original place, we had to chop it out of the tree. It only took a couple of rolls of extra wire to complete the job and Papa was right, the land did produce better than where the land had not rested.

When we planted corn, Papa laid out the rows with Nell using one point of a double shovel plow, and I followed with Kate, pulling a seed drill. It was important to keep an eye on the spout where the grains of seed corn dropped because if it failed to drop seeds, a long vacant place in the row would result. Once while I was operating the drill, I saw a red grain of corn drop and wondered how it got into the seed corn. Next Fall when Lynn Love and I were gathering the corn, there was a red ear, and I remarked to Lynn and Papa that I had seen the red grain drop back in the Spring. He never did believe that I had an eye and memory to recall such a thing.

Tie Hackers and Sawmills

In the early and mid-twenties the woods around Blue Spring were full of tie hackers and sawmills because there were thousands of acres of hardwood, much of it owned by the Ayer and Lord Tie Company. They owned the White Hills and thousands of acres surrounding them, where I spent much of my young life. Many of the farmers either hewed crossties or worked at a sawmill for extra cash and it was not uncommon to hear several hackers hewing ties as you walked along the roads. Wheeler and Lynn Love made their living hewing ties for many years, until the timber was cut off. They earned from ten to twenty cents per tie and could make up to twenty ties a day, but they were mostly in the ten-to-fifteen cent range. The tie hackers went in pairs, because it took two people to saw down the trees and then cut them into eight foot lengths. After a day's supply was cut, each hacker squared the logs with a buzzard-wing broad-

Bill Biggs' sawmill crew about 1910. Tot Lyon, Papa, Wheeler Love, Uncle Milford and Ivey Lyon

axe. It took a good eye and steady hands to make the ties square and smooth or otherwise they would be rejected and no pay would be received. A tie buyer came through the woods every week or two, inspected the ties, and paid off the hackers in cash. He carried hundreds of dollars on him, but there was no danger of being robbed because he was responsible for their means of living.

There were several sawmills in the area at any given time, especially in Winter when farmers were available to work them. One was located at the Boyd Pond, about a mile out the ridge from our house and operated off and on for several years. The mills were a source of tie lumber, the rough planks cut from the logs while trimming off the bark. Many of the rough "slabs", the first cut from the log, were used to fire the boiler and make steam to power the sawmill. The ties were hauled to the Tennessee River and stacked, to wait for barges to take them to Paducah.

"Jack-O-Lanterns"

Jack-O-Lantern was the name we called a strange light of unknown origin at the time that floated in the air as one would expect a ghost to do. This light is also known as Will-O-the-Wisp and Saint Elmo's fire. They were more often seen in the same area from time to time and usually on damp nights when there was little or no breeze. The area between us and the Nances, where Owl and Stilly Hollows came together, was one of the places where Jack-O-Lanterns could be seen more often, and many times I would sit on our back porch and watch for hours and wonder what they were. Sometimes such unknown phenomena were considered an act of God, and it was better to leave them alone.

One night Jack and Gaynell Herndon, who lived farther up the hollow at the Louis Herndon farm, were visiting us, and while they were there, a Jack-O-Lantern appeared in the usual place, and all of us were in the back yard watching as it moved, first one way and then another. After a while the light started moving up Owl Hollow toward where Jack and Gaynell lived, and Jack began to get a little nervous. He was one of those people who didn't really believe in ghost but liked to keep some distance between him and some unknown object that moved around in the air. Papa was never one to let a good opportunity pass, and started talking seriously about ghosts, and wondering out loud if that could be the ghost of some long-gone person searching the hollow for something it lost while alive. He said it just might be the ghost of Jack's grandfather, Louis Herndon, who settled the place where Jack and Gaynell were living, and maybe he had come back for a visit. You could tell that Jack was not too happy about the light going toward the Herndon place. We continued to watch as the light floated across the field toward a tobacco barn just down the road from where Jack and Gaynell lived, and just as it seemed to reach the barn, it abruptly turned upward and was gone from sight. Papa suggested that the ghost had gone up in the barn to roost for the night. Jack refused to go home that night, and he and Gaynell spent the night at our place.

I suppose it was that incident that started me to wondering what those floating lights really were, and I made up my mind that the next time one appeared, I was going to find out . It wasn't that I was all that brave, but I was just curious and did not believe in ghosts. I recalled the story when Grandpa Barbee saw a large white object moving around in the road in front of him one dark night, and found it to be only a newspaper the breeze was playing with. I don't remember how long afterward it was before another light appeared, but I do recall that I was not as anxious as I had been before to investigate it, but curiosity won out and I decided to take a chance. I believe that was the only time that Papa and Mama ever cautioned me to be careful, and it was probably because I was not carrying a light.

Heading down the road toward the light, the pitch-black darkness took the edge off any bravery I might have had, and I recall that at one time I considering turning around and going back to the house. A wooded point divided the two hollows and when I got to where the light should have been, there was nothing to be seen and I walked across to the next creek but still saw nothing. Turning back toward the house, I spotted the thing at the edge of a field about 200 yards away and wondered how I had missed it when I came through that area. It seemed to be moving slowly in my direction, and the thought of leaving there certainly crossed my mind, but I stood still for a moment and the light changed course and started across the field toward Owl Hollow creek. Walking slowly toward it until it was thirty or forty feet away, I could tell that it was something like a ball of fire about 3 to 5 feet across and was making a low hissing noise. It moved with the breeze, and I was glad because if it had gone against the breeze, I'm pretty sure that I would not have stayed around. I followed it for about half an hour until it suddenly vanished.

Trapping For Furs

Trapping animals for their fur, using steel traps, was a way of life in the early twenties. Certainly it was cruel, and now, about 70 years later, I look back on the practice with horror, but at the time it was just the natural thing to do and was accepted by the public as a method of making a living. Some years my trapping would bring in almost as much money as we received for the tobacco crop. A big possum pelt could bring as much as $2.50 and a skunk pelt, if it was almost solid black, could bring up to $4.50. A red fox skin would run as high as $20 and a mink about the same. A coon fur might bring as much as $10. Twenty dollars then was about equal to $300 in the 1990s and gave a lot of buying power. Many people considered hunting, fishing, trapping, or making moonshine as a part of their God-given rights, and it was not in the best interest of your health to challenge them.

I don't remember who it was, but somebody gave me a couple of single-spring steel traps when I was eight or nine years old. I do recall that it was summertime, and Papa told me I would have to wait until the weather got cold before I could start trapping. He said the summer coats of fur were thin and no good for selling. When cold weather did arrive, I went down to the creek between us and the Nances and set my traps at the entrance to a couple of dens I had found earlier. Papa had warned me that anytime I failed to check my traps every morning I would have to give up trapping. He said it was bad enough to catch an animal, but it was even worse to let it stay in the trap longer than necessary and suffer. Next morning I checked my traps early and found that while one had not been disturbed, the other one was holding a big, almost solid black skunk; and knowing the defensive powers of the animal, I went to the house to get Papa. He picked up his rifle and followed me across the field to where the unhappy skunk was pointing his business end in our direction. Papa realized the value of the fur and decided to shoot the skunk but there was a problem -- how to shoot a skunk in the head when the other end was all he could see. He told me to go around to one side and when I did, the cat followed the moving object. When the head came into view, Papa placed a bullet in a vital spot and the animal lay dead. I learned a lot by watching Papa, and it came in handy in later years.

We carefully removed the animal from the trap but as careful as we were, some of that well-known odor invaded our clothes and Mama had to boil them in lye soap several times before they smelled normal again. Papa helped me skin the skunk by slitting the pelt from one hind foot to the other and peeling the hide off the flesh about the same way one would remove a stocking. Once off, the pelt is inside out, and a pointed board just the width of the pelt is inserted, and it is hung in a dry place to cure. Every day the raw side of the pelt was rubbed with cornmeal to absorb any oil that might seep out;   This also had a drying effect.   Before the Winter was over, I had trapped or captured another skunk and several possums which were shipped to Maas & Stevens in St. Louis, Missouri; They sent me a check for over $20.   Mama used most of the money to order clothes for me from Sears & Roebuck.

As the years went by, my collection of steel traps grew until I owned a dozen; Three or four of them were double-spring, strong enough to hold a bobcat, coon, or fox.   Trapping season usually ran from November until the end of March.   Because the furs were more valuable, I made an effort to trap mink and red foxes, but it was a complete flop except for one mink, and I decided it was too much trouble and gave up.   To trap for mink I had to set my traps down on Panther Creek, using a minnow for bait.   The water was cold and the walk of over two miles each day was just too much, especially when the weather was too cold for fishing.

Red foxes were also too much trouble to try to trap, even though they were closer to home.   They proved to be a lot smarter than I, and after a couple of years without catching one, I gave up, but have always admired their intelligence.   I spent days trying to outsmart the foxes and sometimes wondered if they were off somewhere, watching and laughing at my efforts.   A red fox even turned one of my traps upside down one night, and I decided I was wasting my time with the critters.

There is one trapping experience that has caused more regret than all the others, and I have spent some sleepless nights because of it, although at the time I was considered a hero.   It involved an owl, and at the time owls and hawks were considered fair game because it was believed they caught a lot of chickens.   For many years there was a contest in the community and a prize was given on a set day to the person who could produce the most hawk and owl feet.   The prize was that each family in the community gave a chicken to the winner, and that was a valuable prize to work for. Even though I killed a lot of birds, I never won a prize, but I sure did try because at that time it was an honor.

The regrettable episode began when I found a young owl in a hollow tree not more than a quarter-mile from our house and brought it home alive. I thought the owl might make a good pet and placed it in a chicken coop in the front yard where there would be protection until we decided what to do with it. During the first night the young owl was in the yard I could hear it making some sort of noise that made me curious and while watching from the door, the mama owl flew down and fed her youngster. Because owls were considered our enemies, it was my first instinct to catch and kill the mama owl, although I should have admired her for taking care of her offspring that had been taken from her nest. I set a couple of traps, and she came in the following night, fed her young one and flew off, avoiding my traps. Each night I added more traps, and each night she outsmarted me and remained free. At last I set the entire dozen traps and caught her and although I was proud of my feat at the time it wasn't long until I began to wish that I had just let her feed the young one and be on her way. We fed the young owl until it was big enough to be on his own and then took it up in Hickory Hollow and set it free.

Hunting for Furs and Food

Although steel traps played a large part in catching fur-bearing animals, it was not the only method I used. In the Fall when persimmons were ripe, I would take a gunny sack and go out to old abandoned farms in the hills where persimmon trees were plentiful and look for possums feeding in the trees. The best time was after midnight when it seemed the biggest ones liked to feed, and sometimes I might not get home until three o'clock in the morning, and I might have as many as half a dozen live possums in the gunny sack. When there were several to kill and skin, Papa would get up and help me.

A few times when there was a snow on the ground, I would be out in the hills and come upon a coon's tracks and follow them to the den. The den was usually a hollow tree and might be a large one, too big to chop down. If it were small enough to chop down, I would climb the tree and cram a couple of gloves into the hole to keep the animal from escaping.

The Big Bobcat

Bobcats began to be plentiful in the early and mid-twenties and soon wiped out the brown hill rabbits, and were even taking a young pig now and then. For three or four years I had seen the tracks of a huge bobcat, and the more I saw them, the more I wanted to capture him. I wanted the pelt to ship to Maas & Stevens because I was on their mailing list for fur prices and bobcats could bring up to a couple of dollars. I had never tried to trap a bobcat because there were too few of them to fool with. Papa and I had talked about the big cat, but Papa didn't know anymore about bobcats than I did because they had not been around our area long. I had made up my mind that when we got a good tracking snow, I would try to track the cat down. When that day came, I didn't have to tell Papa and Mama what I was up to because parents have a way of knowing in advance when kids are up to something special.

In Winter the weather became an important factor in hunting and without any kind of forecast available, people had to be their own weathermen. One afternoon I was out back of the house and got a whiff of coal smoke, coming in on a southerly wind from either a steamboat or a train somewhere up the river around Danville. When the smoke hung on the ground, it was a good indication there would be snow or rain falling within a day or two. I could also hear the men chopping firewood at the Nance and Boyd Farms over half a mile away. Low in the sky to the northwest was a dark, bluish line of clouds in the sky, and putting all the signs together, we knew it would be snowing next morning. As expected, by daylight next morning it had turned cold and a strong wind out of the northwest was blowing snow, By that evening there was a good six inches on the ground and the wind was out of the north.

When I was a youngster, it seemed that all the good snows fell on Saturday and I was not allowed to hunt on Sunday, so it wou'd be Monday before I could go looking for the big bobcat. I didn't mind much because the weather was too cold for animals to be out anyway. On Sunday I made my plans so everything would be ready, and I brought my ax inside so it would stay warm.

Monday morning was cold and windy and a good day for tracking if an animal had ventured out the night before. Only a few of the braver animals would have ventured out on such a cold night, and this big cat was just the one to go looking for something to eat. I was never one to eat a big breakfast and had just as soon go without it, but that morning I ate a hearty meal. Clothed in heavy long-johns, two pairs of wool socks under high-top leather shoes, with overalls tucked inside, a heavy jumper and wool toboggan, I could go all day through the hills and not get too cold. Carrying a small two-bladed ax, the handle stuck down my collar back of my neck, and my rifle, I was set for the day. I had two gloves on my left hand for carrying the gun and my right hand was in my pocket to keep it warm. You needed to have the right hand free to pull the trigger in a hurry if needed.

As cold as the weather was, I thought that if the bobcat became hungry, he would head for the fields where rabbits were more plentiful. I walked down the road past Hickory Hollow creek, over the hill to Pond Hollow, past Mr. Lane's farm, and on to the Graveyard Hollow, but there was no sign of the cat. Finding no tracks, I turned up the hollow and followed an old road across the hills to the Lum Wallace farm and on down to Bailey's Creek. Turning up the creek and following it for about half a mile, I came upon the bobcat's tracks and soon found a spot where he had caught and eaten a rabbit. I was almost certain that he would hole up soon to digest his meal, but I was wrong. He spent the rest of the day marking his territory, and he sure did claim a lot of it. From the fields of Bailey's Creek, the cat went up a hollow as if he were heading back to where I lived, but at the top of the hill, he turned toward the White Hills, zig-zagging back and forth through a lot of underbrush that made following his tracks difficult. Lucky for me the cat went near a bee tree where the entrance was close to the ground with a big enough hole for me to get a hand through. Papa and I knew about the tree and would sometimes steal a lunch from the bees but we never robbed it otherwise. I removed the rock that was wedged in the hole to keep coons out, reached in and brought out a handfull of honeycomb and honey, replaced the rock, sat down, and ate lunch.

Now that both of us had full bellies, I picked up the cat's tracks again with better spirit. It is not easy to follow a bobcat over rough hills and hollows in six inches of new snow, and I was getting a little tired. The animal worked his way along the ridges toward the Boyd Pond and about an hour before sundown, I came upon a big hollow log, where the snow around it had been beaten down by what appeared to be several skunks. I lost the bobcat's trail among the skunk tracks, and circling, could not pick it up again, and I wondered where he had gone from there. I thought he had to be in the log, but if he were, where were all the skunks? It was a puzzle that did not make sense, which is often the case when dealing with wild animals in their own home territory.

Taking the ax from my jumper collar, I cut a hole in the hollow log ten or twelve feet from the open end and peered into the darkness. Reflecting in the light from the hole I had just cut were two big yellow eyes peering back at me, and they did not belong to a skunk! Knowing that bobcats can be dangerous when cornered, I was scared out of my wits for a moment, but I soon collected enough thought to cram a big rock into the opening so the cat could not escape or get to me. With the rock secure, I took my rifle -- inserted the barrel through the opening beside the rock, aimed as best I could in the dark at a spot between the yellow eyes, and pulled the trigger. I have never in all my life, heard so much growling and carrying on coming from one animal, and when it became quiet, I aimed and fired a second shot. There was no sound or movement and I felt sure he was dead. Cutting a bigger hole in the log, I pulled the cat out of the log, and I found him to be even larger than I had thought. Holding his back feet in my hand, I swung the cat over my shoulder; and his front paws came to the back of my knees.

When I got home, Papa was doing my chore of bringing in wood for the fireplace. As cold as it was, we burned a lot of wood every day. He examined the bobcat and said it was by far the biggest he had ever seen. The retractable claws were more than an inch long and each was as sharp as a razor. Neither of us knew whether the animal should be skinned like a possum or a coon so we decided to skin him like a coon. Later after I shipped the pelt to Maas & Stevens, they wrote me a letter and told me it was the biggest bobcat skin they had ever received. Even though it was skinned wrong, they paid me a dollar above the top listed price and said they would pay me three dollars above the market price for any more that big that were skinned correctly. The bobcat was the last one I ever saw near that size, and it probably got that big because there was so much food available at that time. Papa kept one of the feet, with the retractable claws, but I don't know what happened to it.

My Worst Scare

I have sometimes wondered if my determination to track down the bobcat was the result of an experience I had a few years before. Lynn and Alma Love had moved over to the Cumberland River side of the divide and I decided to visit them. It was dark when I left home for the two mile walk through the hills. I enjoyed walking through the woods after dark because it was an altogether different world from walking in daylight. At night you have to rely on your ears to tell what is going on around you and the sounds can be interesting. I was not prepared for what was ahead that night and don't recall being more scared at any other time in my life. I had just passed Grandpappy's old place in Owl Hollow when I realized that some sort of animal had began to circle me, staying about fifty feet away.

I could hear it in the leaves, and when I came to where it had crossed the path ahead of me, there was some dust in the air, indicating the animal was upset and had clawed the dirt. I had not gone far when the animal let out a scream that could curdle the blood, and I knew then it was a bobcat. This was not normal behavior for a cat, and I had never heard of one attacking except to protect its young or when cornered. There was no doubt in my mind that this cat was mad about something, and not knowing what it was, I was plenty scared. I thought about turning and going back, but if the cat was protecting its young, maybe I had passed near them, and I didn't want to trust my luck again. I was traveling a trail that had once been a wagon road over to Brandon Springs but was now used by both people and animals as a trail. I picked up a couple of rocks and a large stick that gave me a little confidence, but I knew these would be of little use if the cat attacked me in the darkness. The animal followed me all the way to the cleared fields on the Cumberland River side but for some reason, decided to stay in the woods, for which I was very grateful. Returning home a day or two later, I made sure there was time to make it through the woods in broad daylight and I didn't see or hear any sign of the bobcat.

The White Hills

The White Hills were a series of ridges separating Bailey's Creek and Owl Hollow that were covered with white rocks. It was an area used as a marker when describing the location of something that was in the area between the two hollows. A road ran along the ridge, and was used by wagons hauling logs or crossties, and was also used as an animal trail. Once when I was about nine years old, I went up Hickory Hollow and followed an old road that led to the White Hills. While I was walking along the ridge, Nature made a call and I went off the road about fifty yards to answer the call, because no self-respecting person would answer Nature's call near the road where it might offend someone. While away from the road I noticed two animals that looked like a couple of big dogs coming along the trail side by side, in my direction. I stood still while they passed by and when they reached the spot where I had left the road, they stopped for a moment, sniffed the air, and looked in my direction and trotted on down the trail. The animals looked a lot like German Shepherds, except they were larger, and had big bushy tails. I told Papa about what I had seen, and after describing them to him he believed I had seen a pair of wolves that were traveling to some other area.

The Wild Boar

Ever since I sent an accidental bullet across in front of Papa, he was reluctant to hunt with me, but he had little doubt about my ability to kill game because I brought in a lot of meat for the table. His faith in me was put to the test when I was 11 or 12 years old. There were wild hogs in the hills that were descendents of domestic animals that had wandered off from their owners many years before. Each year they multiplied and grew more wild and sometimes dangerous. Most of the time they stayed back in the hills and were no threat to people except when they had young pigs to protect. There was a huge black boar that liked to show his authority by acting as protector of the entire hog population, and as he got older he became cranky and dangerous. He was lean and equipped with the longest tusk I have ever seen, and he could have ripped a person to shreds.

180

A COUNTRY BOY *From Owl Hollow*

Mr. Lane, who lived down the hollow from us, almost became a victim of the black boar, but fortunately he was near a strong fence and made it to the other side and safety. That scare alerted the neighborhood and it was decided that it was time to get rid of the danger. Women and children were warned to stay near home but if they must travel, to take someone with a gun along. A posse was formed to hunt down and kill the wild boar. There were about half a dozen in the group, and Papa said that it became more of a sporting event than a serious hunt. The noise of a bunch of men tramping through the woods, talking loudly and yelling at dogs, was enough to warn every hog in that part of the county, and of course, they disappeared into some unknown corner of the hills. Papa knew they would never get the job done and somebody suggested to the group that the only way to kill the old boar was to slip up on him and bring him down with a well-placed bullet. Only because I was more acquainted with the habits of the animal, it was suggested that I was the one for the job. The next day Papa put 11 long rifle shells in the magazine of his Remington pump and another in the barrel and handed it to me and said he hoped I could find the boar. It was not bravery on my part, but rather confidence that I could locate the animal and get a shot off before he knew I was anywhere around but better yet, Papa must have believed it also.

It was Fall and there were two favorite feeding places for wild hogs at that time of the year. One was an area where there were several "pig" hickorynut trees, loaded with the small thin-shelled nuts that had a bitter taste and which only hogs and squirrels ate. The other place was an area where lots of mountain oaks grew, and the acorns were starting to fall. The first choice was where the acorns were because it was closer. I planned to go out the road past the Boyd Pond and follow the ridges, keeping a sharp lookout for signs of the hogs. Right off I broke one of the most important rules of a hunt of this nature by being careless -- by taking for granted that the hogs would be feeding beyond the pond and that the old boar would be with them. Walking along the road near the pond less than a mile from home, a rustling of leaves to my right drew my attention and I expected to see a deer or squirrel. My guardian angel must have been with me, because about 50 feet away there was the boar, rooting for roots and grubs, and he had not seen me. Knowing what could have happened made chills run down my spine, and I stopped and stood perfectly still, (except for some shaking from being scared). I knew

I had to calm down because the first shot was going to be the important one; otherwise there could be real trouble. The hog was sideways to me and that is a difficult shot to make, even in a hog pen. I waited until he turned toward me, then aimed at a spot I had used many times when killing hogs, and pulled the trigger. The old boar didn't even grunt, but fell to his knees and rolled over on his side. I was so shaken that I had to sit for awhile and collect my wits because I was shaking like a leaf and was still scared. After a while I went home, and Papa hitched up Kate and Nell and he and two or three other men went out and brought the old boar home. Later the carcuss was hauled out into the woods and dumped.

Squirrel Hunting and Whiskey Stills

You never knew what to expect when hunting in the hills, especially around the Bailey's Creek area. On more than one occasion I came upon whiskey stills or sites that had not been operating for several days or weeks, but once I came upon one that was still hot and producing the local white lightning. There was no one in sight, but I was certain that I was being watched by eyes I could not see, and acting nonchalantly, I inspected the entire layout and then proceeded on down the hollow looking for squirrels. Several weeks later Uncle Dave Champion told me all about

Whiskey Still similar to those used in the 1920s.

my activities around the still and said there had been three of them watching me. They were not afraid I might report the still, but they did not want me to see them while at work, in the event they were raided and I might be asked to identify them. It was a compliment, and they were right because I didn't even tell Papa or Mama about the still.

Squirrel hunting had no set pattern, like hunting rabbits, because it could take you to many parts of the hills and hollows. Sometimes I went hunting and planned to be gone all day, and Mama never knew if I would bring in half a dozen squirrels or none at all. Another time I might go into an area just beyond the Boyd Pond to look for fox squirrels. They were much larger than the greys and their living area seemed to be limited for some reason, and many hunters had a tendency to protect them. There was also the "winter hunt" when as many as four or five men got together on a cold day and went through the woods looking for dens in hollow trees where several squirrels would stay together, probably to keep warm. One man climbed up the tree to where the den was and closed the hole with a glove, a piece of wood, or some other object. The tree was then cut down and the squirrels, trapped inside the tree, were easily captured and killed. It sounds cruel, but at the time it was food on the table and seemed okay.

Rabbit hunting with a 22 rifle was a matter of outwitting the animal, You had to spot the rabbit in his nest before he decided you were too close and take off for parts unknown. If the rabbit was facing you and the bullet hit the proper place, the animal would leap two or three feet toward you. If it was a sideways shot, you would aim for the eye, and instead of leaping forward, he would jump straight up a couple of feet. I have never figured out why there were different reactions when shot from the front or from the side. When using a shotgun, no honest hunter would shoot a rabbit in its nest because it was not sporting, and besides, too much of the meat was ruined. It was the custom to make the animal jump and then shoot while he was in motion.

A Brother Arrives!

I don't recall what I did on January 22, 1924, but I do remember that late in the afternoon somebody suggested that I go spend the night with a friend, Louie Hosford, who lived across the hollow on the Nance farm. I knew that Mama had put on a lot of weight, especially around the stomach, and was looking forward to my having a brother or sister around the house. I had been an only child for eleven years and had envied the Simpson family and my cousins because they had brothers or sisters to play with. At that time I had only one girl cousin, Pauline, Aunt Gertie's daughter, who was just six months younger than me but I seldom got to visit her. I spent the night with Louie and next morning hurried home to see my new brother or sister and found a wrinkled little brother who had already been named Charles Douglas. I was no longer an only child, and I was proud of my little brother.

It took me a while to piece together the events of the night Douglas came into the world. Uncle Dave Champion and Grandmammy had stayed with Mama while Papa rode Mag, a horse on the farm, to Dover to get Dr. Crow. Douglas arrived sometime in the morning of January 23rd while I slept about half a mile away. I thought it would be interesting to watch him grow up and maybe it would give me an idea of what I was like before I could remember things.

Douglas' arrival did not change my life-style as to working, hunting, and fishing because he was so much younger than I. Maybe if we had stayed on the farm, we would have had the opportunity to enjoy the bounties of Nature together. About the only change around the house was that Uncle Frank Champion visited us more often and stayed longer. Uncle Frank was blind but was a great baby sitter when Douglas was young. In Summer he would sit in the porch swing and talk to Douglas for hours and both of them seemed to love it. He told Douglas about the animals and what each one did and every word was absorbed and remembered and retold to anyone who would listen. Once Uncle Frank told him about the redbirds and put words to the songs the redbird sang. He said the bird said "Jethro, Jethro, Jim, Jim." When Douglas repeated the story, it became "Jethro, Jethro, two Jims".

I never knew where it came from, but when Douglas was a small boy, he had the worst fear of snakes of anybody I have ever seen. Just mention the word snake and he would almost get hysterical so we all avoided the word when possible. Things really got out of hand one day when he was playing in the yard near where Mama was doing the laundry and wandered off into some weeds toward the stables. Apparently he saw a snake, and according to Mama, who was not one to exaggerate, came out of there so fast that it looked almost as if he was walking on top of the weeds.

His fear of snakes was the only fear Douglas showed, and he was not beyond getting into things that he couldn't get out of alone. Once when the family was at Blue Spring on a sort of picnic, he showed absolutely no fear of the water. A few feet below the spring was a deep hole, and Papa had put several watermelons in the cold water the day before and we were enjoying them at our picnic. He always left plenty of melons in case somebody came by and wanted to eat one. It was what might be called a tradition, and he did it several times during the watermelon season. Douglas was standing on the gravel bank, throwing rocks into the water, when suddenly he started laughing and ran full speed down the steep bank into the water. The water was deep and he went under like the rocks he was throwing. I was several feet away and by the time I reached him, he had been under the water for several seconds. We were afraid he would get strangled and we would have to get the water out of him, but as I brought him to the dry land, soaking wet myself, he was still laughing as if nothing had happened, and he was fine. Douglas had nearly six years on the farm, and the experience of living with Nature has stayed with him even until now.

Interesting Country People

People who have grown up in the city, where formal education is taken for granted, are not aware there are people with little or no schooling who have some sort of super-intelligence. Uncle Frank Champion was one of the most well-read and intelligent persons I have ever known, and his entire formal education consisted of one half-day at school. When he was six or seven years old, he went to school but by noon was so bored that he went home and never went to school again. Later he taught himself to read and he read every book and magazine he could lay his hands on. Not only did he read a lot, his fantastic memory retained ever word he ever read.

Uncle Frank was Grandmammy's brother who lost his eye-sight during the flu epidemic of 1917-18 and spent the rest of his life living with relatives. He had married Mama's aunt and considered himself to be related to us on both sides of the family. He was always a welcomed visitor, and there were many jobs he could do, including baby-sitting, stripping tobacco, hulling beans, and churning the milk. He chewed small amounts of tobacco, but I never saw him spit. Not being able to see, he was afraid he might spit in the wrong place so he just swallowed the juice. It was a happy time when someone yelled that Uncle Frank was coming up the road for a visit.

Uncle Frank always seemed to enjoy visiting at our house and we enjoyed having him. A visit might be a few days or weeks, and no one ever asked him how long he was going to stay. When they were available, Mama would have turnip greens, cooked with a piece of pork, his favorite dish. He said that when he was to be buried, if there was any doubt as to whether or not he was dead, we should hold some turnip greens close to his face; if he didn't open his mouth, go ahead and bury him. Next to turnip greens Uncle Frank liked fresh tomatoes and regretted that when he was a young boy, people believed they were poison and he was cheated out of a lot of enjoyment. Another favorite food was butter that was so old that it might be moldy, and said that it tasted almost like cheese.

I spent many an evening in front of our fireplace listening to Uncle Frank tell stories about the past. His memory was exceptional, and he could tell you the date in the Spring when he heard the first whipperwill or bobwhite of each year for a long time back. He told me once about having a tooth pulled and after carrying it around in his pocket for awhile, buried it at the base of an oak along side the road in the White Hills. He was so exact in describing the location that later I went out to the hills, found the tooth, and brought it to him. After that he never doubted that I could find my way around in the woods.

Once he told me about when he was a boy, going with his father to a hollow that led off Bailey's Creek toward the White Hills to get lead for making Minie balls for his muzzle-loading rifle. He said there was a big chunk of lead, exposed in the bank of a gully and that his father would cut off pieces with an ax and take the lead home to melt into bullets. I spent many hours searching for the lead but was never able to find it. I suspect the gully had filled up or changed location over the years and the lead deposit was hidden from view. I will always believe the lead is there somewhere under the ground.

Uncle Frank was twelve years old during the Civil War and told me a story of how the Yankee soldiers held him by his feet and swung him back and forth, head down, over a hand dug-well. He said it was the most frightening experience of his life. He had a wonderful sense of humor and chuckled when he told about the time he answered an advertisement and ordered "a sure way to get rid of bed bugs". The company said it would guarantee its method to kill the pest or would refund your money. He sent the fifty cents that was required and several weeks later received a package from the company. Inside the package were two blocks of wood that were numbered 1 and 2, with instructions to catch the bed bug, put it on block number 1, and mash him with block number 2.

He told about the time he taught his son, Albert, how to load crossties onto the wagon. Albert was the biggest and strongest man in our part of the country and must have been very strong, even when he was young. Uncle Frank said he showed Albert how to upended a crosstie and let it fall gently across the shoulder. Uncle Frank took his load to the wagon and after dumping it, looked back and saw Albert coming behind him with a crosstie on his shoulder and another under his arm.

The most fascinating thing about Uncle Frank was his memory of what he had read, some of it going back fifty years. After reading a book or magazine just one time, he could quote it word for word, even after he had been blind for several years. He read the Old and New Testaments all the way through and knew both by heart. Many times I have gotten Mama's bible out and just let it fall open and read a verse to him. He could always quote the verse above and the verse below the one I had read and then name the book, chapter, and verse. I used to sit and listen to him recite poetry hour after hour from some book he had read when he was a young man. I have often wondered what would have happened if Uncle Frank had lived where his photographic memory could have been put to commercial use.

Aunt Sally Ann

Aunt Sally Ann Lyon was the widow of Grandpappy's brother, Jim, and was a few years older than Uncle Frank. About once a year the two of them would be at our house together for several days, and I spent every moment possible sitting at their feet, listening to them talk about when they were young. Aunt Sally Ann was of courting age during the Civil War and dated a Yankee soldier while the Federal Army was camped in the area between the battles of Fort Henry and Fort Donelson. She told about him visiting her one Sunday when a swarm of bees gathered on the branch of an oak in front of their house. Her Yankee boyfriend climbed the tree and cut off the branch and lowered it to the ground where the bees were put into a hive. Many times when I passed the oak, I looked at the stub where the branch had been cut off many years before and wondered if the soldier lived through the war.

My Cousin Walter

Walter was "deaf and dumb", as they called it in the twenties, and although he was considered strange by some, he was not dumb by any means. He was the son of Uncle John Lyon who lived across the river in Calloway County, Kentucky. His reaction to people ranged from being friendly to being hostile, but fortunately he and I were close friends and although he was several years older than me, he visited us often. He was deaf and unable to converse with most people, but we got along fine and when he visited us, wherever I went he went along and helped with whatever I was doing.

One time while Walter was visiting us, Mama needed some honey and asked me to go out in the woods and cut a bee tree. I explained to him what I was going to do, and he was happy to go along, even though he knew bees could sting. He sat down on a log some distance away from where the tree would fall and watched as I chopped down the tree. My face and hands were protected, but it was not unusual for bees to sting through a person's clothing. These were the little black bees that put up a fight to the last and may have been what they call "killer bees" today. They would follow you a long distance from their home, fighting every step of the way. Knowing they were the little black bees, I had warned Walter to stay at a safe distance while I collected the honey.

The bees nest was 30 or 40 feet up in the tree, but before I had chopped half, way through the tree they were swarming all around me, and a few were getting under my overalls and stinging me. My antics in reaction to the stings were amusing to Walter, and he was having a great time and laughing at my predicament. I could see that several of the bees had located him and were flying around over his head, and I made a sign for him to look up. When he saw what was going on right over him, he took off through the bushes and didn't stop until he got home. He had tried to tell Mama about me and the bees, but she was not sure what he was saying and became scared that I had been hurt.

Walter couldn't talk, but he sure could laugh as loudly as anybody I ever heard. Once when he was helping me feed the stock, I found an egg in the stable where some old hen had left it because she was too lazy to go up to the henhouse. I dropped the egg in my jumper pocket and proceeded to forget about it and went on with my business of feeding Kate and Nell and Red, the cow. On our way to the house I ran my hand into the pocket and felt egg in the liquid form. Somewhere it had broken and spilled out of the shell into my jumper pocket. Walter saw me pull out my hand covered with egg and he thought it was funny and actually got down on the ground and laughed until I was afraid he was going to be sick. For several days every time he would think of the broken egg, he would start laughing again.

Walter came to visit us one hot and dry summer and when he got to our house he was wringing wet. We knew he couldn't swim and thought he had gotten into the water to cool off, but he had a different story. By using signs and motions I could understand, he told me that he had waded the Tennessee River. That was hard to believe, but Walter did not know how to lie, and I believed what he had told us and that he did wade across the Tennessee River. At that time the water was lower than we had ever seen it, and boats that were pushing barges were unable to make it past the Government Light. The water was swift and dangerous and even though I could swim, I would never have attempted to wade across. He may have used a piece of wood to help keep him afloat in the swift water but I'll always believe he is probably the only person to ever wade the Tennessee River.

Walter was visiting us once when he became very sick, and we had no idea what was wrong with him. He did smoke roll-your-own cigarettes and was coughing a lot, but for all we knew he just had a bad cold. His fever started to climb higher and higher and Papa notified Uncle John who had Dr. Blalock of Concord, Kentucky, come over to see him. He told us that Walter was very sick with pneumonia, which at that time meant almost certain death. All we could do was try to make him as comfortable as possible, but his suffering was terrible. My rifle hung on the wall just above where he lay, and he begged for someone to load it and hand it to him so he could shoot himself. We removed the gun, but he would still beg for it. He died in my bed, and I lost one of the best friends I ever had.

Papa Quits Farming

Albert Champion was a big man in stature and heart and was known for his honesty and sincerity. Papa and Albert were cousins, and when Albert decided to build a new house, he asked Papa to build it for him. Building a new house to replace the old log buildings was quite an event at the time and news spread all over the area. Papa was a good carpenter and enjoyed the work a lot more than farming and agreed to build the house for Albert.

Albert explained what kind of house he wanted, and Papa drew the plans and figured the amount of materials that would be needed, including doors, windows, weather boarding, tin roofing, and even the amount of brick for the chimney. The new location would be on a point near the stables and overlooking the Tennessee River bottoms. Papa looked forward to building the house, especially because it had features he had never tackled. He had never built a brick chimney or finished the inside of a house with tongue and grooved materials before. It was a challenge and he was happier when there was something in his work that presented a challenge.

One Thursday Albert and Papa rode the steamboat *Paducah* down to Paducah, Kentucky, where they bought the materials for the house. They went to one of the large lumber companies and Papa gave a man in the office a list of the things they wanted. It would have to be delivered to the wharf that Friday afternoon or Saturday morning so it could be loaded on the boat for the trip up the river to Boswell Landing on Sunday morning.

190

Papa said that after the man totaled the amount, he asked about payment and Albert said he would give him a check for the full amount and that he did not want any credit. The amount was almost $800 and the fellow seemed a bit nervous about taking a check from an unknown person on an unknown bank located in a town he had never heard of.

One of them suggested the man call Bill Brandon, cashier of The Dover Bank & Trust Company in Dover to verify the check's worth and the fellow agreed he would feel better about it that way. The call was put through, and after going through half a dozen cities, a voice finally admitted she was in Dover. He asked for the Dover Bank and when someone answered, asked if a check for $800 on A. W. Champion for materials at his company in Paducah was good; then there was silence. Bill Brandon was a man of few words and sometimes they could be kinda rough. The fellow listened a few seconds, smiled, and hung up the receiver and said the material would be sent to the wharf that afternoon. Papa was curious as to what the person at the bank had told the fellow and asked about it. He told them that a Mr. Brandon had said "Sell him your whole goddam works and we will stand for it".

Papa went to work on the house immediately and even poured concrete for the foundation instead of using an assortment of rocks as was the custom. Papa had been a carpenter for the Illinois Central Railroad in Paducah and had a good set of tools and knew how to use them. As the building progressed, a lot of people came to look and marvel at all the new materials being used. Most houses had been built out of logs or tie lumber because it was the cheapest material available. City folks often complained that country people didn't paint their houses, not realizing that it was cheaper to replace the tie lumber than it was to buy paint. Building the house for Albert was the beginning of the end of Papa's farming. There would be other houses to build, and he was happier doing the work that he loved. It was left up to me to do the farming.

More Houses

In 1927-28 Papa worked most of the time building houses for other people and I did the farming. He helped build a nice house for Gaylon Miller at Fort Henry and did repair work on others. I was 14 and now my own boss most of the time and started planning what crops would be planted where. Papa was there to help me when I needed him, but I could tell he had lost most of his interest in farming. Lynn Love stayed with us a lot and helped me when the work got too much for me. I remember him helping me gather corn one Fall, probably because we lived near the Simpsons. He was courting Alma Simpson at the time. Lynn was good to have around, for he had a wonderful sense of humor that came in handy many times. After he and Alma married, they lived with us for several months and he helped me with the farming.

The Boy Who Loved Bees

Albert Champion's oldest boy, Corbin, took a liking to honeybees and started fooling around with them when he was real young. He read everything he could lay his hands on about taking care of bees and soon had beehives all over the place. For some reason, bees seemed to like Corbin and seldom stung him, and if they did, it didn't even swell. He built fancy hives from pictures he had seen and even made a honey extractor that worked as good as the bought ones. Papa said Corbin knew more about honeybees than anybody he had ever seen and would someday make lots of money with bees, and Papa was right. Corbin decided to go out to Oregon where some relatives lived and maybe get a job working with bees. He did well and after a couple of years, took a job with some outfit in New Zealand and spent two or three years there. I could spend hours listening to Corbin talk about New Zealand and what a beautiful land it was and that they always had plenty of rain where he worked. Corbin did become famous in the honeybee industry and was recognized for his many improvements in the queen bees.

Fighting Forest Fires

There were other duties that I assumed when Papa was building houses for other people. Forest fires were always a threat, and I can remember watching the reflection of one on the clouds and feeling sorry for all the animals that were in the path of the fire. Like hog-killings and tobacco-cuttings, neighbors got together and fought the fires as best they could, using one of two methods at that time. One, if there was no wind, a wide "path" was swept clean of leaves and underbrush so the blaze would die out when it reached the cleaned area. If the wind was blowing, one person would go ahead, setting fires, and those following would extinguish the blaze on the outside and let the inside burn to meet the oncoming forest fire. Spring fires, when the sap was rising in the trees, was destructive, and most of the small timber was killed. I was not only the farmer but was also the fire fighter of the family.

I was not allowed to fight fires before I was 14 unless I was with Papa and had only helped in fighting one fire. Six or seven miles east of us was an area of pine forest where Grandpappy would go in the Fall and collect a load of pine knots to use as kindling for starting fires in the fireplace. One time a fire raged through the pines and the people in that area sent out a call for help, and Papa took me with him. Night was the best time for fighting forest fires, and we arrived on the scene about nine o'clock at night. The needles were dry, and it was the biggest and hottest fire I had ever seen and was a bit scary. Papa and I worked all night, through the next day and another night. Local people brought us food and water, but after walking several miles home, we were both exhausted.

Another of Papa's jobs that I inherited was working on the county roads two days each year. In the twenties every able-bodied man in the county had to work two days on the public roads or pay a dollar a day for someone else to work in his place. One year I spent the two days on the business end of a pick and shovel and that was no fun. We filled in the ruts on a stretch of road between Clem Hensley and where the Morgans lived. I never understood this practice because the first hard rain washed the dirt away and the ruts were as bad as they were before. The second year they had me hauling gravel from Panther Creek and putting it in mudholes along the road between the creek and where Tince and Buster lived. This work did some good, and after several loads of gravel, the mudholes were gone for good. Also, it was more fun driving Kate and Nell than handling a pick and shovel. It was a new era, and roads now had to be good enough for cars to use them all the year round.

The worst farm work I was ever called on to do when Papa was away, was to help dehorn some cattle. The younger calves with small horns were no more trouble than trimming a toenail, but there were some older cattle with well developed horns. When their horns were severed near the head, blood gushed out, and anyone nearby got splattered. The animals, judging from their cries, were in great pain.

The Walking Man

Charlie Reeder was the walkingest man I have ever known. He was a restless sort of person and was always looking for the end of the rainbow with its legendary pot of gold, but it always seemed to elude him. In the early -- or mid-twenties Charlie, decided that Florida held the pot of gold, and he set out on foot to find it. He did get a little help along the way, but I am not sure where or how much. He could walk 30 to 40 miles a day and made the trip from Blue Spring to the south end of Lake Okeechobee in less than a month. Charlie said that when he got there, the Fall weather was so beautiful that he made up his mind right then to send for the family and make his home in Florida. Before he could get a letter off to his family, clouds began to build up and there were rain showers off and on, but he didn't mind because it was warm. When he got up about the third morning, the wind was blowing at a brisk rate and the rain was coming down in sheets. Either that day or during the night, he said things really got rough, and the house he was in started to shake and a window blew out. He saw water flowing outside the window where there was not supposed to be water, and he went out side to investigate. Before he could get back in the house, it took off and was suddenly gone. The water was up to his knees and he was scared. He remembered a huge liveoak near the house and tried to reach it, and after a lot of effort succeeded. He climbed the tree, expecting to be killed by the lightening, and sat down on one of the large branches. He spent almost two days in the tree while the waters from Lake Okeechobee swirled beneath him, and he saw several bodies being carried along in the water.

A hurricane had just about emptied Lake Okeechobee and several hundred were drowned or killed in the storm. As soon as Charlie was able to come down out of the liveoak, he started walking back to Tennessee and Blue Spring, and this time made it in about 20 days. From that time on, Charlie called the people who lived in Florida, "Floridiots" and he lived out the rest of his life around Blue Spring. He did take a little walk out to Oregon and back to visit relatives and look the country over. He said it was a beautiful country but felt safer living where he had always lived -- in between the rivers.

A Cold Front Sneaks In

When we needed something from Miller Brothers or Ben Wofford's store, I was usually the one to go after it, and I tried to go a different route every time. Sometimes I went the normal way, following the roads, but more often took some untraveled animal trail that was a lot more interesting. One beautiful winter day I was sent to Fort Henry, about 3 miles away, and when I left home, there were no signs that a change in the weather was in the making. By the time I reached the store, a cold north wind was blowing and dark clouds were building up in the northwest. My light clothing was starting to let the colder air through, and I could not walk or run fast enough to keep warm. I had cut through the woods and the cold was beginning to hurt when I decided to head for Albert Champion's place and try to get warm. Snow had started to come down so thick that it was difficult to see where I was going, and the wind was driving it like little pellets of sand instead of the soft stuff I was used to. When I got to Albert's, they saw I was about frozen and wrapped me in blankets and quilts and stood me up in front of the fireplace to thaw out. Thawing out was painful, and I remember wondering if I could make it home in that kind of weather and thought Papa and Mama would be worried if I didn't come home. After about an hour, Albert and Hattie put some of their son Corbin's heavy clothes on me, and I headed for home. It was difficult to follow the road because of the heavy snow, but the extra clothes kept me warm and comfortable. Papa and Mama were surprised to see me because they thought I would stop at Grandpappy's and wait until the weather got better, and of course, I should have.

Virgin Timber

I was fortunate to see a track of timber that had never been touched by an ax or saw since time began. It was known as The Brandon tract and was located near the Cumberland River near what is known as Brandon Springs. I don't know how many acres there were in the tract but remember that it was a large area and was a great place for hunting squirrels. I went with Papa and two or three others and recall that some of the trees were so tall that if a squirrel was in the very top, a shotgun could not reach it. A 22-rifle had to be used instead. There was no undergrowth because of the heavy canopy that would not permit sunlight through. Standing anywhere in the timber one could see a long distance away until the trunks of the trees cut off your vision. Lynn Love, who helped with cutting the timber, told me there were oak, hickory, gum, and poplar trees that measured more than nine feet in diameter, and it might be fifty feet to the first limb on some of the trees.

Ice "Sliding"

I don't recall ever seeing a pair of ice skates in our community, but that didn't keep us kids from having fun sliding on the ice with regular shoes. Often in winter the ice was thick enough on our pond for me to slide on it, and that was one of the things I enjoyed most. My one goal was to be able to slide from one end of the pond to the other, without stopping, and I tried it many times but never made it. One afternoon late, when the ice was thick, I made up my mind that this was the time to reach my goal. Backing up to the corncrib, about 50 feet from the pond, I lowered my head like a bull and with all my strength, started my run to the ice. In the dusk of the evening I had not seen that Papa had cut a big hole in the ice so the mules could get water and it was right where I wanted to start my slide to the far end. I was going full speed when I discovered the obstacle confronting me, and it was too late to stop. I did the next best thing and tried to jump over the hole and land right side up. My feet touched down just as I had planned, but what I had not realized was that my feet decided to go faster than the rest of me and my behind hit the ice so hard that cracks from my point of contact went in all directions. To my surprise, even in an awkward position, I made it all the way to the far end, but I don't remember what part of me touch the bank first.

Uncle Dave Champion loved to act the fool and could laugh loud enough to be heard a mile away. One cold night his son and another boy were complaining about some sort of rash which we called "the itch" (before doctors got fancy and started calling it fancy names). Every home had at least one bottle of Watkins liniment, and it was considered an essential item to have around the house, like rubbing alcohol is today. Uncle Dave told the boys that if they wanted to get rid of the itch, to pour a bottle of the Watkins liniment in a pan of warm water, and using a wash cloth, rub their bodies with the concoction. There was about a minute's delay between the time the liniment was applied and when it started to burn. It was like rubbing the infected places with liquid fire, and soon both boys were outside rolling in the snow without their clothes. Uncle Dave thought that was about the funniest thing he had ever seen.

Nobody Went Hungry

There has been so much written about the poor people on farms that the younger generation might think we went hungry. Nothing could be further from the truth. Those writers are basing their thoughts on dollars without giving any consideration to food and contentment, two things that are mighty important to living. If anybody went hungry around Blue Spring, it was simply because they were too lazy to go out and get the food. If someone was too ill to work, then the neighbors pitched in and divided with the unfortunate family. A good example of neighbor helping neighbor was the Hardy Sills family.

The Hardy Sills family lived in an old building near the spring when tragedy hit them. The building had been a grist mill at one time but had been made into living quarters, and several families had lived there. Mrs. Sills was stricken with tuberculosis and then other members of the family came down with the disease, and the family needed help. The women of the neighborhood took care of the cooking and laundry while the men did Hardy's farming for him. There was no fanfair because it was just the normal thing to do. Dr. Ryan did all he could for the family and probably never got any money for his services. He advised those who came to help to stick their tongues to turpentine before entering the house. He believed it would keep others from contacting the dreaded disease, and to my knowledge no other person was affected.

Some People Were Lazy

Everybody had a garden and grew almost everything needed for food. There were plenty of fish in the creeks and river and wild game was in abundance. Cartridges for a 22-rifle were 20 cents for a box of fifty and if you were a fair marksman, that meant you could have close to fifty rabbits or squirrels for twenty cents and that's pretty cheap eating. Hogs could run out in the hills until a few weeks before they were to be killed, giving a cheap supply of pork and lard. Chickens required very little attention, and they furnished meat and eggs for the table.

There were many kinds of fruits and nuts growing wild and were free for the taking. They included muscadines, grapes, huckleberries, blackberries, dewberries, plums, hickorynuts, butternuts, and hazelnuts. Mama always kept a two-year supply of canned fruits, jams, preserves, dried fruits, and several kind of vegetables. If a family went hungry, it was because they were too lazy to work, and they got little sympathy from their neighbors. Neighbors were reluctant to interfere with other people's affairs, but if there were small children involved when the father was too lazy to work, a group might go to him and tell him to get out and work or they would make him wish he had.

The Chicken Thief

In the mid-twenties a family moved into our neighborhood from some place up the river, and right away people started missing chickens. It was noted that this fellow sold a lot more chickens than were seen running around his house. He even bought chicken wire and fenced in about an acre near the road, and people passing by sometimes saw their chickens in his pen.

This went on for a couple of years and was tolerated because the fellow did have a bunch of children to feed. When there was no sign of him changing his method of living, a man in the neighborhood joined him, and they really got busy. His new partner told a few of the solid citizens that they were going to raid a certain henhouse on a certain night and that they should be there ahead of them and hide in the dark. The chicken thief was caught red-handed and while looking down the business end of a shotgun barrel, was told that it would be a good idea for him to be in some other neighborhood by sundown next day. By noon they had moved and we never saw the family again.

One fellow over on Panther Creek broke a fellow from stealing, and he later became a good solid citizen. This farmer noticed corn was missing from his corn crib and discovered there was a small hole in the wall of the crib where the corn was missing. He set a steel trap just inside where the hole was, and next morning when he went to feed his stock, there was the neighbor standing by the crib with one arm through the hole. The hole was too small for two hands to get through, and he had to stand there until someone came to feed the livestock. He took the man to the house, treated his wounds, gave him a hardy breakfast, and sent him home with the understanding the incident would never be mentioned again. It worked and the man was never in trouble again.

Offbeat Cooking

Mama was an excellent cook, but there were specials that stick in my mind that were offbeat cooking. Like sweet potatoes baked in hot ashes in the fireplace. Those baked in an oven were good eating, but when cooked in hot ashes, they were delicious and had a flavor that cannot be duplicated any other way. Then there was the winter day when I had been out in the hills all day hunting and without a bite of food. I came in before supper time, and Mama had an iron pot full of cold turnips sitting on the stove. A layer of hardened lard covered the turnips and had to be spooned aside. I filled a bowl with those cold turnips, and with a piece of cold cornbread, enjoyed one of the finest meals I have ever had.

Sometimes in cold weather Mama would make flapjacks, Papa's name for pancakes. She made them for supper, and watching her fry them one at a time until she had a stack of about a dozen was one of the most tantalizing periods of my young life. Nobody touched them until they were all cooked, stacked, and quartered. There was plenty of sorghum molasses and butter to put over them, and it was a meal to remember. Other times she might make cornmeal mush, and we would have it in sweet milk.

If there were vitamin pills in the twenties, they had not reached Blue Spring and were not needed. Fresh fruits and vegetables furnished vitamins in summer and in winter they were plentiful in the canned ones. Nuts were a good source of minerals. There would be times in the winter months when I would get a craving for canned tomatoes or kraut, and both were always available. When I craved a certain food, I ate it and that took care of vitamins in the natural way. Mother Nature was an excellent guide to good health, and we got along very well without the multitude of cures that have been produced and promoted by the drug companies.

Most folks think of cold foods as a summertime treat, but we enjoyed them anytime they were available. In winter when there came a good snow, Mama would have me go out and get a dishpan full of clean snow, and she made snow cream with it. She added some milk and vanilla extract and it made a treat almost as good as ice cream.

Papa, the Weatherman

Papa was a good forecaster of the weather, and I would venture to say that for a 24-hour period, he was more accurate than the weathermen today. Farmers depended on the weather more then than now because there were no irrigation systems then. One year we had our plant beds and field ready to set out tobacco, but the necessary rains never came. On July Fourth Papa and I went over the field, dropping three grains of corn in each tobacco hill because it was too late to put out tobacco. When the rains did come and the corn sprouted, it was getting along toward August. The corn thrived on the specially prepared soil until frost came just as the corn was in the roasting ear stage. Papa decided to cut the corn and shock it, and maybe it could be used for feeding Kate and Nell and Red. It kept so well that we continued to get roasting ears from the shocks up until Christmas Day. It was the only time we ever had corn on the cob for Christmas dinner.

Papa would complain about the weather but never said much around people except the family because to do so would be considered complaining about the way God was running things. He knew that in late Fall when there was a chill in the air and white fluffy clouds were racing out of the north, there was going to be frost that night. He had also been keeping an eye on the cockleburrs and even when the youngest plants had matured, it was a sure sign that a frost was not far off. We would set about doing the chores that were necessary before a frost came. He knew that during a dry spell of weather, if his banjo had a sharper tone than usual, rain was on the way, and he was nearly always right. His banjo told him only of an approaching drought breaker and not of the regular summer thunderstorm.

One hot and dry summer we watched as thunderstorms formed in the southwest, and there were times I was certain we were going to get wet but we kept on working in the field and the rain would go around us. There was one time that the weather got completely out of hand, and it was just too much for Papa to accept. We were working in the tobacco field when a big black thunderstorm formed in the southwest. It got bigger and blacker, and all of a sudden was headed right toward us, and we rushed to get Kate and Nell unhitched and into the stables. We could see the rain not more than a couple of miles down the hollow and still coming toward us. Suddenly the cloud split into two clouds and one went across the upper part of Hickory Hollow and the other went up Panther Creek. Later the two clouds came back together over around Tharpe and gave them a regular gully-washer, while we didn't get enough rain to settle the dust. I never knew for sure who Papa blamed but he didn't go to church that Sunday. I am almost certain that incident was what started Papa to thinking about some other way of making a living and convinced him that somebody was trying to tell him something.

Airplanes

In the early twenties it was rare to see an automobile so you can imagine the excitement when an airplane had to make a forced landing just across the river in Kentucky. Ray Lyon and I were the first from our side of the river to go over to see the contraption. I had seen one in Paducah but was too young at the time to remember much about it. Ray had never seen one so it didn't take us long to get to the other side to inspect the plane. It was a World War I Spade that had been forced down in a small field and had gone through a fence and damaged the wooden propeller. There was no one around so we got to go over every inch of the machine. The engine was a liquid-cooled type and from the looks of it the radiator had been leaking. There were struts that were fastened on with bailing wire like a farmer might fix a piece of farm equipment, one wing had a hole in it, and the tires were almost flat. We learned later that the pilot had taken the propeller to Murray to try to get it repaired. We wanted to be there when the fellow took off, but that was several days later and we missed the event.

A few weeks after the airplane was forced down across the river, a group of four planes flew right over Fort Henry and Blue Spring going north. They were just above the tree tops and the noise played havoc with livestock in the area. Kate and Nell were in the pasture, but by the time the planes were out of sight, they were headed farther up Owl Hollow. We found them at the Herndon place and had some trouble getting them back into the pasture. It was two or three days before Old Red gave any milk. Livestock was not alone in being frightened for there were some people who became hysterical and believed the world was coming to an end. Apparently the pilots were following the Tennessee River.

My First French Harp

Sometime after we had moved to The Point, somebody gave me a French harp, but I have forgotten who it was. For more than a year I went around with that thing in my mouth trying to coax a tune out of it, but it refused to turn one loose. All that happened was the old familiar seesaw noise with no sign of a melody. Papa and Mama got to the point that they forbid me to blow "that thing" around the house, and I had to take to the woods and fields to do my coaxing. Even Kate and Nell went to other parts of the pasture if I got too close to them. I was about ready to give up when one day, for no particular reason, some noise came out that sounded almost like a melody. Within a few days I was playing that harmonica like a pro, and within a month could play any tune I could whistle. Before long I was being asked to play my harp inside the house and later was asked to play certain songs. Mama liked sad songs like "Rosewood Casket" or "The Letter Edged In Black", but Papa wanted to hear peppy tunes like "Them Golden Slippers" or "Dark Town Strutters Ball". Both of them liked Negro Spirituals like "Nobody Knows the Trouble I've Seen" or "Swing Low Sweet Chariot".

In only a few weeks I went from pest to star and, of course, loved it. Kids love to do things that please their parents for it is a great ego-builder. I began to play such tunes as "Indian Love Call", "Wreck Of Old 97", "The Fox Chase" and a lot of Jimmy Rodgers' songs that I had heard on Grandpappy's radio. Jimmy Rodgers was my idol and anybody who could not yodel was a square. A lot of my songs came from the graph-o-phone that Papa had bought while we lived in Paducah. That Fall when Mama sent her order to Sears and Roebuck, she included two harmonicas for me.. One was long and sounded much like a violin, and the other was the regular type except in a different key.

Ready-Rolled Cigarettes

One Christmas Eve Carlos Lancaster and I decided to go to Fort Henry to get some shells for our guns. We took the guns with us and planned to do some hunting on the way back home. After buying our shells we had 15 cents left between us and squandered it on a pack of Camel ready-rolled cigarettes. We had been used to home-grown dark-fired tobacco, and the taste of those Camels was like candy over dried beans. We walked down the river bottoms, and not being familiar with them in that area, we ran into all kinds of trouble fording streams and picking our way through the underbrush. We smoked one cigarette after another and by the time we reached Boswell Landing, they were all gone, and we were too sick to go home. If our parents had known that we spent money on cigarettes, we would have gotten a scolding, and we were in no mood to face them. We laid down in a canebrake for a couple of hours and then went on home after dark.

Many of the young boys in the neighborhood either smoked or chewed tobacco although, in most cases, the parents forbid it. Tobacco barns were full of tobacco and anyone could help himself to all he wanted. Papa and Mama also forbad me to drink coffee, believing that coffee or tobacco would "stunt" your growth, and no farmer wanted a stunted son helping out in the fields. The only time I was allowed to drink coffee was when we had fresh fish. It was the general belief that drinking milk with fish would kill you, and besides, what is fish without coffee? For my smoking, most of the time I would slip around and buy nickel sacks of Bull Durham, Stud, Dukes Mixture, or Golden Grain. I hid it out in the woods, and after supper would go out and have a smoke. If cigarette papers were not available, people used the thin sheets from some mail order catalog.

Shot Eagle

One day when Mama was looking out the kitchen window, she saw a huge bird land in a tree about 100 yards down the road toward the Nances. Thinking it was a large squirrel hawk after her chickens, she asked me to try to kill it. Using Papa's Remington rifle, I laid the barrel on the window sill and took aim, allowing for the bullet to fall a little at that distance. I pulled the trigger and the bird fell to the ground. I brought it to the house, and when Papa came home, he inspected it and said it was an eagle, for he had seen pictures of them. The wing span measured about seven feet, too much for even the biggest hawk. We were all sorry that I had killed the eagle, but considered it a natural mistake.

Another time while working on a shotgun that had been given to me by Wheeler Love, I saw a hawk flying low over the sage grass field next to our house and saw it dive on some sort of prey. I didn't have time to assemble the gun and holding it together with my hands, put a shell in it, and headed to where the hawk had dived into the grass. I was within a few feet of the spot when the hawk flew up, and I fired almost point blank at the fleeing bird. The shotgun went in as many directions as there were parts, but the hawk went down. After locating the parts to the gun, I went to pick up the bird, but before reaching it, the hawk flew up again, and I rushed ahead and using the gun barrel, killed the hawk. On examining the bird, we could find no sign that any of the shot had hit him, but the concussion had probably stunned him momentarily.

Mama was an Angel

I have not told as much about Mama as I should, perhaps because I was not around her as much because I was either working outside or was out in the hills or down on the creek fishing. I do know that she did the laundry every week by hand. She drew water from the cistern and put some in a big iron pot and some in two wash tubs. A fire was built under the iron pot and some of the clothes were boiled. Using a sharp knife, she would shave thin slices of P&G soap into the hot water and some in one of the wash tubs. A scrub board was placed in the tub and the clothes rubbed against it until they were clean. The second tub was used for rinsing.

Mama always had a meal ready and on the table when it was supposed to be there. She put up hundreds of cans of fruits and vegetables each year and worked her garden in the summer in addition to doing all the cooking laundry and dish washing. When a neighbor was real sick, the other neighbors took turns sitting with the sick person during the night. Many times I have known Mama to cook our supper, wash the dishes, and walk more than a mile to sit with some sick person, and then return home in time to have our breakfast on the table at the regular time. In winter she sewed and quilted a lot. Mama could look at a picture of a dress in a catalog and reproduce it perfectly for herself or someone else. Mama had a Singer sewing machine that was powered by her foot and could sure make it hum. Most every day Mama read at least one chapter from her bible and often read it out loud so that I could hear it. She was the greatest woman I have ever known.

I Stole an Apple

Often when I went to the river to do some fishing I took a shortcut through the hills that brought me by the Moody Mathis place. Moody had an apple orchard beside the road and when fruit was plentiful, I thought nothing of picking one and eating it. One year the cold must have killed all the apples, all that is, except one. That one apple was just over the fence, and I spotted it before it was half-grown, and watched as it got bigger and bigger. As Fall came, I watched it turn to a beautiful red color. Nobody took the apple so one day I couldn't stand it any longer, climbed the fence, and stole the beautiful fruit. I could not help wondering if Adam and Eve had the same feeling about the forbidden fruit. It was just right to eat and was the best apple I have ever tasted. As time went on, my conscience started to bother me and got so bad that I had to go to Moody and confess to what had happened. He said he was real proud of me for confessing but that he didn't know there was an apple in the orchard that Fall. For a long time I wondered if my confessing was worthwhile since he never knew the fruit was there, but I was glad I told him about the theft.

Papa Makes a Horse Whip

In the early and mid-twenties there was a fad that the driver of a wagon must have a whip to crack over the team. Papa decided to make a real fancy one and ordered the leather strips from one of the mail order houses. Most whips were three plait but Papa made a four plait that was the best one around. It was seven or eight feet long with about two feet of popper on the end. He whittled a fancy whip stock out of hickory and practiced until he could crack the whip every time and loud enough to hear across the hollow. One day he was helping Lohman Nance haul hay, and the ground being soft, the wagon was pulling rather hard. Kate and Nell were doing their job but not fast enough to suit Papa so he cracked the whip right over the mule's ears. There were four or five men working, and it took every one of them to stop Kate and Nell. They almost tore up the hay field, and after they were subdued, Papa put his whip away and never used it again.

The Bell Buzzard

Sometime in the early twenties Papa noticed that one of the buzzards that spent the summer in our area was different from the others. Buzzards don't often flap their wings while flying and can soar for hours in noiseless flight without any apparent effort. There was one however, that wore a bell around its neck and when it flapped its wings, the bell would ring. If there was one thing that the people around Blue Spring had plenty of, it was curiosity, and each spring we all looked for "The Bell Buzzard" to return. The bird returned in the Spring of 1928, and I have wondered how many more years it returned to soar in the skies over Hickory Hollow.

Radio Inventor?

Papa told me a story he had heard many years before about a fellow by the name of Stubblefield that lived out in the country from Murray, Kentucky, and he had electricity all over his farm and lots of it The strange thing about it was that there was no power lines for many miles from the farm, and it was believed that he got his supply of electricity from metal posts that he had driven into the ground at several locations. Papa said that a man had told him that when he was a boy, he approached the fence that protected the property, and when he came near the fence an alarm went off, and one of the wires at the top of the fence became red hot. There were stories about Mr. Stubblefield working on a gadget that

206

sent messages through the air and that the thing had been stolen from him. Before he died, he had destroyed all the secrets and he had been dead several days before he was found.. There is a statute of some kind on the campus of Murray State University that indicates that Mr. Stubblefield did, indeed invent the radio.

Last Year in Paradise

The year 1928, when I was fifteen years old and the last year I would spend in Owl Hollow, holds many memories, but they were more adult and lack the excitement of the younger years. Ray Lyon and I were close, even though he was a few years older. It seems that I put away childish things too early and became an grownup at fifteen.

I had my first date in the Spring of 1928. Dorothy Rowlett was a pretty girl and we had known each other all our lives, but at fifteen, girls begin to look better than they did a few years back. One night when Dorothy came out of the church, I asked if I could walk her home, and to my surprise, she agreed. She lived beyond Fort Henry, at least two miles, so when Corbin Champion asked if we wanted to ride with him and his girl, Elsie Sills, we gladly accepted the offer.

Dorothy lived about a quarter mile past where Elsie lived, and we had to walk from Elsie's house. I don't recall what we talked about, but I do remember that I was uneasy about us walking the distance alone and wondered what her parents would have to say about it. Dorothy's father and mother had known me all my life, and if there was anything dark in my past to cause suspicion, I didn't know it. Her father, Mr. Joe Rowlett, was a pillar in the church and often led the singing, and I was thinking he had always been nice to me and maybe he would think nothing of me walking with his daughter. We were standing on the porch with plenty of distance between us when the door opened and out came Mr. Joe and his wife in their night clothes and carrying a lantern. He didn't ask who I was, but instead held the lantern in my face to see for himself who was courting his daughter. Mr. Rowlett was nearsighted and wore thick glasses and when we were looking at each other eye to eye, his eyes looked so big and dangerous that I quickly made my getaway. He said later that he was glad to see it was me, but on a first date things have a tendency not to look normal.

A Busy Night

Ray Lyon and I did a lot of crazy things that would be dull today. Like the time three of Uncle John Lyon's daughters, our cousins who lived across the river in Calloway County, wrote and asked if we would ferry them and two or three girlfriends over the river so they could attend a revival that was going on at Blue Spring.

On the day they had selected, Ray and I went to the mouth of Panther Creek where there were always several jon boats tied up, chose one, and headed across the river to Kentucky. Panther Creek island lay between us and our destination, and we had to go around the lower end of the island and row up the shoot to where the girls would be waiting. It was mid-afternoon when we loaded our cargo of six giggling girls into the boat and headed back to Tennessee. Because Ray was stronger than I, he did the rowing while I guided the boat where the water was not as swift along the island and then across to dry land.

There were still about two miles to walk through woods and fields to reach the church where the revival was being held. When we got there, others were also arriving, and there was plenty of time for visiting or flirting, depending on who the visitor was. A revival preacher could go on for hours, and when it came time to sing the invitation song, that could be repeated several times. It was after nine before the preacher let the crowd out, and we headed back to the river to ferry the girls back to Kentucky. Ray or I walked in front, carrying a lantern and a big stick, just in case there was a cottonmouth or copperhead in the path. For some reason girls always shied away from snakes, and the river bottoms were known to have some big ones. However, we did not see one that night.

When we reached the river, there was a big stern wheel towboat about a mile down stream pushing several barges, and we had no choice but to wait until it passed before starting across the river. The waves from the barges were small, but that big stern wheel made waves that could easily capsize our boat. It was about an hour before we ventured out into the river and the darkness. On the darkest nights there is always enough light to outline the trees along the bank of the river, and we had no trouble finding our way around the island. The current of the shoot slowed us down but Ray was able to row us to our landing where we put the girls ashore. We walked them to Uncle John's house and then returned to the

Tennessee side of the river. Daylight was breaking by the time I got home and Papa and Mama were up, and I was soon in the field working.

Another time Ray and I decided to attend a revival at a church over on Nevels Creek between Tharpe and Model. We started a little after noon and walked through the hills to Tharpe and then down the Model road to Nevels Creek. After the services that night, we walked back home the same way. The distance must have been about ten miles for the round trip, but we enjoyed it.

Paradise Slips Away

Sometime in 1928 I started to think about getting an education. Because of problems with my eyes I had not been to school in more than two years and was now fifteen years old, over six feet tall, and strong as a bull. I kept my ideas to myself until I could give Papa and Mama a clear picture of what I had in mind. I remembered living in Paducah and somehow got the idea that if I could go to the city, I could work during the day and go to school at night. I don't recall where the idea came from. I had been wearing glasses a couple of years, and when the light was good, I could read up to an hour before my eyes began to water. The idea of a six-foot boy starting out again in the sixth grade was not very appealing. After all, I had even had a date with a girl and that was a sure sign I was "growing up". I figured it took more courage to ask a girl for a date than it would to ask somebody for a job.

Thesbie Wallace and his family had moved to Nashville a few years before, and I wondered if they would let me room and board with them. They had lived in the upper Panther Creek area and were members of the Blue Spring Church and came almost every Sunday. The family included Mr. and Mrs. Wallace, three girls and a boy. The youngest girl was about my age. Without Papa or Mama knowing it, I got their address from someone and wrote and told them my plans. Later I got a letter telling me that they would be glad to have me board with them and that the prospects of finding a job were good. My hopes were fired up now, and it was time to tell Papa and Mama about my plans. They listened as I outlined my desire to get an education, and I showed them the letter I had received from the Wallace family in Nashville. How would I get the money to live on until I could find a job? They explained that room and board had to be paid ever week whether I was working or not and that I would need some money. Otherwise, they didn't seem to have any serious objections.

Lohman Nance had bought a sawmill and planned to set it up on a ridge between Stilly Hollow and Panther Creek. Offbearing at a sawmill was hard work, but the pay was better than most farm jobs, and the winter days were shorter, too. I asked Lohman about working at the mill, and he agreed because he knew I was used to hard work and long hours. He told me he would pay me the same wage as he paid the older men, $1.25 a day, and that I would be expected to be at the mill and ready to work as soon as there was enough daylight for him to read the gauges. Sometime around the first of December of 1928 I started my first job for pay.

Somehow Mama managed to get me up early and insisted I eat a good breakfast. Papa was always up before me, and this morning was no exception. A big lunch was packed and with no fanfare I was ready for the long walk to the sawmill. I was surprised when Papa walked with me to the gate and, putting a hand on my shoulder, spoke words that would become a part of my working life. He said,"Always remember when you are working for someone that as long as you make money for them, you will both have a job". Papa was so right.

There were four of us in the sawmill crew; Lohman was the sawyer, Mack Hosford, Lynn Love, and myself. One crew member rolled the logs to the "carrier" and helped place them in position to be cut into slabs, tie lumber, and crossties. The other two were "offbearers", removing the finished product from the carrier and carrying the slabs, lumber, and crossties to their respective piles. Offbearing was much harder work because some of the crossties weighed well over 100 pounds. Mack, Lynn, and I took turns at the easier job of keeping the logs ready to roll on to the carrier. Handling a crosstie was not a bad job if you knew how to handle them, but could be a back-breaking job otherwise. We worked 20 days before Christmas and Lohman paid me $25. I was rich now and ready for the trip to Nashville.

I had written the Wallace family a second letter that I planned to arrive in Nashville soon after the first of the year. Between Christmas and the New Year I received a letter from them advising me not to come to Nashville because jobs were getting scarce and doubting that I could find work. Fortunately I went to the mail box that day and kept the letter a secret because I was afraid Papa and Mama would change their minds if they saw the letter. With almost thirty dollars in my pocket and a cardboard box full of clothes, on the morning of January 3, 1929, I said goodbye and headed across Owl Hollow and toward Dover. Looking back I could see Mama standing on the back porch watching until I was out of sight. I had the feeling that Papa was watching me also but would never let me see him doing it. My brother Douglas was almost five and did not fully realize what was going on.

I had planned to pay the fifty cents and ride with the mail carrier to Dover, but when he came by, he was already overloaded with mail and passengers. I. could either wait until the next day or start walking the ten miles to Dover. I got to Dover in early afternoon and looked up Bro. Allison who had been our First Sunday preacher at Blue Spring for longer than I could remember. He and Mrs. Allison had a house full of children but said I could spend the night if I didn't mind sleeping on a pallet on the floor. That was no problem because I had slept on pallets many times before. Next day I rode the Dover-to-Clarksville mail truck to Clarksville and then took a bus to Nashville. I had spent a dollar of my money already on getting to the city.

I brought a letter I had received from the Wallaces with directions on how to find their house at 830 Joseph Avenue, between First and Second Streets in East Nashville. There was no problem finding the place but they were surprised to see me after writing me not to come, but they seemed happy that I was there. Everything was arranged, and I would pay $5 a week for room and board. The family operated a restaurant in North Nashville near the Jefferson Street bridge, and they told me I could take my meals either at the house or the restaurant. They said there were some places near the restaurant where I might find a job.

Wednesday morning I was up early. I dressed in overalls and walked across the bridge and ate breakfast at the restaurant. After eating I walked around the area and saw a group of men working and asked to see the foreman. He gave me a suspicious look and wanted to know my age. I lied and said I was 21 years old. He pointed to a wheelbarrow and told me to grab it and start pushing cement. I fell in line, got my load and pushed it to where it was dumped into a footing, thinking to myself that this was a lot easier than carrying crossties. A few minutes later the foreman came and said that he did not need me but wanted to see if I really wanted to work. He said that a friend of his needed me and was on his way over to pick me up. Soon a big car pulled in, and I was on my way to Old Hickory to work for the T. L. Herbert Company. Before we got there, I wondered if Old Hickory was in the same state as Nashville. We crossed over the Cumberland River on a swinging bridge where traffic would go one way for ten minutes and then, the other direction. A few weeks later a two-lane bridge opened, and we were among the first cars to cross on it.

The company was building some sand bins, and I was given a fresh wheelbarrow and a load of cement to push. These loads had to be pushed up a ramp and dumped into the footing. I was later promoted to carpenter's helper and spent most of my time pulling nails out of the lumber that was being used for forms. I was paid 30 cents an hour for nine hours a day. The foreman let me ride with him free of charge, but I had to meet him at First Street and Woodland Avenue about daylight each morning. I was making $11 a week after room and board, and before January was over I bought a new suit of clothes and a new shirt. It was the first suit I ever owned. A tie was thrown in and now I could go to church if I could get somebody to show me how to tie a necktie. One of the Wallace girls helped me pick the suit out, and showed me how to tie a necktie, the only piece of clothing I consider a curse.

The cement bins were completed in late February and I was laid off. Fortunately, the oldest Wallace girl had a boyfriend who was a foreman at the Jarman Shoe Factory and he got me a job there. Jarman at that time made the popular "Friendly Five" shoes that sold for $5. On my new job I would not be paid by the hour, but instead, would be paid by the piece. I was assigned to a big piece of wood (that to me looked like a huge stump), and given a gadget that cut a small patch of leather out of pieces of scrap. The work required nimble fingers and that was not one of my better traits. After a few weeks I was not doing much better than paying my room and board, and my slow pace was noticed by the younger Mr. Jarman who was of the opinion I should do better. The elder Mr. Jarman was friendly and would often stop and chat with the workers. His son was more interested in production, and we started having a few words that were not the friendly type. One day when I was sure he came down to fire me, I said "I quit" and that ended my work at the shoe factory. Someone in the payroll did have a sense of humor, and one Friday instead if my envelope reading "C. Lyon" it was "Sea Lion", and I have used that name at times ever since.

Because I felt my job at the Jarman Shoe Factory was not secure, I had been going by the H. G. Hill Stores hiring office every morning, and after they were through hiring for the day, I would still have time to get to my job at the shoe factory. One morning shortly after I had "left" Jarman's, the man who did the hiring, I believe his name was Hudson and he always wore a black hat, picked me out of a lineup of about twenty-five and sent me to their store at 15th and Cedar Streets. I gave the manager the note Mr. Hudson had handed me, and he began showing me around. I recall him taking me by the candy case and telling me that he didn't want to see me snitching candy so anytime I wanted some candy to help myself and nobody would say anything to me. I did help myself and by noon I didn't care if I ever saw another piece of candy. He knew how to handle new employees and that was probably why he was a store manager. When we closed, we had sold over $500 worth of groceries. We waited on each customer, item by item, and then went to another customer. Our special that day was large Florida oranges for one cent each or ten cents for a dozen. The manager said it cost more freight to get them to Nashville than the grower received. I also worked at the 8th and South Street H. G. Hill Store, where a man and his wife operated it. I was not permitted to handle the money as I had at 15th and Cedar, but that was ok with me. Soon the Cumberland River went on a binge, flooding several of the stores, and I was out of work again. The river flooded Sulphur Dell and the ball games were played in Centennial Park.

Before I could find another job, Papa showed up in Nashville unannounced, and before he knew I was out of work made me an offer. He said that he and Mama were considering moving to Dover and that they were hoping I would come home and go to high school there. It was the answer to all my wishes, and next day we caught a bus back to Dover and Blue Spring.

From the News Media

Bob Battle, Senior Business Editor, Nashville, Tenn., Banner: "His book - now in its second printing - is a masterpiece at returning the reader to country life the way it was lo those many years ago when hay rakes were pulled by two mules, neighbors helped kill hogs and plowing looked easy until you tried it and had to be rescued by your dad."

Bonnie Lill, Stewart-Houston Times, Dover, Tenn.: "What was there for a Tennessee farm boy to do in the 1920's before television, video games, electricity, and even running water? Stewart County native Clyde Lyon answers this question, and more, in his newly published book A Country Boy From Owl Hollow."

Jeannie Brandsetter, Paducah, Kentucky, Sun: "Lyon remembers a great deal about the first six years of his life on Guthrie Avenue in Paducah . . . Our running water supply was a hydrant in the back yard, and our plumbing was an outhouse back of the lot. There's the time (in Tennessee) he got tipsy from eating too much soured New Orleans molasses; the episode when he hid his prized duck egg in his grandmammy's parasol, only to have it break over her head; and the day he and his Aunt Tince decided hoecake-making was boring and fried a mouse instead."

Pettus Read, Editor, Tennessee Farm Bureau News: "He began his 82 years using a slate and slate pencil in his first school year and progressed to the computer to do his book. Quite a change in writing in one lifetime, but the results are still a work of art. A Country Boy From Owl Hollow is a masterful job of returning the reader to country life the way it was lived at the turn of the century. It will bring you back on the farm when life was not controlled by a clock but by the sun. The book has stories that are both funny and sad. Mr. Lyon has tried to include it all."

Tracy Sherrill, Kentucky New Era, Hopkinsville, KY: "His memories of growing up in the country in the early part of this century are of taming foxes, hunting bee trees, fishing and trapping. Although he is impressed with the sales of his book, Lyon isn't sure if he will write another . . . For now, Lyon is content to enjoy his new success as an author and let people know how enjoyable life was in the early 1900s."

Ann Cline, The Sunday News, Tullahoma, Tenn.: "Author Clyde Lyon, of Nashville, grew up in the early part of the century near old Fort Henry in the land between the Cumberland and Tennessee Rivers. Childhood as he knew it, like Fort Henry itself, has ceased to exist. As a child he enjoyed a freedom and sense of security that seems to have been lost. Roaming the hills and hollows and exploring the backwoods around his grandhather's farm in Owl Hollow, a rural community in the Tennessee portion of The Land Between the Lakes, Lyon developed an independence and curiosity which have motivated him throughout his 82 years."

Letters From Readers

"I just finished reading your book, "A Country Boy", and I wanted to let you know how much I enjoyed it. I was engrossed with the tales of adventure and strong sense of community and family you expressed throughout the text. Being a 26 yr. old woman, born and raised in the city, I appreciate a glimpse into a real lifestyle--where priorities settled around people and survival, not economic advancement." E.H. (Tennessee)

"I finished reading your book . . . I'm glad you preserved those memories." J.A.H. (KY)

"I read part of your book, A Country Boy, while in Tennessee recently. Enclosed is check . . . please send a copy so I can finish it." R.V.M. (California)

"Enclosed is a check to cover purchase and mailing of 3 copies of your book, A Country Boy . . . We plan to pass the book along to our children to serve as a piece of the puzzle to their past." P.W. (Michigan)

"I want two more books . . . please send to the addresses below." A.C. (Kentucky

" . . . you sold another book by me letting a friend read my book. When she brought the book back she asked me if I'd order one for her, which I was glad to do. She gave me her check made out to Country Life Publishers." M.G. (Florida)

"Thank you so much for the book. ------ and I are enjoying it so much. ------ is almost blind but I read to him every day." M. & J.S. (Missouri)

"I just recently acquired and read your book, A Country Boy From Owl Hollow, and thoroughly enjoyed it . . . It is humorous and informative . . . This book will be something I can pass on to my children that in years to come will be worth more than money. When reading a book like this, it sometimes makes me wish I were born forty years earlier . . . I wish my dad could have read this book." H.K.H. (Kentucky)

"When I showed the book to my daughters (ages 9 and 6), we sat down and read several stories from it. The girls were quite interested in the stories and also found some very funny. I explained to them the author was a real person telling about his childhood . . . . I particularly like reading to them from your book because I can open it anywhere and just start in. We negotiate how many stories we will read that evening, depending on the time, degree of tiredness . . . well, you probably remember how that goes! I feel the girls (and myself, for that matter) are getting a history lesson in a way they can truly enjoy. N.S. (Tennessee)